THE BOOK THAT CAN CHANGE YOUR LIFE!

Garbo, Jennifer Jones, and David Ben-Gurion are among
the many devotees of Yoga, the ancient science which
restores health, vigor and youth to the practitioner!
Now YOU can enjoy the bountiful benefits of this exciting
physical and spiritual experience . . .

YOGA, YOUTH, AND REINCARNATION
by JESS STEARN

Here is the full, fascinating story of a sceptical journal-
ist who found that Yoga could not only cure his physical
ailments but lead to new inner security as well.
Jess Stearn's remarkable story includes diagrams and
descriptions of exercises to build and restore vitality,
body harmony, and sexual potential.
"A more peaceful attitude toward life is the second
'wonder ingredient' of the Yoga approach, which insists
on keeping you young!"

—New York Daily News

YOGA,
YOUTH,
AND REINCARNATION
JESS STEARN

Photographs of Marcia Moore
by Frank Stork

Drawings by Goldie Libson
author of *Rejuvenation Through Yoga*

*This low-priced Bantam Book
has been completely reset in a type face
designed for easy reading, and was printed
from new plates. It contains the complete
text of the original hard-cover edition.*
NOT ONE WORD HAS BEEN OMITTED.

YOGA, YOUTH, AND REINCARNATION
*A Bantam Book / published by arrangement with
Doubleday & Company, Inc.*

PRINTING HISTORY

Doubleday edition published July 1965
2nd printing . September 1965   4th printing .. December 1965
3rd printing .... October 1965   5th printing ..... March 1966
6th printing .. September 1966
*Bantam edition / January 1968
22 printings through April 1978*

Bantam Books are published by Bantam Books, Inc. Its trademark, consisting of the words "Bantam Books" and the portrayal of a bantam, is registered in the United States Patent Office and in other countries. Marca Registrada. Bantam Books, Inc., 666 Fifth Avenue, New York, New York 10019.

PRINTED IN THE UNITED STATES OF AMERICA

CONTENTS

		Foreword	vii
Chapter	1	GETTING TO KNOW YOU!	1
Chapter	2	MY GURU	14
Chapter	3	CLOUDS OVER CONCORD	24
Chapter	4	WE START	39
Chapter	5	ONWARD	52
Chapter	6	CARRY ON	64
Chapter	7	THREE MONTHS	75
Chapter	8	MEDITATION	88
Chapter	9	DIET YOUNG	109
Chapter	10	SEX, ALAS	123
Chapter	11	CLASS-CONSCIOUS	135
Chapter	12	ASTROLOGY À LA LOUIS	151
Chapter	13	POINTERS AND HEALTH TIPS	165
Chapter	14	STEPMOTHER INDIA	181
Chapter	15	REINCARNATION	193

Chapter 16   REINCARNATION,
              ANYBODY?   218
Chapter 17   SPIRITS AND SPOOKS   228
Chapter 18   CONCLUSION   243

              Appendix

              Tips for Students   261
              Yoga Warm-ups   264
              Basic Yoga Postures   283
              Pranayama:
                 Breath Control   315
              Purifying Exercises
                 (Kriyas)   326
              Tips for Teachers   328
              Training Pages   331

Glossary of Sanskrit Terms   339

Foreword

This is the story not only of my experience with Yoga, but of Yoga's experience with me. It is the story of an old physical and mental discipline and of the Boston Brahmin who was to become my guru—and of the wonderful collection of students, psychics, astrologers, and modern transcendentalists that passed through her Concord ashram. As for me, I feel that if an old beat-up sedentary like myself could do it, anybody can. And this book is an effort to get just about everybody to help themselves get young, slim, and energetic with Yoga, while showing them how they can do it themselves. For this reason, the exercises—conditioners and postures with the deep breathing—are fully detailed in the Appendix, with a Training Table as a working guide. Before I undertook my own Yoga experience, a noted teacher told me: "Some come for lunch and stay for life." I am one of those, I hope, who will stay for life.

"In three months," Marcia said, "you'll be a new person. I guarantee it."

I must admit I was getting rather tired of the old person —and my body seemed to be tiring of me—but there didn't seem to be anything I could do about it short of rebirth.

"Don't you care about staying young and vital?" she urged.

I shrugged. "So who's young and vital?"

She smiled. "You are a perfect subject: you're nervous, tense, run-down, and your body, from the look of you, is about ready to give up. It is later than you think."

"You're not very flattering."

"I'm being honest—that's one of the requisites of Yoga. It leads to truth."

And what did Yoga have to do with it?

"Come up to Concord, Massachusetts, take our Yoga course, and in three months, I guarantee, you'll be a new person."

I sniffed. "Everybody's pretty used to me the way I am."

"You're not bad for middle age, but before you know it, unless you reverse the aging process, you'll be passing out of your prime."

I had not known Marcia long, and I wondered if she approached everybody with such startling directness.

She gave me an impish look. "Call it my woman's intuition, if you like, but I think you're the one to introduce Yoga to a much larger audience in America. And it will be a wonderful experience for you."

My meeting with Marcia Moore had been as unexpected as it was electric. I had just finished a talk on psychic phenomena before a staid Boston group, when a slim, boyish-looking girl with straight hair and regular features approached with outstretched hand. She appeared to be in her early twenties. We chatted casually for a few minutes and I learned that she was rather versatile. She had become interested in the mystic in India, did her graduation thesis at Radcliffe on, of all things, astrology, and she taught Yoga.

I had not given her an answer, but she could not tarry. Looking at her watch with a small cry of horror, she announced, "I must get home to the children."

She hardly looked old enough to be married.

"I have three," she said, "and the oldest is fifteen." She ran off, calling over her shoulder, "Now don't forget, think it over and vote aye—for yourself."

We corresponded irregularly, as she was kind enough to help me in some research on astrology. And then we met in New York one day. She was in town, she explained, for a lecture on Yoga, and she had brought her lavender leotard along to make it living color.

She seemed to have endless facets: mother, mystic, astrologer, housewife, and now a yogi or yogin, an expert on Yoga.

As I stood musing, she eyed me reflectively. "You really ought to try it. It would bring you a greater grasp of life, and help your writing."

"But I already go to a gym," I said.

She smiled. "In Western calisthenics, one depletes his energy; in Yoga, he renews it. But the physical is only part of it." She looked me in the face. "You can't find peace and contentment in the gym."

I looked up rather sharply. "What has that to do with Yoga?"

"Most of my students come for relaxation, but they're looking for peace of mind."

And did they find it?

"Come and find out for yourself."

The next time I was in Boston, I visited Marcia and her most recent husband, Louis Acker, at their Concord ashram—ashram being a Sanskrit term for a shelter in the forest; its modern equivalent, a Yoga studio. Louis, a hulking giant of a man, was twenty-three, some twelve years younger than Marcia. But standing on their heads, a frequent posture in the Moore-Acker household, they seemed in complete accord.

It was an unusual household, even considering the rugged individualism of New England. Fifteen-year-old Louisa, who sang folk songs while strumming the guitar, was an adept at the highly esoteric tarot cards, and was studying Hebrew so she could better explore the Cabala, the ancient book of Jewish lore. The boys, Chris, thirteen, and Jonathan, eleven, fancied themselves Beatles, and treated Louis like a junior Beatle.

Louis was also an astrologer and a teacher of Yoga, and he made telescopes in the one-car garage, while still trying to graduate from Boston University. He was strangely unimpressed by my lank figure and stringy muscles. And when I complained of fatigue after a trying day, he said with quiet disdain, "With Yoga, you'd be able to work twenty hours a day."

Marcia laughed. "But who wants to work twenty hours a day, Louis?" She explained, "What Louis means is that you'd be full of drive and all sorts of energy." She regarded me with a solicitous eye. "In our culture we're all much too cerebral. We have to stop thinking once in a while, so we can learn what kind of people we are and where we are going."

It was still difficult for me to decide. I had contracts for two books, was about to undertake a syndicated newspaper column, and being of a pessimistic nature I felt that anything promising as much as Yoga could only turn out badly. I needed more time to explore.

I knew of Yoga and its claimed wonders, of course, but I had never been able to work up an interest in something that seemed so alien to my own life. When anybody mentioned Yoga, my imagination mustered up a Gandhi-like figure sitting impassively with legs crossed, staring at his navel, or some Indian fakir shuffling placidly over a white-hot bed of coals.

If Yoga, as a branch of the Hindu philosophy, was of any purpose, why was it that India, the land of its origin, was marked with poverty, squalor, and disease at every turn? Why was it then that this cult had made so little impact on a caste system which had helped keep India backward for centuries?

And yet perfectly reasonable men and women of the Western world appeared enamored of Yoga. I encountered beautiful young girls who said it kept them slim, trim, and happy. I knew that silent-screen star Martha Sleeper and long-retired Lili Damita insisted it kept them young and vital. It seemed almost a specific for the apostles of perpetual beauty: Jennifer Jones, Olivia de Havilland, Dolores Del Rio, Garbo, Gloria Swanson. Septuagenarian David Ben-Gurion of Israel did headstands to keep up his vigor and clarity of mind. It apparently helped Yehudi Menuhin's violin fingers stay nimble. Former model Dorian Leigh, a much older sister of actress Suzie Parker, looked as young as any of the girls modeling for her Parisian agency—and attributed it to Yoga. And it kept model mogul Gerard Ford as sleek as any of his models, and looking ten years younger.

I wondered how an Oriental ritual, smacking so much of the Eastern mystique, could be adapted to the hurly-burly of the West and the more aggressive temperament of its people. And what could it do for me?

Could one be Christian or Jew, or whatever, and still make use of Yoga, without affecting one's own faith? It seemed likely. Tony Soma, proprietor of Tony's Wife, a popular Manhattan bistro, remained a Catholic, while standing on his head and singing operatic arias in a remarkable demonstration of vitality at seventy-three. But Yoga was far more to him than a dramatic headstand. He had taken it up after his first wife's death, and it had helped him through a period of tension and sorrow. And now he stood on his head five minutes every day, and let the world do as it pleased. A United States senator from Massachusetts, a Catholic like Tony, had once demanded, "How can you say Yoga is superior to your own religion?"

Tony smiled. "I don't say it's superior—just different."

John F. Kennedy returned to his dinner, apparently mollified.

As I looked about me, I noted with surprise that many people I knew had been using Yoga to good effect, though each, curiously, seemed to have a rather different idea of what it was for. Suzy Wright, an attractive young dress designer, used the Yoga she had absorbed in a New York studio to keep her slim body strong and flexible and compose her thinking under the pressures of starting a new business, and going through a divorce.

A dear friend, Virginia Belmont, sat an hour a day deep breathing and meditating, and was the envy of Hollywood stars who made expensive pilgrimages to Switzerland for rejuvenating injections. Free of wrinkles, firm of muscle, this Bird Woman of Rockefeller Center looked some thirty-five or forty years old at most. Yet, she was, incredibly, past sixty. For years, her own husband, who ran their bird shop with her, had been taken by many as her father, though they were of an age.

Yet Yoga seemed rather vague and disjointed and hopelessly abstract. In my own way, I strove to resist the alarms of middle age, living one day at a time and occasionally working off steam at a gym. I told myself I was getting too old for new tricks. And then occurred one of those chance encounters that so often shape our actions. One day, at the gym, as I went through my routine of sit-ups and toe-touchings, I noticed a spry little man, with a cherubic face and wavy iron-gray hair, striking a pose that even I knew to be a classic Lotus posture.

He saw my look of inquiry and smiled.

His name, it developed, was Charles Weiser. Though small in stature, he was, it seemed, a big-business type. But unlike most tycoons, habitually pressed for time, he was friendly and engaging.

"Yes," he said, "that's a bit of Yoga. I practice a few basic postures just to keep fit."

He threw an apologetic look at the physical instructor, who was eying him quizzically. "It isn't so much the physical side of Yoga that I'm interested in," he said. "There's a mental aspect far more important."

He looked down at his trim figure. "I lost twenty pounds in six months with Yoga."

"Did you diet?" I asked.

"Not consciously. I just got detached from food."

I didn't understand.

He explained patiently. "After a while, meditating about things, getting detached in your thinking, you begin to realize that much of the eating you do is an outlet, a nervous reaction. You start thinking of food as fuel, though you still enjoy it. Without thinking about it, I found myself cutting out desserts." He had not become a vegetarian, as some yogis insist upon, but he had cut down on meat. "I found I could go farther on less food."

He had never felt better, more physically capable, though he was now in his fifties. "I can do things," he said, "that I couldn't do since I was a kid." But the temperament changes had brought him greatest satisfaction. He had become a man with a new outlook and personality.

"Everything used to excite me once," he said. "Now I remain calm and composed. I am more compassionate, and can detach my ego from situations. I was always having trouble with my employees. I would discover somebody had misrepresented something or fallen down on the job, and I would call him in and begin storming at him. He would get upset and start shaking, and I'd get so upset I couldn't sleep at night. But now, if a man isn't working out, I call him in, reasonably go over his deficiency, and then if we don't see eye to eye, I give him a few weeks to look for another job."

I failed to see how this miracle had been wrought by staring off into space and musing dreamily of some vague cosmic consciousness.

He smiled. "I know it seems hard to believe. When I first started, my family and friends laughed at me. But now that they see what it's done, they just keep quiet and let it go at that. In fact, a few friends have tried it themselves."

"But how does it work? What happens that triggers this change?"

"I think of pleasant things, a garden perhaps, or I may visualize God, and as I meditate, I find myself growing calmer and stronger inside. I feel more in tune with the world, and of course I'm more relaxed from the exercises, and that helps me concentrate. I find myself looking at people, including myself, from a sort of mountaintop, and all their striving and struggling becomes so clear and evident."

I still didn't understand how he had gained great insight and peace of mind.

He shrugged. "I don't think anybody can spell it out for you. It's like a drug experience, I suppose; you have to go through it yourself to know how it works."

Peace of mind in a world that knew no peace? How many people of untold riches would exchange everything for this precious commodity!

I kept reading about Yoga, and talking to people who seemed to know something about it. In its Oriental context, it embraced vegetarianism, reincarnation, meditation, and spiritism. Deep breathing was integral to the discipline, and Pranayama, breath control, was the key not only to bodily stamina but supersensory development. Some regarded Yoga as a religion, others as an art or science. C. G. Jung, the eminent Swiss psychoanalyst and philosopher, observed after study: "Every religious or philosophical practice means a psychological discipline, that is, a method of mental hygiene. The manifold, purely bodily procedures of Yoga also means a physiological hygiene which is superior to ordinary gymnastic and breathing exercise, inasmuch as it is not merely mechanistic and scientific but also philosophical. In its training of the parts of the body, it unites them with the whole of the spirit."

I was more impressed by the report of a distinguished American physician who had tried Yoga himself. In *Yoga for Today*, by Spring and Goss, Dr. Franklyn Thorpe pointed out that he had been practicing Hatha Yoga, the purely physical Yoga, for forty minutes a day for ten years. His was a resounding testimonial. Yoga not only made a new man of him, but a new doctor. "During this period, I have rarely had a cold and no disease of any kind. What has been perhaps of even greater value to me in this confused, fear-ridden world is my concomitant sensitive improvement in mental and emotional control and self-knowledge. It has given me a reserve of mental and physical energy and an inner harmony and poise. While saving myself much useless emotional wear and tear during trying and difficult times, the equanimity and imperturbability I have gained has enabled me, through a more patient and sympathetic understanding to be of infinitely more help to my patients."

That was quite a breathful. But I still couldn't help wondering how Yoga differed from pure calisthenics. There were points of similarity overlaying fundamental differences, it seemed.

"They get into meditations and mind control," reported Harold J. Reilly, Rockefeller Center's famed physical culturist. "Still many of our exercises are similar, particularly the slow, stretching routines, where you must concentrate." He looked up with a smile. "But why don't you sit down with Madam Blanche DeVries; she's been teaching Yoga for forty years, and knows all about it."

The name seemed familiar.

"Do you remember Oom the Omnipotent?"

I did vaguely. The tabloids had irreverently given this name to the late Pierre Bernard because he had led his students in meditation with the chant of the sacred word *om* or *aum*, the Sanskrit sound signifying God or creation.

Madam DeVries was his widow, and their nephew Theos Bernard, also a yogi, had died on a mission to Tibet. As an advanced yogi, who had won his Ph.D. at Columbia University via Hatha Yoga, he had been able to stand motionless on his head for three hours, irrigate his colon sitting in a shallow basin of water, and swallow yards of gauze tape as part of an internal purifying process. This was a little extreme for my taste, but as a scientific experiment illustrated the potentialities of the body.

Mrs. DeVries was an apostle of moderation—and a remarkably informative hostess. Looking out on the splendor of the Hudson, at the angle of the Tappan Zee Bridge at Nyack, where she maintained her ashram, we had a relaxing lunch that included meat and fowl and pearls of wisdom. "Vegetarianism is fine if you can manage it," Mrs. DeVries said, "but in the temperate climes a little meat now and then is quite useful."

She quoted from the Bhagavad-Gita, the bible of the great Indian yogin and of Emerson, Thoreau, and Bronson Alcott: "Yoga is impossible for the man who over-

eats or for the man who starves, or for the man who
sleeps too much, or for the man who does not sleep
enough. The Yoga which dispels sorrow is for the man
who is temperate in his food, recreation, activity and
sleep."

It was another way perhaps of saying, "As a man thinks
so he becomes," a cardinal maxim of Yoga.

It was hard to realize that she had been a teacher so
long. Her eyes were brightly expressive, her voice resonant,
her underarms firm, and she had the calves of a prima
ballerina. She sat straight in her chair, presiding over the
table. There were perhaps six other guests, including
Reilly and a young dancer with emotional problems.

"Yoga," Mrs. DeVries was saying in her melodious
voice, "is the only religion that doesn't reject. In this way
it is somewhat Christlike, without being Christian, since
Christ didn't reject anyone, not even those who took him
to the Cross."

Yoga a religion?

"It's a way of life," she observed, "and what else, properly, is religion? Yoga is a union of body and mind with
the supreme spirit. It is clear, simple and direct, and there
are no mysteries to it, except those planted merely to
create mystery."

We talked of people standing on their heads, restaurateur
Tony Soma, and David Ben-Gurion, the elder statesman,
who had been photographed upside down on a beach with
a telescopic lens. Mrs. DeVries smiled. "Headstanding,"
she said, "has certain physical advantages. It changes the
flow of blood, refreshing the brain and easing the mind.
But even more it is a discipline, making one gently aware
of the authority of mind and body."

In a way Yoga was dedicated to the young in heart.
"We keep youthful, body and mind, by maintaining elasticity. We are in a state of senility when we can't change
either our attitudes or our bodies. Then we are drying up
for sure."

The dancer with the creamy complexion and restless
disposition pouted. "You mentioned that you can develop
such control over the body that different muscles can be
isolated." She frowned, "But we do that in ballet."

Mrs. DeVries nodded. "Yoga is a method, not just exercise. There are five basic principles. Silence is the first
of these; keeping our mind quiet so thoughts can enter;
then listening, so that we can learn; remembering, so that
we can consider; understanding, so it will have meaning;

and then acting." She eyed the young dancer evenly. "So often we just act first, getting all stirred up to no avail."

I regarded her placid features curiously. "Don't you ever get stirred up?"

She pursed her lips. "Anger should be simulated only for effect. But real anger dissipates energies, and causes innumerable little internal explosions damaging to body and mind."

Her words seemed directed at the girl. "Thinking with a disturbed mind is no thinking at all. Don't act first and regret later. Don't get upset or concerned by actions of others, by criticism or flattery. Practice the detachment that comes with Yoga. When the mind is calm and quiet, truth enters unsought." A kindly smile took the edge from her words.

"The need for self-discipline was never greater," she went on. "Lawlessness and delinquency stem from lack of self-discipline. We are living in a world which has abandoned the old standards, and needs self-discipline—control—more than ever. Since it is impossible to live by old patterns when they have disappeared, the problem is to know yourself—a supreme function of Yoga—and make the necessary adjustments."

Not only the have-nots, resorting to mob violence in their frustrations, but the rich and the overprivileged could profit by this discipline. It was remarkable how many people acted without reflection—with disastrous results.

Mrs. DeVries recalled the wealthy woman who had arrived at the ashram for her first lesson. Without bothering to say hello, she had slipped off an expensive mink wrap and thrown it on a chair. It slid off to the floor.

"Let's get on with the lesson," the woman said.

"Aren't you going to pick up the coat?" Mrs. DeVries asked.

The woman shrugged. "When do we start?"

"I think you should pick up your coat first."

"It doesn't matter to me," the woman said carelessly, "but if it bothers you that much, you pick it up."

The Yoga teacher retained her customary calm "That coat should represent something to you," she said mildly. "It took the lives of a good many innocent animals, it required a great deal of labor, and it was undoubtedly given with affection or love."

"Never mind the lecture," the woman said. "When do we start?"

As we listened bemused, Mrs. DeVries broke off and

looked around the table with an even smile. "I could have told her that the first lesson had started, and that she had failed, but it would have served no purpose." Even Yoga couldn't penetrate a closed mind.

Mrs. DeVries had never known illness, not even a head-ache, and had never taken a drug or medicine. And Yoga had helped others as it had her. People with sinus condi-tions, for instance, could lie out flat, their heads and necks over the side of a bed, and lower their heads to the floor, with some hand support, if necessary. After a week many no longer had a sinus complaint.

Even as she spoke, I recalled a newspaper colleague, Sidney Shalit, telling me that his doctor had prescribed a similar remedy. "I couldn't believe the mucus that poured out of me," he had said, "and in a few days I had no more chronic sinus." It had plagued him all his adult life.

Yoga was diagnostic. "It is one of the tricks of Yoga," Mrs. DeVries said, "to discover the habits opposed to good health. People usually sit on their stomachs with everything pushing down. Through standing or sitting im-properly, the abdominal organs are pushed down and out, pressing against the transverse colon, which becomes pen-dulous and hangs down languidly. With Yoga we strengthen the holding muscles and reverse the downward pull of gravity. Even in the bending exercises, we stretch and lift; otherwise there is constriction. All this lifts the organs and helps put them back in place—opens the body so the heart and vital organs have room to work."

Some people took to Yoga more quickly than others because they were already yogi-like in the performance of everyday duties. An art teacher, for instance, was so hobbled with a sacroiliac condition that initially he had to do his exercises lying down. But he had cultivated a certain patience and detachment as an artist and was able to concentrate almost at will, which facilitated his progress. At first he could only raise his legs and elongate his back; but gradually strengthening the shoulders and upper back, which affected the lower areas, he cautiously moved on to general exercises, and in three months his ligaments and muscles were fully repaired and the condition had disappeared.

Roughly, Yoga fell into two broad areas. There was Hatha Yoga, which developed the physical side. And there was the meditative, apparently enhanced by the mind control developed through the physical exercises. The meditative included Karma Yoga, Bhakti Yoga, Jnana

Yoga, and Raja Yoga (the ruling Yoga). They stressed meditating in relation, respectively, to one's work, devotions, mental processes, and spirit. And they were all more or less commingled, and were mostly for students who had already achieved some proficiency in the physical aspects.

The stage had to be carefully prepared for productive meditation. "At first," Mrs. DeVries observed, "we will settle for concentration, then maybe they can contemplate." There was a difference. "In concentration we see the drops of water coming from a hose, in contemplation the constant flow." In meditation, the highest level, which comparatively few achieve, the individual attains unity with the infinite that governs the universe. "Until the Lord is known as one's own self," she quoted the great teacher Prasad Shastri, "there is no freedom from fear and no real wisdom."

As part of their spiritual development, the yogis, Mrs. DeVries pointed out, believe in a Universal Order, and strive for attunement with this order and a continuous cycle of life they feel to be part of the order.

I had been interested in the psychic for some time, but considered reincarnation so much wishful thinking by people who had seen their best of this life, and were catching at straws to avoid the darkness beyond.

Mrs. DeVries smiled. "Yes, I believe in reincarnation. But that doesn't alter the eternal now. What we do in this world is as important as in any other life. We cannot shirk or excuse our behavior by lamely saying all will be forgotten. On the contrary, it may be very much remembered."

I asked a skeptical reporter's inevitable question: "Where does the spirit go when it leaves one body, and how does it find its way back into another?"

She laughed good-humoredly. But her reply was solemnly given. "The brook knows how to find the river, and the river the sea."

I mentioned that I was considering studying Yoga in Concord, in the heart of the transcendentalist country. She was a great fan of Concordian Ralph Waldo Emerson. "Emerson's essays on character, obedience, self-reliance are virtually models of the meditative aspects of Yoga. He thought everything through with such detachment, yet with such inner spirituality that he stands as a great exponent of Raja Yoga."

She was all for my Concord experiment.

"Intellectual grasp is not enough; you will never understand Yoga completely from outside; it has to happen to you. Only in this way will you get to know your weaknesses and strengths, and with the right teacher, correct and perfect yourself."

How would I know the teacher was right?

"The student must feel inspired by his teacher. Just as the sunrise, stars, flowers, and forests inspire, the teacher, or guru, inspires the pupil with his own strength, purpose, and serenity. And this transmits the power needed to follow his—or her—teachings."

She gave me a gentle smile. "If the pupil is ready, the master will appear."

Never before as a reporter had I directly experienced the strange and esoteric that I researched and wrote about. Otherwise, I might well have been a juvenile delinquent, prostitute, drug addict, homosexual. Exploring the psychic, I had surprisingly experienced certain intuitive flashes of my own, but this was without design. Instead of observing from the outside, for a change I would be on the inside looking out—or in. Needless to say, I had my misgivings, professionally and personally.

Admittedly, I had aging problems. Who didn't? My neck and shoulders still ached recurringly from an old whiplash injury, and X rays showed a traumatic arthritic formation in the neck area. A chronic sinus condition made breathing difficult at times, and I felt a shortness of breath in the subways, where the air was close and the steps steep.

I could sit at the typewriter for only an hour or two without my lower back stiffening so that I had to edge myself slowly out of my chair and gradually unwind.

Intermittently, I had a nervous stomach, gas pains, indigestion, and headaches from strain. I was edgy and irascible, often couldn't concentrate, and didn't sleep well. I seemed heir to all the pesky little ills that the boiler-plate ads promised to relieve—irregularity, sluggishness, lack of pep.

As to sex, for which Yoga was slyly recommended, I felt no concern about that. I rarely even thought about it.

For the first time in my life, I was beginning to think of myself as at a certain age; this bothered my vanity, for I had always thought of myself as youthful.

But with it all, grown accustomed to my failings, I still thought of myself as physically fit. Yet I did have the uneasy feeling that I would like to know more about where I was going, before the race was run. My body was not as important as my mind, nor my mind as important as my spirit. I wanted most of all to be in tune with a world which at times seemed darkly hostile and frightening.

I didn't know really what Yoga could do for me. It seemed to have helped a good many people. I was rather repelled, aesthetically, by the grotesque postures that so many Indian gurus seemed to feature in the courses they charted. But in Marcia I would have a distinctly American guru, often goddess-like in posture, who would consider the Occidental temperament at every learning level, though I suspected at times that her only regret was that she wasn't born a Hindu. "It will make a new man of you, mentally and physically," she had said.

And so I went to Concord to relax and seek peace of mind. If Yoga could do it for little Charlie Weiser, maybe it could do it for me.

"You will resist the exercises in the beginning," Marcia warned, "and will think of a dozen reasons for dropping out, just as the person first going to an analyst tries to rationalize quitting because of cost and time."

"Why should I quit before I've even started?" I asked.

"Your body is used to being treated a certain way, and at your age is in a process of ossification. Your shoulders and neck are rigid, and the arthritis that comes with the middle years is forming." She looked up. "Incidentally, as this rigidity disappears, the rigidity of temperament that accompanies this physical phase will also disappear."

I had not been aware my neck was that rigid.

"Why should I resist anything so obviously helpful?"

"Yoga," she said, "makes people live longer, as it strengthens body and mind. And your body, which has a life pattern of its own, an established aging process, will resist any move to change the established order.

"You are going to be young again. Look at the people taking Yoga as you go along. None will appear old, no matter their age. My own teacher in India was fifty, and looked thirty, because nerves, muscles, and mind were those of a man of thirty. With Yoga people get to look ageless, of indeterminate age, as you will find for yourself."

"All in three months?" I said.

"If it happens at all, the transformation should be well on the way in six weeks. All you have to do is want it."

It was an old truism that a man was as young as his spine. "As you stretch and loosen your back, so will your inner self stretch and loosen," Marcia said. "As a rejuvenator, Yoga stimulates abdominal muscles, spine, lungs, pelvic area, and refreshes the glands and nerve centers with pranic energy from the disciplined breathing. In their study of old people in Czechoslovakia, researchists observed noticeable debility in just these areas that Yoga keeps flexible and pliant."

Marcia had first studied Yoga in India. But she had continued her instruction under Swami Vishnudevananda near Montreal, and was conversant with the leading Indian gurus in America, including the outspoken Yogi Vithaldas and the scientifically oriented R. S. Mishra, physician, surgeon, and psychiatrist.

Vithaldas, teacher of Nehru, violinist Yehudi Menuhin,

and actress Dolores Del Rio, once likened Yoga to psycho-analysis, aimed at bringing the individual "to a full realization of his true self and his vast potentialities."

Marcia herself, struck by the self-analysis achieved through Yoga, had written a monograph comparing the two disciplines. It was somewhat similar to Vithaldas' summary of why a jittery, anxiety-ridden world could find comfort in Yoga. In his instructive volume, *The Yoga System of Health and Relief from Tension,* he had observed, "Half the sterile lives in the world are due to the unconscious (or the sometimes conscious) realization of the inadequacy of the individual to reconcile his life with what he feels should be the true method of living. The result is a sense of frustration, for the individual wants something which he cannot identify. A knowledge of what man wants is gained only after searching self-analysis, and the true self is only revealed when its potentialities are made apparent. The postures, breathing exercises and objectification of the body induced by Yoga therapy automatically bring into being a state of mind perfectly attuned to the world around. In other words, Yoga makes the patient his own psycho-analyst."

I couldn't help wondering how a few exercises, simple or complex, would do all this for me, and I really didn't know how much of it was pertinent.

I was after greater stamina, for which Yoga was supposedly a specific, greater emotional endurance, mental detachment so that I could work more productively free of stress, and if a sense of tranquillity could be thrown in, all the better. But it hardly seemed likely.

Marcia had encountered these misgivings before. "Even if you're only interested in Hatha Yoga, it still will do wonders for you, not only physically, but emotionally and spiritually," she said. "In disciplining yourself to do the exercises properly, you cannot help but bring about an integration of personality which is of paramount importance. The word *Yoga,* from the Sanskrit, the classical language of the Hindu, is responsible for our own wo.d *yoke,* meaning *to join together.* It is a union of body and mind."

Marcia had met me at the Boston airport, and we talked about Yoga and our project while driving through city streets, past the ivied walls of Harvard and the Crimson crews idling on the Charles. As we headed for the pastoral pleasantness of Concord, which oddly meant peace and harmony, she observed with a smile:

"Don't try thinking about it too much; you don't learn

about Yoga, you experience it. You've heard about detachment, separation, and withdrawal in connection with Yoga. Actually, you completely separate the various forces—the physical, mental, and spiritual—before bringing them together in a unified whole."

It would have been unthinkable at this point for any neophyte to fully grasp what she meant. She anticipated my perplexity. "The whole point of Yoga is that you never hurry or force anything. So"—she laughed—"let's not throw too much at you at one time."

She now spoke of the meditations, which many teachers felt were as important as the exercises in the search for self-knowledge. I was to meditate fifteen minutes a day, trying to achieve a mindless state.

I was most dubious, oriented to the West as I was. "You must still think about things to begin to understand them," I said.

"What we are trying for," she explained, "is the opening of the subconscious. Through the subconscious we get the highest superconscious experience and become in tune with the universe. Now, to get from the conscious ego to the higher awareness via the subconscious we do use the mind as a raft, crossing the gulf dividing the two, but when we get to the subconscious bank, we discard the raft; it has served its purpose and is no longer of use."

She shrugged. "There is nothing mysterious about Yoga, except for that which the uninformed put there. It is a way perhaps of seeing more clearly. Through Yoga, a reintegration begins to take place—we come to know ourselves acutely through the exercises and the meditation, and then, knowing, become gradually aware of unsuspected forces within. A regeneration takes place, as the separate forces begin to merge in a meaningful manner, because we have achieved control."

"Exactly how do these wonderful things happen?" I asked.

"By not thinking of them too much, and just doing the various exercises that bring fresh oxygen, blood, and stimulation to our bodies and our souls, call it the subconscious, if you like." She sighed. "If I had my way, instead of the sign THINK, I would hang up a DON'T THINK. So many of our so-called intellectual thinkers dissect and analyze so much that they chew everything up, without learning or experiencing anything of the subconscious. The intellectuals notoriously have little experience in the psychic field, which works out of the subconscious. In India they have a saying that the mind is the slayer of the real—the real of course being the nonintellectual. The child sees more clearly than the adult because he hasn't yet learned to judge. The Chinese have a saying: 'The child looks at the mountain and sees a mountain, the grownup looks at the mountain and sees many things, the sage looks at the mountain, and sees a mountain.'

"In other words, through a process of development the sage has gone back to seeing things with the unconfused, intuitive directness of the child."

"How," I asked, "is the subconscious affected through exercise or meditation?"

"It is hard to verbalize what we see and experience through the subconscious. As the subconscious opens, it comes in intuitive flashes and in images; so we train ourselves to meditate in terms of images.

"Then, through the exercises, we learn control, as we discipline ourselves, doing things with a sense of purpose. As part of our body control, we begin to control our emotions automatically. With control comes detachment, and we detach ourselves not from life, but from the fears that make living difficult and becloud our purpose."

And this purpose?

"To constantly seek knowledge of ourselves, and the world about us, in a controlled way, so as to achieve independence in ultimate freedom and perhaps even unveil the meaning of existence."

"Have you got there yet?" I smiled.

She shook her head. "All we hope for is progress, the sort of progress, that gives every day a fresh meaning. We breathe deeply, feeling union with Nature, strain our bodies, arms, legs, and the rest to develop our latent powers, physically and spiritually, to the fullest potential."

"How do you recognize this progress?"

She smiled. "It will sneak up on you. First to be affected will be the nerves. When you begin to have tranquil periods, you will realize you are making progress."

"I understand," I said, "that some Yoga positions, or asanas, are maintained for ten minutes."

"That is sometimes the Indian practice," she said, "but in adapting Yoga for the American way, we find that unnecessary. Actually in holding postures two or three minutes, there is enough muscle stretch to permit an even flow of blood and to develop the smooth suppleness that makes the body responsive to a variety of demands."

Her brow furled in a small frown. "It is sufficient, I feel, to discipline the body to a point where it becomes immobile on demand, thus curbing a restlessness which dissipates vital energy."

She looked at me curiously. "More important than anything to the success of this project is your wanting to do it. It may be to strengthen your body, release inner tensions, or just slim down. But there must be some purpose in mind to give you the resolution to follow through."

And there must be a recognizable pattern to fit into.

"In an experiment with mice recently, the mice were shown a cluster of circles and squares. They came to learn after a while that there was food in the circles and an electric shock in the squares. They responded to the circles, and were able to accept the disappointment of the squares with tranquillity, knowing what to expect. But then the role of the circles and squares was confused, with the food shifted from one to the other, and pretty soon they didn't know what to expect. They became frantic, as they threw themselves in confusion against their cages. They were completely out of control, because there was no longer any order in their world. They were at their wit's end, just as people are when their standards are taken away and they have nothing to replace them with."

Motivation was obviously important. At one time Marcia had taught Yoga in a beauty parlor. It had not been one of her more successful projects. "A few were interested for the sake of improving their looks," she said, "but that wasn't motivation enough for fifteen minutes a day. Health proved more of a motivating force than beauty.

"But those interested in peace, in the peace that, as the Bible says, passeth all understanding, were the only ones who really stuck with it. Unfortunately, few people were looking for peace in beauty parlors."

She had other failures. At Framingham Reformatory, near Concord, she taught the wayward for five months. Many of the teen-agers, particularly Negro girls with little family structure, were not sufficiently disciplined to do the simplest exercises reflecting mind control. They found it difficult to breathe slowly and rhythmically. And they did not have the patience to practice an exercise. "They had to be moving arms and legs all the time, without any thought to what they were about, a reflection, I suppose, of the lack of discipline which had put them in the reformatory in the first place."

Their efforts at the shoulder stand, one of the most tranquilizing exercises, was a nightmare for even a modest disciplinarian such as Marcia. "They would get up on their shoulders, and instead of holding legs still, would wave them about and giggle madly. They had not the slightest conception of what we were trying to accomplish."

Couldn't they have achieved discipline through practice?

Marcia smiled. "I thought so at the beginning. But I was forced to the realization that Yoga is only for people who have had some discipline in their lives. Actually, ordinary calisthenics would have been far better for these girls, as they move quickly and spasmodically, and pass from one exercise to another, without any capability for prolonged control."

Ironically, the best pupil was a young woman who had killed her husband. Her crime was one of passion, but was marked by a curious discipline under trying circumstances. "She had shot her husband," Marcia recalled, "and carefully trussed up the body and deposited it in the river. All this took unusual nerve control."

The prize student was in her late thirties, twice the age of the teen-agers, and not as strong and well-muscled. But she could concentrate, and so she could cultivate control.

She did the shoulder stand well, rearing up backside and legs perfectly with practice, and she did the breathing deeply and rhythmically. She enjoyed the exercises tremendously, expressing regret when Marcia withdrew from reformatory instruction. "Please come back," she said.

Of all those behind bars, the drug addicts appreciated the exercises most—surprisingly, since they were not exponents of any discipline except drug-taking. But they did have a purpose. "They enjoyed the deep breathing, finding that by hyperventilating themselves with oxygen, they got a high feeling comparable to the ecstasy of drugs."

Average persons had no trouble accepting the Yoga discipline since most knew some form of discipline at one time. In significant contrast to Framingham was Marcia's experience with the Shakers. Only nine of these celibates remained in the Shaker colony in East Canterbury, New Hampshire; all were women some sixty-five years and older. But Marcia had found them ready pupils. Sister Bertha, for instance, lightly threw herself on the floor, and did the forward and side bends. Others practiced the deep breathing, and neck and back stretching; and some with arthritis tensed their hands, slowly curling the fingers, in an exercise to relieve stiffness.

"Even at advanced ages, they could show progress," Marcia observed, "because their lives had been dedicated

to practical disciplines. The Shakers built their own communities, manufactured what they needed, sold off the rest,
and maintained a rigorous celibacy, a prime tenet of their
faith."

Now facing extinction, there were only twenty-three
Shakers, split between two colonies. They had once re-
cruited young orphans, willing, as they came of age, to
take the vow of celibacy for the satisfaction of communal
living in an enterprising, spiritually oriented community.
"But today," one Shaker pointed out, "the young people
just want to get into their cars and go, free of responsibility."

Believing in reincarnation, the Shaker ladies felt at home
with an Oriental philosophy which conceives of many lives.
"Actually," Marcia said, "they had been practicing Yoga
—Karma Yoga, devotion to duty and work—since they
were children, and their meditations, rooted in spiritualism,
made them yogic in their detachment."

Even married couples, forsaking the flesh, had become
Shakers, Marcia pointed out, living in separate dormitories,
but working together productively as they sublimated the
sexual drive by creativity in other fields. But, inevitably,
this sublimation, together with a world of changing mores,
foreshadowed their end.

Absorbed in the Shakers, I had not realized that we were
already in Concord. There was the snap of a late New
England spring in the air, the quietude of sleeping greenery,
and a blessed concord of the old and the new in land
where American transcendentalists once steeped themselves
in the Bhagavad-Gita, India's Song of God.

As we clambered out of the car, Louis Acker, Marcia's
husband, took my bags. He had been tussling with a huge
boulder, and was a little red of face, but breathing easily
with disciplined intakes of air, like a good yogi should.

Louis was well over six feet, and bountifully muscled.
"He is the strongest man I ever saw," Marcia said proudly.
"Right now, he is moving some boulders to an area back
of the house."

The boulders looked almost as big as the house. "How
do you move them?" I asked, nodding at a two-ton monster
which looked like it hadn't been budged since the glacial
age.

Louis wore a distracted look. "Oh, I just roll the bigger
ones. Once you get them moving, they go right along."

Louis, too, taught Yoga and like Marcia was an astrologer—their marriage apparently prospering because of

their common inclinations despite Louis being only twenty-three and a senior at Boston University, while Marcia, at thirty-five, was the divorced mother of three.

Louis was also interested in astronomy, in almost anything celestial; he taught the Astronomy Club at the local high school, and for a year had been busily making a man-sized telescope of his own with which he could roam the skies on starlit nights. He had the reputation of being quite a martinet, as a Yoga teacher, while Marcia was of the gentler school, careful not to push the beginner.

As big as life he trooped after us into the house, handily carrying the bags. I got the impression that he had something on his mind. Marcia apparently had the same feeling.

"How did the experiment go?" she asked.

"Splendid," he said, with a pleased smile. "I fooled the polygraph machine completely." He turned to me. "That's a lie detector, you know."

"Louis," Marcia put in, "had been a volunteer at the research center at a mental hospital in Boston."

"I made four dollars and fifty cents accelerating and decelerating my heart beat ninety times," Louis said happily. "They pay you five cents each time you do it, and my doing Yoga made it relatively simple."

"Did they know about your Yoga?" I asked.

"Oh, yes, it was very apparent, as it couldn't have been done otherwise. I would simply relax myself completely to slow the beat. To accelerate it, I would sit still and hold my breath, and it would step up slightly, then by breathing again, deeply, it would accelerate even more. Or I would visualize myself doing hard physical work, chopping wood or pushing boulders, and it would jump up." He had tried still another method. "I would concentrate on my heart, actually feel it beating, get the sound of a drumbeat, and then try to step up the tempo with concentration."

It seemed a hard way to make four dollars and fifty cents.

"That wasn't the idea at all," Louis said. "I was testing myself, as well as showing the scientists what Yoga could do."

"But how did you beat the lie detector?" I asked.

A big grin spread over Louis' face, revealing a healthy set of teeth. "We were supposed to read from a crime story for five minutes; then they questioned us. But remaining detached and relaxed I kept my autonomic nervous responses from changing, and they didn't know what story I had read."

"How did this reflect itself on the machine?"

Louis beamed. "When I gave an incorrect answer, I suppressed my galvanic skin responses, such as sweating, by withdrawing all consciousness from my trunk and limbs and focusing on my forehead. My hands became weightless and lost all sensation. If I wanted to sweat, I would focus on my hands."

Marcia received the tidings casually. "This is just an extreme example of what yogi-like concentration can do for the individual. Through exercising with control, and practicing deep breathing, Louis has built up such detachment that he can isolate virtually any area of his body and make it respond at will."

It seemed incredible that I should ever reach a similar stage.

"Don't worry about it," Marcia said. "Patience and persistence is all that's required. It isn't what's accomplished, but how you go at it."

She showed me to my room, mentioned I would be taking my meals with the family, then hesitated slightly. "I would like very much," she said, "if you gave vegetarianism a try. If it doesn't agree, I won't push it. But I have a feeling that it will help with the exercises, besides improving health and energies, generally."

I wondered what had made the two vegetarians, though they were moderate enough, it seemed, not inflict their views on the children.

"We feel that meat, so near decomposition as it is, adds to the toxic load of the body, producing harmful uremic acid," Marcia said. "Secondly, and most important, I don't like the thought of any living thing being killed because of me. Third, I feel better inwardly and psychic sensitivity is also somewhat heightened."

None of this had ever bothered me. I had not killed an animal since a bullet from a boyhood air rifle had left a feathered creature palpitating in my guilt-stricken hand, and I had not fished since that same boyhood. Yet I felt no compunction about eating meat or fish, since it was an approved way of maintaining strength, and certainly heartening to the taste.

However, in the interest of giving Yoga its all, I shruggingly went along with her suggestion. As far as I knew, fruits, vegetables, cheeses, nuts, etc., had never killed anyone.

Marcia now looked me over. "We won't do much for the first few days," she said.

"I feel fine," I said. "I've been going to the gym, getting prepared, and I'm set to start."

She smiled. "There is the right time, and the right place, that's what Yoga tells you. We will start tomorrow, but slightly, with much breathing and long periods of rest and relaxation. You must learn to relax."

"I feel fine," I said, "perhaps a little tired from the trip up, that's all."

"You have layers of fatigue around you, and we'll try to peel off one layer at a time. Let's not move any faster than you are ready to go."

She hesitated a moment. "I only have one injunction, a sort of cautionary note. The thought will pass through your mind, as you search around for reasons to give up on the exercises, that you are devoting too much time to your body. As we grow older we all spend more time on our bodies, and it's better to spend this time on the exercise mat than in doctors' offices and hospitals."

It seemed unlikely that I would give up because my body was getting younger, when I found the very thought of rejuvenation so immensely refreshing.

"A good night's sleep," I said, "and I'll be ready."

She shook her head. "Believe me, you are more tired than you think.'"

She seemed unduly persistent.

"How can you say that?" I asked.

"Not particularly by the way you look, though your eyes are puffy and a little tired." She looked up quickly. "We will do eye exercises for that." She regarded me speculatively. "But when people are very, very tired, I get a funny feeling here." She poked a finger at her solar plexus. "It's a sort of fluttery feeling." She laughed. "I suppose I have my solar plexus so well developed from Yoga that my subconscious is able to receive and record your own vibratory force—which isn't terribly strong at the present time."

Suddenly, her face became radiant with confidence. "However, you will be all right, in two or three weeks, with proper exercise and diet. Besides," and her eyes twinkled, "as a Taurus, your Uranus transiting through Virgo is in trine to the Sun, and there couldn't be a more auspicious sign, astrologically, for a new venture."

I had almost forgotten that my guru was also an astrologer.

Actually, Marcia was no pioneer; she had only brought Yoga back to Concord. It was old stuff to the hardy transcendentalists immersed in the Bhagavad-Gita and Raja Yoga, without, so far as I know, their finding it necessary to squeeze, stretch, pull, and twist themselves into the pretzel shapes of this Oriental discipline.

Though these distinguished leaders of American letters, generally Unitarian by persuasion, sat around and discussed Yoga's preoccupation with God, destiny, and reincarnation, not once, Marcia conceded, did Emerson say to Thoreau, "Now Henry, a headstand, please." And from his austere mien, I doubt that Amos Bronson Alcott, the father of the author of *Little Women,* would have contorted himself under any circumstances into the postures that American yogis know as the Eagle or the Crow.

Here in Concord, Yoga thought was introduced to America. Thoreau had owned the largest Oriental library in America, the gift of an English admirer, Thomas Cholmondeley, and had loaned the books freely to Emerson and Bronson Alcott. In his *Journals,* Alcott called the "Geeta" "the best of books—containing a wisdom blander and far more sane than that of the Hebrews, whether in the mind of Moses or Him of Nazareth."

Alcott, a brooding mystic, had foreseen the day when the spirit would one day rule the mind, and the mind the body. He saw life with a clearness that stamped him Concord's greatest guru. "The chaos about thee is but the confusion within thee." That was Alcott.

Marcia came by this yogi-like tradition honestly. At seven, she had been struck by mention of the word reincarnation, and couldn't turn it out of her mind. At fourteen, she had read Paul Brunton's *A Search in Secret India,* and dreamed of the day she would settle in the Himalayas—the Abode of the Snow. Growing up, she steeped herself in the transcendentalists. She lived in the libraries where their works were, and in the woods where they drew their inspiration. There were other influences. Before Radcliffe, she attended Concord Academy, locally proclaimed "the third best girls' school in the country." In the family were ministers and artists, preoccupied with the mystic brew of the transcendentalists. Grandfather James Moore was the biographer of America's leading mystic, Andrew Jackson Davis; and his widow Jane, in her seventies, traveled to Duke University to study psychic phenomena. Great-grandfather Newell, pastor of Cambridge's First Church for forty-nine years, knew the transcendentalists by their Chistian names. This was her tradition.

In the woods behind Marcia's home, Thoreau had tramped with his thoughts, and Marcia often had the feeling that the sardonic apostle of solitude was peering over her shoulder, lending encouragement in the search for self-reliance and freedom. They were the same sort of rebels.

"As rebels," Marcia said, "the transcendentalists believed more could be realized with the spirit than the mind —that in the search for life's meaning the intuitive transcended the rational."

Transcendentalism and Yoga were one. "The transcendentalists saw man as having a threefold nature: animal, reasoning, and spiritual, the spiritual transcending all. Consequently no transcendentalist was concerned with making money. It was Gandhi again, only a hundred years earlier."

Concord saw Marcia as an eccentric, just as contemporaries once regarded Thoreau and Alcott. But she was unabashed. "Like Thoreau, I'm trying to keep Concord from becoming suburbia."

It was a losing fight, of course, but roaming the meadows and idling by the trees that nurtured Thoreau and Emerson, Hawthorne and Alcott, I seemed almost aware of their presence. Thoreau and Alcott were the free spirits, Emerson and Hawthorne the conformists standing by a system they sought only to improve. Alcott had gone to jail for a principle, and Thoreau followed. Thoreau was unique in a community that took pride in the unique. "Thoreau," Marcia observed, "was locked up in the local jail for not paying taxes to a government that sanctioned slavery." The jailer offered to pay his tax, which only came to a dollar and a half, but Thoreau was determined to register his protest. Emerson came to visit asking, "What, Henry, are you doing in there?"

Civil Disobedience contemplated Character and Self-Reliance reproachfully. "And what, Waldo, are you doing out there?"

For the many who came to Concord every year to view the birthplace of American freedom, Thoreau was the magnet. For East Indians, the trip to Walden Pond was a pilgrimage. They would stand reverently and meditate at the site where the solitary hut once was. With great tenderness they would add a stone to the mound marking the holy spot, and then ask where the Great Individualist had been incarcerated for freedom's sake. They seemed shocked that he had been jailed but one night for his Civil Disobedience, could actually have left whenever he wanted, and was in no way mistreated or tormented.

"So that is where they kept him?" An Indian lady's face drooped in disappointment. "There were no irons or chains?" She looked up hopefully. "He did not suffer?"

An American guide shook her head. "Oh, no, Henry had the best of everything. He was just being stubborn —a typical Concordian."

The Indian visitor left, mumbling to herself over these inconceivable New Englanders who did not appreciate martyrdom, if only for a day.

There was little to mark where the jail one stood. "Thoreau was not very important in those days," a Concord librarian explained. Behind a clump of buildings in downtown Concord, near the Colonial Inn, I found a marker in a tuft of grass: "Henry David Thoreau was imprisoned one night in jail on this site, July, 1846, for refusing to recognize the right of the state to collect taxes from him."

Ironically, across the way was an imposing monument to the dead of World War I, with a tribute to Civil Obedience from Emerson, the "merchant-genius" of his time:

> So nigh is grandeur to our dust
> So near is God to man,
> When Duty whispers low, *Thou must,*
> The youth replies, *I can.*

This was a sharp contrast to the jolting cry of "Civil Disobedience": "Unjust laws exist: shall we be content to obey them, or shall we endeavor to amend them, and obey them until we have succeeded, or shall we transgress them at once? . . . those who call themselves Abolitionists should at once effectively withdraw their support, both in person and property, from the government of Massachusetts and not wait till they constitute a majority of one. . . . I think that it is enough if they have God on their side, without waiting for that other one. Moreover, any man more right than his neighbors constitutes a majority of one already."

The trail of freedom had beaten out from Concord,

halfway around the world, and then back again. Jailed in South Africa for protesting discrimination, Mohandas Gandhi received the gift of a book from Prime Minister Jan Smuts of the Union of South Africa. In it was Thoreau's essay on "Civil Disobedience." "It was the first flame," Marcia observed, "of the prairie fire that was to sweep through India as passive resistance."

And here at home, in his college dormitory, a generation later, a young Negro named Martin Luther King was "fascinated" by the fiery message of the New Englander who meditated like a yogi while viewing the world with a fierce detachment. It all came out of Walden. And what was Concord without a trip to Walden?

As we parked near Walden Pond, I wondered what the simple recluse would have thought of the trailer camp gawking gracelessly across the road from the wild preserves where he had roughed it two years.

As we hiked through the woods, catching a glimpse of the famed pond through the foliage, all signs pointed to Thoreau's solitary hut.

Why was it that the simple Thoreau, over the years, had transcended his mentor Emerson?

Marcia thought a moment. "Emerson was a brilliant observer of his times. But Thoreau made the one great timeless gesture, experiencing for himself the nature of existence in complete detachment." She smiled. "I don't imagine there's a person today who wouldn't like to crawl into his own little Walden for a while."

Still, Emerson was precious in his own way. "One day," Marcia said, "one of the Millerites, a bygone cult believing in an appointed doomsday, rushed up to Emerson in alarm, warning the world was coming to an end.

"Emerson smiled benignly, not even taking his eyes from his book. 'I can do without it,' he said pleasantly."

We did not walk far before we came to the Thoreau memorial. A plaque announced that the cabin site had been reliably established in 1945, one hundred years after Thoreau, only twenty-eight, had taken to the woods in search of independence.

A heap of small stones rose at the front of the hut site. Like a small boy dropping a penny into a wishing well, I added my rock to the collection.

We roamed on through Walden, scrambling to the end of the pond where Thoreau caught his breakfast and made his morning ablutions. By his solitary campfire he meditated, gaining impressions for *Walden*, his masterpiece.

"In searching for truth," Marcia pointed out, "the true yogi often concentrates on the flame of a candle just as Thoreau gazed on the flames of his campfire. It can be very effective."

Mistily she quoted, "Why should we be in such desperate haste to succeed and in such desperate enterprises? If a man does not keep pace with his companions, perhaps it is because he hears a different drummer. Let him step to the music which he hears, however measured or far away."

It was *Walden*.

Reluctantly, we bid good-bye to the weekday serenity of Walden, passed the trailer camp and piled back into our horseless carriage.

Soon, with Marcia at the wheel, we came to Emerson's house, staidly white and respectable, just as Emerson must have seemed to even his wife and children.

But Emerson had other points. Near the neatly manicured homestead stood Old North Bridge. There the Massachusetts minutemen had hurled back the redcoats. There beyond the bridge—hardly more than a foot's span over a sluggish river—stood a statue to the brave band who had gallantly taken up arms for freedom. On that statue were deathless words, Emerson's words. And they were as much a testimonial to him as the hardy handful who fought there:

> By the rude bridge that arched the flood,
> Their flag to April's breeze unfurled,
> Here once the embattled farmers stood,
> And fired the shot heard round the world.

Leaving the field of glory, we passed the Old Manse, Hawthorne's inspiration for his *Mosses from an Old Manse*. The house was dark and gloomy, like the skeletons the saturnine storyteller exhumed as he skirted the fringe of the transcendentalist movement. He was no Thoreau, or iconoclastic Alcott, who mocked the do-gooders of every age with caustic insight: "The scholars and reformers, if followed into the house, shrink into ordinary if not hideous men."

Alcott's house reflected its master's somber personality and modest materiality. Alcott kept himself in tune with nature, guided by his beloved "Geeta" (the Bhagavad-Gita) in yogi-like communions which conferred sublime self-control and faith in adversity. He was a vegetarian, unwilling, as are other yogis, to take life for his own comfort. "He was so strict," Marcia said with a smile, "that at one period neither he nor his family, including daughter Louisa May, wore leather shoes because the hides came from animals; nor did he use candles, since the wax was made from tallow of whales."

Bronson Alcott founded a school of philosophy, and it provided little more than philosophy to keep body and soul together. But Bronson, beyond poverty, felt a beneficent nature would always provide. And he was rarely wrong.

"In the bitterness of a New England winter," Marcia related, "the Alcotts ran out of firewood. Bronson called the family together one night and asked that they all pray for help to the God that never failed them.

"The next morning, looking out on the snow-covered road, the family saw a huge jumble of tangled firewood. With joyous shouts, Alcott's little women gathered it up. During the night, a cart laden with firewood had collapsed and the carter had gone on empty with his disabled wagon. While it might have seemed an accident to some, to Bronson it was no accident but the hand of God, and he could very well have been right."

Louisa May Alcott's name was posted on the family homestead now, her fame outstripping her father's. As Bronson himself foresaw, he was too much the mystic to be given his due in his time. But the other transcendentalists noted intuitively the greatness in him. Nothing ruffled his yogi-like calm. With William Ellery Channing, Thoreau's bosom friend, he visited the dying Thoreau, then noted placidly, "He is confined to his bed, and has not many days of mortality to give us."

Alcott could not grieve over a friend going to greener pastures. Had not Thoreau said in jail, "I could not help being struck with the foolishness of that institution which treated me as if I were mere flesh and blood and bones to be locked up"? And Alcott believed with him.

The two were sure of their place in an orderly universe. Thus, Thoreau's sardonic humor never left him. Contemplating the flowers, fruits, and notes friends had sent, he remarked wryly, "I should be ashamed to stay in this world after so much had been done to me."

Even at the end, he was pricking platitudes with the old deftness. When a caller said unctuously, "Well, Mr. Thoreau, we must all go," the sick man looked up with a faint smile. "Death," he said, "is as near to you as it is to me."

Henry was uniformly cheerful, for as he told well-wishers, "This is a beautiful world, but I shall see fairer."

"He must have really believed," Marcia said with a faraway look of her own, "for he was in good enough spirits to the end to banter with friends and relatives. When his sister demanded one day, 'Have you made your peace with God?' Thoreau responded mildly, 'I did not know that God and I had quarreled?' "

While I found all this legend entertaining, I couldn't help but wonder why Marcia was exposing me to these faded giants of Concord's golden age.

She had a ready answer. "I just wanted you to know about our real yogis, in the hope that you might get in the proper yogic mood."

Her car stopped in front of a large frame house of General Grant vintage. "Walt Whitman slept in this house," she said, "though I'm not quite sure of the room."

"From the looks of things," I said, glancing at the bleak front, "he may still be sleeping there."

"It is now the home of Mrs. Herbert Buttrick Hosmer, the town historian. She knows more about Concord than anybody in the world."

Mrs. Hosmer was a crusty old lady with a determined jaw, and of undetermined age. She smiled at Marcia as at an old friend, and eyed me darkly.

As I furtively cast about, I noticed that the walls of her living room were highlighted by lugubrious portraits of Emerson and Thoreau.

"They look alike," I observed.

She squinted, comparing the portraits. "That's the prominent New England nose," she said with finality.

She had married into the Hosmer family, one of the Hosmers being a crony of the two essayists, while the Buttricks were descendants of the major who led the minutemen at Old North Bridge.

I took on Mrs. Hosmer rather gingerly. "What do you think of Marcia's Yoga classes?" I asked.

"What is there to think about?" she countered.

"Don't you think it a little unusual to find such devotion to East Indian culture amid all this concentration of Americanism?"

She smiled, perhaps a bit smugly. "We in Concord," she said, "find nothing unusual about being unusual. Emerson read from the Gita until the pages were literally so worn that they dropped out of the book. And if Gandhi had not got hold of Thoreau's 'Civil Disobedience,' India might still be an English province."

Her formidable features softened for a moment as she studied Marcia's cool countenance. "We're still a bunch of rebels, who insist on doing things whichever way strikes us."

Then turning directly to Marcia, she said, "I was quite proud of your mother coming out with that declaration on human rights."

I looked up inquiringly.

"Mother tried to keep herself anonymous," Marcia said, "but her identification with the declaration leaked out." It had been essentially an appeal to the New Englander's sense of fair play. "The declaration says in effect that the people of Concord, in accordance with their tradition, welcome all races and creeds to settle down in their midst."

Some thousands had signed the declaration.

"We don't fuss about causes in Concord," Mrs. Hosmer said. "As Negroes move in, nobody is going to get excited, as long as they don't make a cause of it."

Two emissaries for a Negro major seeking a house had approached a Concord real estate agent, interceding for the officer who was stationed nearby.

The agent had asked Mrs. Hosmer's advice. "I told him to advise the major he didn't need advance agents. He could apply like anybody else."

We walked past the room where the poet Whitman had slept. "That was also William Henry Channing's room," Mrs. Hosmer said, "the nephew of William Ellery Channing. He came one night for dinner with a previous owner, Franklin Sanborn, and he stayed ten years."

In Concord, Whitman was known as the "trancendentalist from New York." He had sent his *Leaves of Grass* to Thoreau, and Emerson and Thoreau had visited him in New York. The three felt much in common.

"For one thing," Marcia said, "they all believed in reincarnation."

My eyebrows raised, and Marcia quoted softly from Whitman's "Song of Myself":

> And as to you Life I reckon you are
> the leavings of many deaths,
> (No doubt I have died myself ten thousand
> times before.)

Emerson a reincarnationist? His steady eye saw through

all sham. Marcia closed her eyes, gently reciting from
memory:

> We are driven by instinct to have innumerable
> experiences which are of no visible value,
> and we may revolve through many lives before
> we shall assimilate or exhaust them.

And in every breath of Thoreau was implicit faith that
he would live again as he had before: "I lived in Judea
eighteen hundred years ago, but I never knew there was
such a one as Christ among my contemporaries. . . . But
Hawthorne I remember as one with whom I sauntered in
old heroic times."

As for myself, even after reliving a previous century
with Mrs. Hosmer, I was still very much in this one as
we pulled up to Marcia's modern house. The names on
the mailbox were Roof-Acker. "We're polynomic," Marcia
explained with a laugh. "The children are Roof, Louis is
Acker, and everybody knows me so well as Marcia Moore
that I don't have to hang up a sign."

Clambering out of the Moore-Acker-Roof car, we could
see Louis straining against a huge boulder back of the
house. He looked so big and strong that I could not
visualize even a two-ton boulder standing up to him. "I'm
moving it out with the other boulders to form a boundary
for the outdoor ashram," he said, looking up. Marcia
smiled indulgently.

He seemed a little vague. "I'm really not trying to lift
it. I can't lift more than three hundred pounds or so, but
I can jar it loose and roll it to where I want it."

He looked up, the sun catching his short-cropped red
hair, and cocked an appraising eye at the sky. He stood
motionless for a while, staring directly overhead. All I
could see was blue sky and a cluster of white clouds.

Yet Louis seemed to be straining, as though still locked
in mortal combat with a boulder. His breathing came in
sharp intakes right down to the diaphragm and he was
clearly oblivious of everything but the point in the sky
on which his eyes were trained.

"What is he trying to do?" I asked.

Marcia pointed to a cottonball cloud forming the lower
part of a triangle with two similar clouds. "He's trying to
make that cloud disappear."

"Trying to what?" I thought I had misunderstood.

"Trying to make that cloud disappear," she repeated
casually.

I broke in on Louis' concentration. "Are you trying to say that you can make a cloud disappear by looking at it?"

He turned a mild look on me. "Oh, yes, pick out any cloud, of the cumulus, snowball type, and I'll make it dissolve."

I was beginning to think somebody should see a doctor.

"I've seen clairvoyants read people's minds, and soothsayers predict the future, without understanding how they managed it," I said, "but this is really out of this world."

"Pick out your cloud," Louis said.

"It probably would disappear anyway," I said.

He shrugged. "I'll make it go away in five minutes or less, and the other clouds nearby will still be there." He pointed to an overhead cluster; I selected the cloud at the upper right, a heavy powder-puff type.

"How do you propose to do it—with magic?" I asked.

He shook his head. "By concentration. I will produce an energy force which will create enough heat to vaporize the cloud."

The cloud was several thousand feet in the sky, for all practical purposes miles away. But this didn't faze Louis.

He reared up his head, shaded his eyes for a moment from the sun, and then began to glare. It was like watching an internal combustion engine start up. I thought his eyes would pop from his head and his frame come apart at the joints. His whole body was a-quiver with rapt concentration.

My eyes returned to the cloud. I saw a pocket form at one edge, the edges began to fade, and then the center became filmy and transparent. It was rapidly losing substance. I looked at a watch. Only two minutes had passed.

But Marcia didn't seem impressed. "You'd better hurry, Louis, or you'll be late for your astronomy class."

Louis held up two fingers.

"He can do this any time," she explained. "I don't want him late for his class."

Almost as she spoke, the last filaments of cloud evaporated into thin air. Louis looked up with a smile, and then consulted his watch. "Four minutes," he said quietly.

I shook my head. "That cloud might have been ready to disappear anyway."

He pointed to the sky. "The other clouds in the cluster are still there. But"—he shrugged—"why don't you pick out the cloud, or clouds, and we'll conduct an experiment any time you say?"

Marcia was growing impatient. "Fine," she said, "but you better be off for school. Your class will be waiting."

And so we saved it for another day. In Yoga one learns there is no hurry; the desired end will fall to the deserving.

It was a week before Louis had another crack at the clouds. Some days the skies were completely overcast, but these were not Louis' kind of clouds. "The cumulus, dissolving type are invariably in a blue sky," he reminded me. He did not always have enough power for the solid gray masses.

The Roof children were oddly unimpressed by their youthful stepfather's accomplishment. "I made a face at a cloud the other day," Chris jeered, "and it went away."

Somebody else pointed out that Louis had dissolved three clouds in a cluster of ten, ticking them off consecutively while the others hung on or even grew.

"What do you think of that?" Chris was asked.

"It's just an optical illusion," he said.

"That's something too," a defender of Louis rejoined.

But Louis treated skepticism with the complacency of a man sure of his strength.

As a student at tiny Windham College, in Putney, Vermont, he had also drawn taunts as he wandered the moors dissolving clouds. But with success had come acceptance. "Pretty soon," he recalled, "I had practically the whole student body doing it." Eventually, as the students concentrated noticeably less on books than clouds, the cloud-breaking came to the attention of the faculty. "Seeing all the students standing on the roofs, straining at the clouds, they thought they had rocks in their heads." Louis laughed. "But they soon found out."

"That they had rocks?"

"No, that you can make clouds disappear with the proper energy force."

The day chosen for the second test was ideal except for scattered gusts. We all trotted down to an open field a mile from the Roof-Acker home, so as to be on neutral soil and get away from the distractions of the children.

A few members of the Sunday Yoga class were enlisted as witnesses: Lester Hinds, a retired British Army officer, Nancy Fleisher, an attractive sophomore at Boston University, and electronics scientist Bill Mercer, who questioned the authenticity of an experiment that couldn't be duplicated at will.

The experiment took place opposite a large white house with BRAMHALL on the mailbox; a middle-aged man skipping a power mower over the lawn was the only outsider in sight.

We had agreed to pick out clouds at random, deciding among ourselves, Louis excluded, on the specific cloud to come under attack.

"Any one you like," said Louis. "It doesn't matter to me."

We finally chose a big cloud, white and puffy, just above the horizon, another larger cloud over it. Louis went directly into action, arms akimbo, face lifted to the cloud. He appeared to be concentrating intently, his face purpling with the effort, but the cloud remained unaffected. In fact, it seemed to be getting larger as it merged with the larger cloud above.

Louis shook his head in vexation. "It's that darn wind," he said. "Just as I have a field force of energy worked up in a particular spot, the wind comes along and moves the cloud away from the force."

Nancy Fleisher leaned over and murmured, "Is he serious?"

"Watch and see," I said.

Louis waited for the wind to subside, and then ran off three small clouds in a row. The longest took five minutes to dispose of.

Nancy's eyes bulged. "He can really do it," she whispered. "Now I've seen everything."

"It's not scientific," Bill Mercer observed aloud, "unless he does it every time."

"I admit I missed that once," Louis said apologetically, "but the wind creates problems. Even in Washington, where I first learned about clouds, I had trouble with the wind. But I compensate by concentrating all the more. Besides, I always need a little time to warm up."

Bill Mercer, looking up, indicated two heavy clouds forming almost directly overhead. "How about them, Louis?" he said, with a trace of mockery.

Louis' jaw jutted out. "All right," he said, "it's a rough one but I'll do it."

"Well, you just can't pick and choose your own clouds," Bill Mercer said.

A small cloud—of vexation—darkened Louis' face. "I'm not trying to pick my own clouds; I just pointed out that the wind makes it difficult, and you've picked on two clouds that the wind is knocking together in a big mass, and they may keep moving, that's all."

"We're waiting, Louis," Bill Mercer said stolidly.

Louis took a deep breath, ran forward a few steps into the open field, then drew back a couple of strides, apparently trying to get a better bead on the clouds which had merged and now looked even more formidable.

"It's gotten bigger," Mercer called out.

"I know it," Louis said testily. He was braced for a major effort. His head and neck were arched, his hands laced together behind his back, his buttocks tight with the tension of deep breathing. Two or three witnesses giggled.

Without turning, Louis cried, "Will you please stop that noise. How can I concentrate?"

Bill Mercer laughed. "How about that yogi-like detachment we hear so much about?"

"Please be quiet, all," Louis shot back, "you only make it more difficult."

He was now breathing quite heavily, his face the color of a Concord grape.

"You may as well give up, Louis," I said, "it's just a bad day."

He craned his neck around. "Maybe I should try another cloud. These clouds just don't seem to respond in the wind."

Bill Mercer threw up his hands. "If some do and some don't, then you're not doing anything to them; they're doing whatever they want to do."

"All right," Louis said, "I'll get rid of it; just be quiet, please."

He stood on his toes, in a yogi-like balance, and began breathing deeply from the diaphragm in an effort to send up a head of pranic energy.

By now, other clouds had formed in the area of Louis' target and so we had something to compare with.

Louis puffed a full minute, still on his toes, facing the open field across from the Bramhalls', when lo and behold, a gap formed suddenly in the center of the big cloud. Then the edges began to melt away, and in another minute the cloud had broken up into fragments. In three minutes more, by Bill Mercer's watch, the fragments had vanished.

Louis turned around apologetically. "Sorry I took so long," he said, "but that wind plays all kinds of tricks."

Nancy's jaw dropped. "I would never have believed it," she said, "never in the world."

The cluster of clouds which had surrounded the dissolved cloud was still intact.

But I still had to be convinced, even though the scholars

and scientists were beginning to postulate that man, like the atmosphere, had a magnetic field of his own, and was a potential dynamo.

As I pondered, a middle-aged woman crossing the Bramhall lawn called over good-naturedly, "Could you tell me what you people are looking at?"

"That gentleman"—I pointed at Louis—"is dissolving clouds."

The woman's face dropped. "Is that all?" she said. "I do that every afternoon just lying out in the sun."

The next three or four weeks was great cloud-dissolving weather. The air was cool, and blue skies were almost constantly afloat with puffy white clouds. The papers lamented the singular lack of rain, and the neighbors talked of nothing but the drought. It was the worst in remembered history. But Louis mooned around the house with a long face. He was brooding over his last performance. "I'm not going to feel satisfied until I've run off ten clouds in a row," he said. "That should take care of the skeptics."

Three days later, examining the sky, he suggested a return engagement in the open field.

"Why not in the back yard?" I said.

"The trees get in the way."

So we again adjourned to the meadow opposite the Bramhalls'. I was beginning to think of them as old friends.

"I'll warm up with a few small ones," Louis said. "That was my mistake last time; I took the big ones right off."

In a few minutes he had dissolved four clouds. Scanning the sky, he pointed to a fifth, just over the horizon.

"Getting rid of that one won't prove anything," I said. "There's no cloud nearby to compare it with."

Louis was agreeable. "Whatever you say."

I turned to the opposite sky and spotted a big cloud that looked ideal for an acid test. There were three or four other clouds close by, and then great spaces of azure blue.

Louis drew himself up to his full height, took a deep breath, and braced himself for the test. His face was grave but relaxed as he put his gaze on target. It was the old story of man versus nature.

For a minute or two, it seemed as though Louis would make short work of the cloud. Then, suddenly, the wind came up, whipping through the trees and sending clouds scudding across the sky. As Cloud Five appeared about to join its neighbors, Louis began rubbing his eyes. "This is not an excuse," he said stiffly, "but something blew in my eye, and it makes me blink." He turned to me appealingly. "When I blink, the force of concentration is obviously interrupted."

Looking up, I saw that Number Five had now merged with another cloud.

"I don't think I can do anything with it," Louis said. He was heaving heavily, drawing the oxygen down to the bottom of his lungs, then sending it charging through his body.

"It looks like Yoga is out of tune with nature today," I said drily.

"It's not exactly ideal, particularly when you have to keep blinking." He sounded the least cranky.

"There's nothing to it, unless you can repeat it at will," I said, remembering Bill Mercer.

"All right," said Louis, "I'll get rid of it." His chin jutted out, his jaw clamped down, and he wiped his eye. "Just watch."

For thirty seconds nothing happened, and then, amazingly, blue patches began to appear in the giant cloud. It began to fade before my eyes. Soon there was no trace of it in the sky. Louis, jubilant, gave a cry of triumph and looked at his watch. "Four minutes."

I turned my head to examine the cloud which he had originally wanted to dissolve. The sky was completely blue to the west. There was no sign of any cloud. It had dissolved by itself.

That finished the cloud-breaking for the day, and we went home to read of the drought again.

That evening, a neighbor, Wellesley-bred Frannie Fripp, dropped by for a brief chat.

"It had better start raining soon," she told Marcia, "or everything will dry up. I can't ever remember a drought like it at this time of the year."

She turned to me politely. "How is everything coming along?"

"Fine," I said, "we've been dissolving clouds."

"Dissolving clouds?" Her pretty nose wrinkled in bewilderment.

"Louis stares at the clouds a while and breaks them up with his energy force."

Frannie's face grew suddenly solemn. "So that's what's doing it," she said, her voice rising with indignation. "Well, you better tell Louis to start concentrating on rain, and leave those clouds alone. This drought has gone on long enough."

Marcia brought out the scales.

"Let's weigh you first," she said, "and we'll check each week."

I scaled in at 171 pounds, height six feet one. She tested the scales herself—five three, 105 pounds.

"They're right," she said, with satisfaction.

We stood facing each other on mats, in the ashram-like big room with a picture-window view of the woods where Thoreau and Emerson often strolled, discussing the gifts of the spirit.

"One woman complained recently," Marcia said, "that we pay too much attention to the body." She lifted her eyebrows. "I told her that we pay all this attention to the body in the beginning so that we can forget about the body later."

She turned her attention to me. "We will do a few limbering exercises, so I can get a clearer idea of your flexibility or lack of it, and gauge about how much your body will take."

She gave me a sharp glance. "You are in good shape for your age, but we want you in good shape, period. And once in shape, it will be easy to maintain at home."

"Let's go," I said.

"Breathing, as I told you, is of the utmost importance. You are to consider oxygen more important than food. The body can survive without food for thirty days, without oxygen for hardly four minutes."

And so we spent the first few minutes breathing. "Breathe in and out through the nose, not using the mouth at all. Bring the air all the way down to the diaphragm, pushing the abdomen out with each intake of air. Pull your stomach in tightly, but gradually, breathing out."

This was the reverse, of course, of the normal breathing I had grown accustomed to over the years. It was a little difficult getting used to the idea of not sucking in the stomach—or gut—with each deep breath.

"The lungs are pear-shaped," Marcia pointed out, "and they have greater capacity at the bottom of the sort of triangle they form. Most people breathe shallowly, using the upper narrow portion of the lungs, and don't get enough air to give the blood the oxygen it needs for the stress of living."

Yoga breathing was usually more difficult for women than men in the beginning. "All their lives," Marcia observed, "girls have been told to tuck their tummies in; so the air never gets down to their lower lungs." Girdles, cinches, pantywaists, all contributed to generally ineffective breathing by the female.

All of Marcia's "ladies" worked in loose clothing, fatigue slacks, leotards, or shorts.

I was a bit surprised that a course as spectacular as Yoga should stress rather less than sensational breathing hints. But the phrase "breath of life," as Marcia put it, was no happenstance.

"Breathing will be important in itself, and will be an important part of all exercises. Generally, we shall breathe in coming up, out going down, whether moving arm, leg, neck, or waist. And we shall hold the breath in some exercises, for an extra surge of oxygen."

And so I was introduced to prana, a word untranslatable in the English, but invoking a vital energy force induced by deep breathing.

Marcia breathed in and out to show me how the exercise should be performed. "I live on oxygen myself," she said; "it is my principal food."

She was slim and supple, yet strong, easily doing exercises that left me faltering, frustrated, and muttering angrily to myself.

She laughed at my annoyance in failing to perform even the simplest exercise properly.

"Never be impatient, never discouraged, always concentrate, always realize that whatever you do is more than you did a week ago, a month ago, or even yesterday. It is progress we are concerned with."

That first week was orientation week, with an accent on limbering and the simpler postures or asanas. "After a while," Marcia said, "we can go right into the postures, but I'm not taking any chances with those tired muscles right now."

We were to concern ourselves with only a dozen postures and conditioning exercises in the beginning. "They will get at every part of your body," Marcia observed, "and it's easier for the beginner to remember a few postures, and get them down correctly. Later, to avoid monotony, we vary the postures."

The first instructions were: "Lie on your back, pull knees up to chest, clasp hands under the knees, and gently rock back and forth as though your back were the bottom of a rocker, trying to reach an agreeable rhythm." This was a simple routine—the rock 'n' roll—designed to limber the back for the more basic postures.

It seemed easy as Marcia did it, and it was easy, but, unfortunately, rocking back on my top vertebra a little too enthusiastically, I was brought up with a spurt of pain.

"What's up?" Marcia said.

"My neck—an old whiplash," I said, trying to be casual.

She tested the tender area with her fingers. "You're unusually tense," she said, "we'll have to do a few things to loosen neck and shoulders. We'll do the head rolls now. Normally, we wait until after the shoulder or headstand." She again ran her fingers over my neck. "It's an odd thing, people after forty are invariably round-shouldered, reflecting the burdens of life, and unless they do something about it they'll soon have the undulating spine of a snake."

The head roll was not quite as drastic as Louis the Sixteenth's.

"Imagine your neck a shiny stainless-steel ball bearing," Marcia said, "with no sand or gritty particles to disturb the motion."

She watched me closely. "Let your head droop forward, falling of its own weight, and hold a moment—don't hurry —gently roll to the right. The head hangs sideways, but you keep facing forward, and continue the roll until the head rests back over the shoulders without strain, and then on to the front and reverse."

This was to be done three times.

As I moved my neck, visualizing that ball bearing, there was a tiny grinding sound in the joints of the neck.

"That's only ossification," Marcia said, "it will break up as you exercise. But go slowly," she cautioned, "there's never need for speed. All of Yoga teaches you to act deliberately, with control."

The gravelly, gritty sound was customary, Marcia observed, even among the youthful, but even students in the forties and fifties can get rid of this by-product of aging in a few months. "Just imagine a drop of oil on that ball bearing of yours as you roll your neck."

My own ball bearing was quite tender at the point of the whiplash injury and Marcia suggested my clasping the side of my neck for additional support the first few days of the neck rolls. "We do this when the neck is particularly weak."

And what was the value of all this rolling?

"Besides providing the neck beautiful, removir

tale circles and wrinkles—purely a side effect in Yoga—it releases the tension in the restricted area through which all blood and nerve impulses must flow to the brain. It also tends to correct any small misalignments in the upper vertebrae, permitting nature to make her adjustments naturally.

"And stretching," Marcia pointed out, "is innately tranquilizing."

Breathing was always via the nose. "Yogi Vithaldas says that the mouth is for eating and kissing, the nose for breathing." Marcia smiled.

Many of the limbering exercises were familiar. I had either done them, or seen them done, in gyms. They were old staples, adapted from the 840,000 different exercises the yogis had evolved over the centuries.

In the Pump conditioner, lying flat, I pulled up a leg, stretching it to the sky, yet keeping my back to the floor, breathing in as the leg came up, out as it went down.

All was done slowly, three times with each leg.

"Newcomers," Marcia said, "tend to jerk the leg up by the knee. It takes several sessions before even this simple exercise can be done slowly enough, ten seconds up and ten down."

The combination of exercises was not important, so long as all areas of the body were affected. For Yoga was not essentially a series of exercises, but a principle of exercise, involving concentration, superstretching, and deliberately controlled movements—all visualized by the mind.

"That's what makes Yoga so adaptable to every age."

I was not so sure that the pupil was as adaptable.

But Marcia was optimistic. "We're learning about you with every exercise," she said, "and with self-knowledge comes an awakening, as to both our limits and our potentials. You must know where you are, before you know where you are going."

She smiled. "These first limbering exercises are not only important in loosening the beginner, but they tell the teacher how fast or slow to proceed."

Some of these exercises were similar to calisthenics offered by Harold J. Reilly in his health club in Rockefeller
woven together by Marcia they seemed
greater design. Unlike calisthenics, repeti-
ly with the postures, were not indicative
of apprenticeship. "Once you got a pos-
ectly," Marcia observed, "repetitions be-

come meaningless. We repeat in the beginning only to achieve perfect control. And once a holding exercise, like the shoulder stand, is done perfectly, we know that we have established the desired mental rapport, and repetition would only be depleting. Some mobile exercises may be repeated, but they are done easily and have the added purpose of breath control."

Our opening major posture was the so-called Sun exercise, Suryanamaskar, the Hindu salute to the sun. It began with standing erect, hands folded together, legs close, and facing the sun.

It was a warm-up in itself, for it involved a dozen different movements. I started raising the arms way back over the head and stretching, breathing in deeply; then bending forward and touching the toes, releasing the breath as I did so. Then, forward on one knee, chest, neck, and head tilted upward—toward the sun, of course—again stretching. As I was hoping the exercise was over, came the signal to lie flat, touching feet, knees, chest, and forehead to the mat, but keeping the hips arched upward. Then I flattened out completely, and brought head and chest up. Then—there seemed no end to this one exercise—Marcia ordered me up halfway, feet and palms flat, body hunched up in a pyramid effect, then scrunching forward on the other knee, bringing the feet together between the hands, and finally erect again, arms back over the head, breathing deeply.

It was all as complicated as it sounds, and I couldn't see myself doing it in a million years. "How can I do an exercise when I can't even remember it?" I asked.

We made a few more efforts, all futile, and then Marcia came to a decision. "We'll put Suryanamaskar away for a while, then come back to it later, when the coordination between mind and body has improved. You will be surprised one day that you ever thought this exercise difficult, but meanwhile I don't want to waste time and energy with things you can't begin to do."

"I'll never learn that one," I said.

Marcia smiled. "I predict that in a few weeks you will consider it elementary.

Next, in our cycle of postures, came the shoulder stand, known by the Hindus as Sarvangasana; in Sanskrit, "Good for all of you."

My legs dangled and my lower back sagged, even as I supported it with my hands, but at least I could make a start, and as my chin pressed into the hollow of my throat, I was inspired by the thought of all this was doing for thyroid and my creative libido.

From the shoulder stand, by thrusting first one leg, then the other, stiff-kneed over my head, I was ready for the Plough.

As I brought my legs back over my head, Marcia enjoined: "Stretch, gradually, easily, and try to bring your toes down to the mat."

I missed by a foot, even bending my knees. "Nobody can do that," I wheezed.

She laughed out loud. "A child can, and you will in time."

As well as churning up the glands, and stretching the back from the sacrolumbar area to the top cervical vertebra, the Plough had a tightening effect on the buttocks, and reputedly toned up the male prostate.

For every forward sequence, there was a compensating backward exercise. "It's all part of Yoga's equalization," Marcia explained. "After the forward bend, there's the backward bend, and muscles strained in one direction are stretched back to their normal relaxed status."

The forward bend was done from a sitting position, legs outstretched, spine straight.

"Bend one leg, fit the heel into the crotch, then stretch both hands toward the toe of the extended leg." I could only touch the shinbone on one side, and then, changing legs, could barely grasp the other ankle. Marcia was undisturbed. "One side is always different than the other, because so many activities make us one-sided—bowling, tennis, golf—the resulting unbalance makes it easier to throw out muscles and tendons. But Yoga, every day, will equalize things."

As I stretched vainly for the toes, Marcia stressed that the forward pull should come from the lower spine and that I should visualize every vertebra bending forward pliantly. "Think about it hard enough, and they will do the work for you."

Marcia seemed to ask the impossible.

"Stretch, hold the toe, and relax; maintain the position with easeful exertion."

In time, the teacher assured me, the muscles will respond to this message from the brain; controlled relaxation will be as easy as stretching.

"If you can learn to relax under this kind of stress, you

will relax under any stress brought about by external circumstances."

This "toe-touching" was to be done two or three times for the first few days, and then as I gained control, working slowly, I would do it but once.

And then, the compensating back bend.

"Double your knees under you and sit back on heels, spreading the heels slightly with toes together for greater comfort."

Try as I might to be comfortable, squatting on my heels grated painfully on my ankles.

"Slip back from that position on one elbow," Marcia said. "We'll try to work into this back bend."

I got one elbow back, but I couldn't slide back on the other without losing my balance.

Having watched classmates older than myself slip into the back bend with ease, I was rather irked at my own clumsiness. "What's wrong with me?" I asked, crossly.

"Your back and ankles are stiff that's all, but they'll loosen up; we'll just keep trying, until one day, it will suddenly happen."

I doubted, silently.

Next came a sequence—the Cobra, Locust, and Bow.

In the Cobra, one lay flat like a snake and slowly raised first the head, then neck, chest, and stomach, feeling the undulating rise of each vertebra, and arching the head and eyes toward the sky as a snake would its hood. "Come down just as slowly, reversing the process, and bring the stomach, chest, and face down in that order," Marcia said.

The Cobra not only develops back and neck, but strengthens the abdominal muscles and gives the internal organs, such as the liver, a stimulating massage. "It is particularly good for women," Marcia pointed out, "since it tones up the uterus and ovaries, and the whole reproductive tract."

Marcia thought for a moment. "Many so-called female complaints would be avoided if the average woman in her thirties and forties would do just the Cobra, shoulder stand, and the forward and backward bend every day. They really wouldn't have to do much else, execept a few limbering exercises."

The Locust was done flat on the stomach. It was relatively easy. One leg was raised, than another, simulating the awkward gesture of the grasshopper. Pressure was exerted, gradually bringing the leg up as far as possible and holding it for a couple of seconds.

Then came perhaps the only deliberately convulsive movement in Yoga. "With the hands clenched under the groin, raise both legs with a sudden upward thrust," Marcia said.

I was barely able to get both legs off the mat, three inches at most.

"If you are doing this exercise correctly," Marcia said, "your face should become red from the increased circulation."

Marcia's legs were tilted upward at practically a vertical angle. "When Louis does the Locust," she said, "his face turns purple."

It had helped many students remarkably, considering its simplicity. "It is especially good," Marcia said, "for women with bunchy varicose veins and other circulatory problems." One middle-aged woman had come to her following surgery for hardening of the arteries. She was disciplined enough to give up smoking and drinking at her doctor's orders, and in a few weeks she was sufficiently disciplined to do the headstand. But the Locust was most strikingly beneficial. "Her doctor," Marcia said, "encouraged her to keep at it, particularly the Locust."

I liked the Bow, though I found it quite impossible at first. Still flat on the stomach, I reached back and grabbed my widespread ankles, trying to lift my knees from the mat by the pressure of my outstretched arms.

It took me three or four days to get the knack of this exercise. "Keep the elbows straight," Marcia said, "imagine your arms as the string of the bow, and the body the wood."

That did it, keeping my arms taut from shoulder to wrist.

"It's great for the back and the abdominal muscles," Marcia said, "and good for elimination, indigestion, gas, rheumatism, reducing, and bodily grace."

The way of holding the body was very important in all Yoga exercises.

"Sitting up even, keep the spine straight without noticeable exertion, as this permits the energy to flow to various areas with greater freedom. After concentrating a while, your posture will be correct without your thinking about it."

"How about the headstand?" I asked, inflated by my halfway successful shoulder stand.

"Not until the third or fourth lesson will we try that," she said. "It is a very dramatic accomplishment, besides being good for people who use their brain, but I want to make sure that your neck and shoulder muscles are strong enough to withstand strains from doing the exercise improperly."

We were still in the testing stage, and Marcia directed me to stand on one foot, meanwhile bending the other leg up behind me, and holding the foot. This little exercise is known as the Stork.

It seemed easy as she did it, but I found myself struggling to keep my balance. "You're not supposed to be doing a dance," she drawled good-humoredly, "but standing still."

"Why is it so difficult," I asked, "when it looks so easy?" I had just dropped my upraised foot to avoid falling altogether.

"Lack of motor nerve coordination," she said, "and that is what we are striving for—control of the motor nervous system, and eventually the autonomic nervous system, by which advanced yogis control their breathing rate and even their heartbeat."

She had me repeat the exercise. "With enough concentration, the nervous system will finally obey the signal from the brain, and you will be able to stand still on one leg—and close your eyes at the same time."

I tried it closing my eyes, after I had finally balanced for a few seconds with my eyes open. My foot immediately came down to the floor. It was like trying to walk in the dark.

"This demonstrates," Marcia said, "something that the old Hindu masters have known for five thousand years: that we not only use the brain to think with, but the whole spinal cord, and every nerve."

We had worked for nearly an hour, with long pauses between exercises. Many of the exercises were performed only two or three times, as Marcia guarded against my overdoing. During the longer relaxation periods, lying down, her voice, soft as the Concord breeze, soothed my restless mind and somewhat strained muscles.

Marcia believed in accenting the positive. The Indian gurus, for instance, knew the resting prone position as the Corpse. Marcia called it the Sponge, since a corpse was hardly an inspiring name.

"Picture yourself on a beach, with the golden sun seeping through your pores with its warm, healing rays. Imagine the sun soothing, bathing each tired muscle, each straining nerve, with its warm radiance."

The rest periods were important. "You not only absorb oxygen, but you permit your subconscious to assimilate the exercises you have just performed. Actually, it's a form of hyponosis, and you become both hypnotist and subject after a while, or your own analyst, if you're psychiatrically minded. To be effective, every posture must be accompanied by mental concentration, visualization, and constant autosuggestion, which will reach the subconscious in due time, opening up new channels of communication." She smiled. "That is why it really doesn't matter at first if you succeed in doing the exercise, as long as your concentration is complete. It's method that counts."

I was thinking of the Suryanamaskar. "But some of these postures are so complex," I protested, again.

She laughed. "That's one of the values: you have to concentrate or you can't do most of these exercises—like the Twist, for instance."

In this exercise, by some effort, I had managed in a sitting position to lace my legs together, and then turning from the waist, extend an arm over the opposite shoulder.

Had I thought of anything but my objective, my arms and legs would have become a hopeless tangle.

Most Yoga exercises had a manifold purpose. The so-called topsy-turvy exercises—the headstand and the shoulder stand—were known as the great rejuvenators, not only for their effect on the sex glands but because they helped restore a natural balance throughout the body.

"In old age," Marcia pointed out, "the supply of blood to the brain is drastically reduced, frequently resulting in weakened memory and the inability to concentrate." She frowned. "Man hasn't adjusted completely to the evolutionary change of standing erect on two legs, instead of crawling on all fours—and so his sinuses don't automatically drain as they once did, nor does he normally get the reverse flow to his brain."

There were many oldsters, from fifty-five to seventy-five years old, in her classes, all doing the shoulder stand, if not the more difficult headstand. "With older people, we have to be careful starting them off, as a sudden surge of blood to the small capillaries of the brain might do more harm than good. So we do less drastic things at first, getting them to bend their heads between their legs from a sitting position, or do the neck rolls, which permit them to rotate their heads easily with the help of gravity. And then, if they respond comfortably, we take them into the shoulder stand."

In my first shoulder stands, I had noticed a certain nausea—apparently from an unaccustomed rush of blood to the head.

"This passes in two or three weeks," Marcia said. "The system is merely registering its first small protest at being diverted from its normal aging pattern."

Be that as it may, I felt very conscious of age that first week, as every muscle in my body—including some I hadn't realized owning—registered a dull indignation.

Maybe I was too old a dog to be learning new tricks?

"If I was a psychiatrist," Marcia observed, "I'd say that you were blocking. Just remember, in the interest of maintaining your status quo you will seize all pretexts to give up—but eventually, as you learn to relax, these misgivings will vanish."

For Marcia, the topsy-turvy exercises were an instant redistributor. Some mornings, when rushed for time, the headstands and shoulder stands were all she did—three or four minutes of each.

"They pull everything into place," she said, "head, neck, stomach, and legs." They were almost specifics for body symmetry.

With Yoga, she had added two inches above the waist and dropped two inches below. "In itself, this might not be particularly impressive, but for the fact that I'm reversing a family tendency. Mother and grandmother had a disposition to be heavier through the lower body, and so does my daughter, but this will rectify itself, as it did with me, as she becomes interested in Yoga."

In many cases underweight people gained both in muscle and strength, and poundage melted off the overweights. It was apparently never too late to profit. Mrs. Edna Karmazine, a Brookline, Massachusetts, grandmother, dropped some twenty pounds, and Mrs. Celia Gavin of Portsmouth, New Hampshire, widow of a railroad tycoon, shed fifteen pounds. Marcia assigned the credit to newly activated thyroids.

Though older than myself, in her mid-fifties, Mrs. Gavin did a commendable shoulder stand, along with the dozen or so exercises that Marcia thought sufficient for the yogis of the Western world. And then, apparently renewed, Mrs. Gavin had gone trudging, with the light tread of a teen-ager, through the woods back of the Concord ashram.

"If we had been doing calisthenics," Marcia pointed

out, "all these senior citizens, as my husband Louis calls
them, would be exhausted by now, their brows flushed and
their pulses palpitating. But our slow rhythmical movements build up rather than deplete oxygen reserves—and
minimize the risk of injury inherent in spasmodic motions."

She laughed. "With all my suppleness from Yoga, I
still twisted my back once doing cartwheels in a gym. The
trouble with calisthenics, particularly for the seniors—and
we all start becoming senior at thirty—is that once a swift
motion is started, it usually can't be stopped, passing right
through the danger signal of pain."

Mostly I exercised as a class of one, but occasionally
during the week, and on Sundays, when students like Mrs.
Gavin turned up at the house, I worked out alongside
men and women of every age from sixteen through the
seventies.

It was a little nettling at first to see females in my own
age bracket do so much more than myself. But Marcia
saw only the good side of this.

"If they can do it, surely you can."

Ironically, the last exercise of the day was a usual first
in calisthenics. We reached up, stretching, inhaling deeply,
and then down, grabbing the ankles, holding as we released
our breath. "It serves to put you back on your feet, which
is a good windup, suggestively."

We followed with some deep breathing from the diaphragm, pushing out as we breathed in through the nose,
contracting the stomach, and rolling the breath up and out
—through the nose.

"We will get into alternate breathing after a while,
when your lungs are used to being filled to capacity, instead of one-fifth of capacity as they are during normal
breathing," Marcia said.

As we finished our first sessions, I expressed disappointment at not having performed with greater facility.
"I thought that going to a gym intermittently over the
years would have helped me."

"It's a different thing, and you'll find it more rewarding
and less depleting before long."

She surveyed me appraisingly in my T-shirt and trunks.
"You are at an age where you can live twenty-five or
thirty more productive years, or go as most Americans do,
from a flabby middle age into a doddering old age."

She thought a moment. "The greatest tragedy in the
country today is the decline of the American male in the
forties and the fifties. Though he should be in his prime,

he has already started to give up. He is bogged down with kids in school; the mortgage that never quite gets paid up, and a wife of whom he is beginning to tire, as she gets fatter and more fatuous every day. And he knows in his heart that this is what it's always going to be. That is the real killer."

But women, those not fat or fatuous, were more prone to help themselves. Marcia taught a group of upper middle-class fortyish housewives at her Yoga Center in Boston; their husbands had turned up out of curiosity, but once they saw the ease with which their wives did the exercises they seemed to lose interest. Most had sedentary office jobs, and felt they would lose standing by not being able to compete with the weaker sex in the physical sphere. "They didn't realize, of course, that Yoga is noncompetitive, and that in time, anyway, they would be doing as well, if not better."

Marcia sighed. "And so they went back to their old way of living—and dying."

I couldn't understand why women should want to do more about body and mind than men.

Marcia had the answer. "This is the package they've been selling all their lives, and they don't like to see the wrapping wrinkled and spoiled."

As the month of May drew on, the sun thawing the frosty New England air, the Yoga sessions were transferred to the outdoor ashram back of the house.

But we were not alone. The whole earth seemed trembling with new life—insect life—and everything that crawled, flew, or made one itch seemed determined to take part in the exercises.

"How can anybody concentrate?" I gasped one day, dusting some small flies out of my eyes, as a whole school of red ants insisted on crawling up my trunks.

"We'll have to do something," Marcia agreed. "I admit these bugs call for a bit more detachment than you're up to."

Only Louis, wheeling his huge stones around the glade, appeared to be unmoved by the bugs. As he lovingly rocked a giant boulder into a hollow, Marcia called out, "Louis, don't you think we'd better do something about these bugs?"

"What bugs?" He eyed his wife absently.

Her lips tightened. "The bugs that are eating us up alive."

"Oh, those bugs." Louis didn't appear interested.

"I think we should have the sprayer in," Marcia said. "Will you call and see that he gets here tomorrow?"

Louis withdrew his attention from the boulder. "Do we have to do anything as drastic as all that?"

I noticed now that Louis was sniffing and snorting rather heavily, blowing the bugs away from his head. "I don't see why we can't put up with them for a while," he said plaintively. "They'll go away by themselves or die a natural death."

Marcia's lips drew together.

"Please call Burbank today," Marcia said, Burbank being the sprayer. Her voice was adamant.

An unhappy look came over Louis' face. He shook his head sadly. "If we spray the bugs, then the birds will die from the spray when they eat the bugs."

"It's either the bugs or us, Louis—so please call Burbank."

Louis' face dropped, but his voice rose indignantly. "What would Rachel Carson think about this?" he demanded.

Louis sulked a little until the sprayers came, and then he noticeably brightened after they left. Whatever they put in the spray seemed to have so engaging an effect on the bugs that they brought their friends and relatives to the ashram. There seemed little danger of any bird life being lost.

In my rest periods, between exercises, I watched Louis with fascination. Every time I looked up, it appeared that a new and larger boulder was on the way, gradually forming a circle around the grove.

Marcia was beginning to develop that surrounded look. "If you move any more boulders here," she protested mildly, "this grove will be getting to look like a grotto."

But moving boulders seemed to fire the spirit of adventure in Louis. He attacked them as some men attack wild beasts. With cool deliberation, he launched an assault on two and a half tons of boulder which had not budged for a million years. He threw a lasso around a tree, extended the lariat to a heavy chain, which was in turn attached to a hand winch, which was attached to another chain, which was girded around the boulder. As Louis applied the pressure of the winch, the chain around the boulder would slip off, but he patiently readjusted it. Finally the grip was just right, the lines grew taut, and the boulder stirred and groaned. As the pressure was maintained, I heard another creak of protest. It came from the sturdy pine which was serving as an anchor. The tree bent ever so slightly.

"Won't that tree come down before the boulder comes out?" I asked.

Louis cast an expert eye from boulder to tree. "I've got the line low enough on the tree so it won't pull over," he said. "Marcia wouldn't like anything like that to happen."

Marcia continued to contemplate the rocks with yogi-like detachment, until Louis began digging up a three-ton monster, which he had earmarked for one end of the grove. "One more rock," she said, "and this place will look like Stonehenge."

As Louis' face fell, she quickly relented. "All right," she said, "just this one."

She looked at the boulders circumnavigating the grove with a mildly jaundiced eye. "We can always sink them into the ground," she said, "and grow a little wisteria over them."

We didn't see much of Louis during the day. He attended his classes at Boston University, and some evenings he was busy with his Astronomy Club, or an astrology class. However, peering out of the window of my study, I occasionally caught him ripping through the woods with a rock, or I could hear him moving ponderously through the house. Though a vegetarian, he was a great eater, and when the refrigerator door creaked, I could generally tell he was in the house.

Sometimes there would be a pounding, indicating he was in his workshop, off the garage, putting the finishing touches on his telescope. And then one day the pounding stopped. The telescope was completed. It must have been one of the big days in his life, climaxing a year of work in which he had made virtually everything in the scope except the lens.

And then, as I sat back relishing the glorious silence, I heard the charge of heavy feet, and a voice bellowing through the house, "Open the door, open the door."

I opened my own study door, and down the hall, heading for the front of the house, was Louis' hulking form, struggling with an equally hulking object. It was tall and white and looked like a giant scarecrow. But actually it was a telescope, the fruit of his long labors.

"Will somebody open the door?" Louis was shouting.

Marcia poked her nose out of the kitchen. She eyed her husband with a placid expression. She made no move to go to the door. "You told me," she said, with a trace of reproof, "that it was going to be portable."

In the beginning Louis and I had little to talk about. He was so much younger than I that almost anything dated that I mentioned by way of making a point struck no responsive chord.

Occasionally, raising my stomach or bending my back, I would catch a glimpse of him at his upstairs window, watching us. I could not quite fathom his expression.

One day he offered to do my horoscope, and after I had supplied the date and place of birth, he brought the finished chart to my room.

"What does it add up to, Louis?" I asked cheerfully.

"For one thing," he said, screwing his eyes up at the chart, "I see you running into some difficulties from being overfriendly with a married woman, though it will be no fault of your own."

"Really," I said. "Can you tell me more?"

"No, just that you're going to have to be very careful the way you handle your personal relations for the next two years."

"Thank you, Louis," I said, surveying his broad back as he bade me good night, taking the chart.

Later, I asked Marcia about this rather sinister prognostication.

She laughed gaily. "Oh, Louis calls them the way he sees them."

It was understandably hard for any male animal to get used to the fact that his attractive wife was spending a good deal of her time showing another man what to do with his body and mind. He must have felt a little out of it.

One afternoon, as we were resting outdoors between body bends, Louis emerged as big as all outdoors. He had just returned from his college classes.

"I just took an examination," he announced.

"That's nice, Louis," Marcia said.

"Now," she said, turning to me, "we'll try the Locust; lie down flat, stretch, rest on your arms, and bring one leg up slowly, stretching as high as you can, leaving your stomach flat on the mat."

Louis disappeared into the house.

He re-emerged in a few moments and began appraising the outlying lawn. "Marcia," he said, "what are weeds?"

With her head cradled between her hands, beginning the headstand, Marcia replied evenly, "Anything that aren't roses, asters, or dead pansies are weeds, Louis dear."

"Oh," said Louis. "I'll start after the weeds then as you asked."

"And don't forget to mow the lawn," Marcia said. "The grass is getting to look like weeds, too."

Again Louis disappeared into the house. But a few moments later his voice, which had a curious vibrating quality, carried out to the mat. Marcia was now showing me how to do the Plough, standing on her shoulders and bringing legs, stiff-kneed, back over the head to the mat. Her form was exquisite.

"Can we go to a meeting of the telescope-making club in Boston tomorrow night?" Louis said.

"Of course not," Marcia said, serenely coming to her feet.

"Why not?" Louis asked through the window screen.

"Because, dear, you have your astrology class to teach tomorrow night."

"Oh," said Louis, "I forgot."

It was no wonder that Louis was inclined to forget little things. He had forgotten all about his Astronomy Club class at the high school earlier in the week, and was reminded in time to get there after everybody had left.

But his mind was taken up not only with his college exams, but with earthquakes. In casting his astrological charts, he had seen catastrophic quakes for the years 1964, '65, and '66, and the great Alaskan temblor coming shortly after his first predictions had been announced did nothing to assuage his alarm.

"What do you think of the earthquakes?" he now asked. "I see that your book *The Door to the Future* predicted something like that for Alaska, California, New York, and Connecticut. Do you think it'll get up this far?"

Marcia put her hands on her hips. "Louis," she said, rather sharply for her, "we don't have time for earthquakes right now. Anyway I wish you would mow the lawn first."

"Just think," Louis said mildly, "what an earthquake might do to all those boulders after I had them all nicely lined up."

We eventually got back to the exercises. Marcia promised there would be no more interruptions that day.

But she had reckoned without fate.

The children had retired and I was reading in the study, consulting a book on cosmic consciousness, when the very boards seemed to tremble under my chair, and a cry that could only be described as bloodcurdling rent the night.

I leaped to my feet and dashed out into the hall, arriving just as Marcia pulled up with a look of fright in her eyes.

Groaning, Louis was slowly picking himself off the floor.

"Whatever happened?" she said. "Are you badly hurt?"

"I'll be all right." He had fallen a few steps into the well of a staircase.

He was standing up now, patting himself gingerly, to see if he had any muscle sprains or broken bones. "I guess I'll be all right," he said finally.

"But what happened?" Marcia persisted.

Louis pointed to a steel bar lying nearby.

"I grabbed that chinning bar, like I usually do, and it gave way." He stood looking at the bar contemplatively.

"You what?" Marcia said.

"I grabbed the bar."

"How could you grab the bar," she said, "when I took it down yesterday?"

"You what?" His hurts were forgotten in the face of this new enigma.

"Yes, I took it down." She motioned to me. "I was afraid our guest might hit his head against it."

"Then how in the world . . . ?"

A light suddenly gleamed in Marcia's eye. "I know what must have happened. Chris must have thought that the bar had fallen down, and he screwed it back on."

"Sure," said Louis, "and he couldn't turn those screws far enough, and look what happened."

"He probably tested it," Marcia said, "but he doesn't weigh more than eighty-five or ninety pounds, and it was strong enough only for him."

Louis suddenly moaned. "Well, it wasn't strong enough for me." He retired, limping.

The following morning, after my room had been cleaned and straightened, I noticed a printed legend, apparently clipped from a magazine, pasted on the window ledge over my typewriter. It said, simply, YOGI TAKES OVER. Originally, it had described the assumption of the managerial reins of the New York Yankees by Lawrence (Yogi) Berra. But even so, it appeared to strike a happy note for our project. But it was, alas, a trifle premature—for Berra too, as it developed.

After two weeks, looking and feeling better, I thought I was getting used to the idea of the exercises.

But one day, as Marcia said, "Raise one leg like a pump, and breathe in," I felt a sudden discontent. "All this is very silly," I told myself. "Why don't I just get in my car and drive back to New York, and get on with my work, a book on drugs, my new syndicated column, a new psychic book."

My dissatisfaction must have shown in the reluctance of my movements. For as I went into the shoulder stand—at which I had become respectably adept—Marcia said, "As I told you, you will have good and bad days."

"I had some indigestion last night, didn't sleep well, and I have been thinking of packing it in."

She laughed. "I told you your body would fight bitterly to retain its indispositions—the ossifying lower back, the arthritic lower neck and shoulder, the queasy liver, all signs of aging to which it has unhappily become accustomed. You are lengthening your life span, and your dying body doesn't like it a bit."

I remembered that she was an astrologist, believing in destiny. "Don't you think that my life cycle is pretty well set?"

She smiled. "By the same token your learning Yoga may be the instrument of maintaining the cycle. As you pointed out in your book about prophecy, it could very well be the fixed future that determines the ever-shifting present."

Regardless of all that, I was rather dissatisfied with what was happening. The trouble in my lower back, which had been somnolent for some time, was kicking up. It was awkward, even difficult at times, to get up from the floor or a chair. The area was tender. But in all fairness it had bothered me as much when I sat overlong at the typewriter.

"The weakness is being churned up, and then it will go away," Marcia said. "That's just a sample of what had to happen. You are disintegrating mildly, so to speak, before you reintegrate. You are being churned up, physically, emotionally, and spiritually, and the physical, naturally, is the first to manifest itself."

She may have been right. My body, though aching, seemed aware at times of a new power. Other times I appeared afflicted by a curious lassitude, and wanted to do nothing but sit or lie down. "You are learning to relax for the first time in years," Marcia said, "and you have years of fatigue to overcome."

Even though approaching fifty, I liked to think of myself as chronically youthful. But now, at grips with the Yoga discipline, I wondered whether my supposed youthfulness was not just a veneer, erasable overnight by illness, misfortune, or a flip of the calendar. On the other hand, I knew for sure that my eyes were better. They were clear and almost luminous. A week of eye exercises appeared to have been helpful. They were simple exercises, pulling the eyes up and down, diagonally, and around, just short of muscle strain, but they seemed to restore a sense of well-being to the orbital area.

"We single out the eyes for special exercise," Marcia observed, "because eye fatigue and strain is a major cause of general tension and fatigue. And we are trying to reach a state of body ease where we can forget the body completely."

I took stock of myself.

I was not happy about being a vegetarian. I had gone without meat for a week without discomfort, but I found myself thinking about food constantly. I did not have the motivation that Marcia and Louis had for abstaining, as I favored moderation in all things—including diet. However, I thought I would carry on for experimental purposes, and as a disciplinary measure, since the whole program was a discipline.

After the first few meatless days, my stomach stopped

rumbling, and I made a discovery: it wasn't going without meat that bothered me so much as eating meat substitutes. After two days I was so weary of soybean balls that I preferred not eating to consuming one of these concoctions. Yet other guests at the ashram seemed to regard these ersatz meatballs as rare delicacies.

I could get along with less exotic fare: fresh vegetables, cheeses, milk, baked potatoes, eggs (which Marcia permitted). But something seemed lacking.

"I find myself thinking more of food," I told Marcia, "and I'm sure that's quite the opposite of what you're after."

She offered to put me back on meat, with her children, but I refused to give up that easily. We compromised on an occasional fish dish—fresh fish, of course.

I do not know what was doing it, exercise or diet, but my system was certainly undergoing dramatic changes. In one week, elimination problems common to many aging males had not only disappeared, but I found myself rushing off to the bathroom.

I hesitated to inquire about the reasons for this transformation, but did manage finally to put my curiosity into words.

"That's a common reaction," Marcia said. "It's part of the churning-up process. I remember at Swami's camp in the Laurentians, the women lining up, and giggling, 'Swami, do you know what happened last night . . . ?' They thought it was diarrhea. But actually it was the unaccustomed massaging of the inner organs, including the liver, from all the stretching and squeezing, the increased circulation and metabolism."

"Is there a nervous reaction?" I asked.

"Oh, sure. The psyche is affected by the exercises and all the breathing and meditations. A new personality is emerging."

There were specialized exercises for overcoming constipation too, in the slight event that they were needed.

One served the additional purpose of tightening the abdominal muscles. It was accomplished by hunching over standing, bending the knees slightly, expelling the breath sharply through the mouth to empty the diaphragm; and then, without allowing any air to enter through the mouth or nose, sucking stomach in and holding, the hands resting palms down slightly above the knee.

"On a single exhalation, the stomach is contracted and released four or five times," Marcia instructed.

By the second week, this was one exercise that I was no longer performing.

But as Marcia had predicted, I had normalized toward the middle of the third week, and I was beginning, unbelievably, to look forward to the routine exercises and take pride in my progress.

I was not only performing the shoulder stand without difficulty, but was able to branch out easily into the Plough—bringing the legs gradually back until they were parallel with the mat, though not quite touching it.

"We call this the hang-over exercise," Marcia said, "for two reasons. Your legs hang over the head, and it's good for hangovers. It gets the blood into the head, tones up the system, and gives the victim the dash of confidence he needs to face the rest of the day."

Some exercises seemed to do more for me than others. I enjoyed doing the shoulder stand. But as I looked up, I noticed a fold of fat, like a rubber girdle, around my waist; I had never observed it before. It sort of hung down and looked quite unattractive from where I stood.

"That's a great one for getting really fat people to reduce," Marcia said with a laugh. "Many students remark on the devastating effect of having to watch all that flab jump at them as they rest helplessly upside down.

"It is a very good exercise for redistribution of poundage. Many women announce complacently that they weigh just what they had weighed twenty or thirty years before, as teen-agers. But what had happened was that the weight had left shoulders and bosoms and settled in one huge glob of lard around the hips. The weight chart tells them nothing, but coming face to face with their own fat is a traumatic awakening."

As in the headstand, which I had only made a feeble attempt at as yet, there was a reversal of the downward pull of gravity, and the internal organs, particularly in the abdominal area, had a chance to relax and "bounce back."

Whether the Crow, the Cock, or the Wheel, one complete turn, properly done, was all that Marcia expected. "Yoga is calculated to save energy," Marcia explained. "Actually, we are trying chiefly for a control which will integrate the body and mind in perfect union. Doing it as well as you can do it is enough at the time."

When I did a third shoulder stand, proceeding ambitiously on my own, Marcia reached over and gently stopped me. "You are overdoing," she said. "I am imposing limits in the early stages because you haven't yet learned enough about your new self to know how far you can safely go without damage."

"I feel fine," I said.

"We want to keep you there. For the first two or three weeks, judging from your agility, muscle tension, and the color of your face upside down, I'll have to regulate things. Soon, you will know enough about your own reactions to judge yourself how much you can safely do."

She did not feel that exercises should be charted to the last count for the pupil. "After you have done an exercise with relative ease, you can determine how many you can do and how slowly, increasing resistance by slowing the movement."

"How can I tell that point?" I asked.

"By exerting just short of the strain point, which you will anticipate after a while." She laughed. "When I think of all those charts for beginners, and even advanced pupils, I think of the English diplomat who was asked whether it was necessary to know Greek and Latin to be a statesman. 'Not at all,' he replied. 'It is quite enough to have forgotten them.' "

At the end of two weeks, I was ready to take stock of myself again. I had been ready to quit after a few days. I was stiff; my lower back bothered me so much that I could hardly bend down; my sinus, a problem for years, seemed worse than ever.

And now I wasn't even aware I had sinus, an irritating post-nasal drip had stopped, and I wasn't aware of my lower back even after five straight hours at the typewriter. It seemed a minor miracle. Even my eyestrain had diminished and I read some without reading glasses.

Marcia warned against undue optimism. "There will be ebbs and flows, but each time you will fall back less, until the problems disappear for good."

My flexibility was dramatically better, particularly in my back, and here I was easily brushing my fingers to my toes. Two weeks before I fell short by four inches, and par for my age bracket was six inches from shoe leather.

All this perhaps intensified what calisthenics alone might have done, but I doubted it. I would have been worn out long before I could have completed a steady routine that would have accomplished these wonders.

And I was beginning to notice something else—the power of mind over body. It was a dramatic discovery, and it had come to me while I was meditating, not exercising. As my mind wandered, I recalled with some satisfaction how

I had performed the Twist, a complicated contortion, so well that it had drawn Marcia's surprised approval.

The exercise was so complex that it could not have been done even poorly without concentration, as one leg passed over another, and the arms intertwined, until the individual resembled an Indian fakir begging for alms in front of some mosque. It was a ridiculous posture. But it did bring about perfect rapport between the mind and the body. I discovered myself straining every faculty of my mind to force legs and arms to accomplish their unnatural mission, as I held my spine rigid and managed to breathe properly at the same time. My mind was actually working as much as my body, and I felt that it was doing the job.

I was beginning to be able to isolate muscles or muscular movement for the first time in my life—and after only two weeks, and such a pathetic beginning.

I was doing the Bow when I made this additional discovery. In this exercise I concentrated equally on relaxing the pelvic area so that it would stay down as the lower thigh raised. On the fourth or fifth effort it worked.

"Yes," said Marcia with a smile, "this is progress. Nearly all Westerners think of the mind as something up in their heads, but with Yoga you begin to see that the body is also an integral part of the mind substance."

I was becoming acutely aware of the idiosyncrasies of this mind—or body.

Under the reversed pressure of the shoulder stand, or a simple back bend with the spine arched and the head resting on the mat, I could feel the acids churning in my stomach. It happened, I noticed, only when I had taken coffee in the morning, even six or seven hours before. Testing, I found that without coffee I had no kickup, no heartburn, no caffeine aftertaste.

Yoga was stepping up my reactions. "Under the increased pressures of Yoga," Marcia said, "what might have just been a point of sensitivity becomes virtually an allergy. The body dramatically rejects anything opposed to the disciplined control that Yoga is working toward. You have undoubtedly been doing gradual harm to your system with coffee, but under the stress of Yoga, the reaction was intensified."

Shoulder-standing and head-standing, pushing blood to the head in unaccustomed waves, helped externally as well as internally. "After doing a head-down exercise," Marcia said, "rub your face firmly but gently with your hands, always up, along the cheeks, out from under the eyes, up the temples, and then feel the freshet of blood in the head; it will give the skin a revitalizing blood bath."

I did as directed for the few seconds prescribed. My face was immediately suffused with a glowing warmth. "That's because of all the unaccustomed blood in the head," she said. "Brought to the skin, it can do more good than any cosmetics in any beauty parlor."

We put off my headstand three or four days. "Your Mars is squaring Uranus," Marcia said, "and there is no point to additional stress."

"It's Mars transiting," co-astrologer Louis put in, "so the condition will continue only another two or three days."

"With your neck," Marcia said, "I'm not taking any chances. So, let's do some neck exercises, and we'll practice the Dolphin, which is a sort of launching pad for the head-stand."

I wasn't sure what Mars had to do with it, but I remembered what Marcia had told me earlier: "When the pupil is ready, the teacher will arrive."

Marcia was my guru—and I was hers for the duration.

"Another thing about Yoga," Marcia was saying. "Until you get an exercise perfect don't worry about it. Experiencing an exercise is the important thing. A very wise man in India said once that the yogi reaches his goal when the means and the ends are one. You concentrate, visualizing every movement, emphasize the breathing, but don't dissect or analyze. Don't try to gauge progress as they do in calisthenics, where they increase repetitions or weights."

I was only to think of doing—not the result.

In the Dolphin position, I cradled my head between my hands and did my best to jacknife my hips, so that my body formed an inverted V.

"We'll do this for about a week," Marcia said, "resting weight on arms and elbows, rather than the head and neck." It was a preliminary for the headstand.

She came forward, rocked my neck gently, testing its flexibility. "Still rigid," she said.

I did my neck exercises faithfully, stretching my neck straight up and down as far as it would go, craning it to one side and then the other, ten times for each movement. Then I slowly revolved my neck, five times in each direction, hoping that practice would make perfect. There was nothing complex about it. Yet these simple exercises affecting the throat area had an almost miraculous effect. Although I still heard the cricks as I kept rotating my neck, I noticed my jowl leaving me and my jaw line becoming lean and hard.

In the last few years, I had developed three middle-age

rings around my throat. They vanished completely after four weeks from the front of the throat, though some lines were still faintly visible at the side.

"In another two weeks," Marcia promised, "they'll be gone, too. I tell women that Yoga is the best beauty course they can get, but only those who do it are convinced. The exercises you do are the ones that help you."

There were a number of gratifying results. I could now sit at the typewriter all day without the slightest backache or rheumatic cramp at the base of the spine, my usual trouble spot.

I had discovered, as do many Yoga students, that certain exercises did wonders for me while others expended more energy than they were worth.

I found a variation of the Cobra or Snake just what the doctor ordered for my lower back, weak because of my preoccupation with the typewriter. As I raised head and shoulders from the mat, stretching each vertebra in succession, I bent my legs upward at the knee. There was an instant tug at the lower spine, which robbed it of an ache built up from years of stiffening.

The exercise was known as the Swan.

It seemed remarkable that such a slight variation could produce so drastice a result.

"Backs are what people have most trouble with," Marcia observed, "and Yoga has so many different back-stretching exercises that one is bound to do the trick. One girl's back was killing her. She tried every intricate exercise; then one day, I had her lift her legs about three inches from the ground, and then do the same with head and shoulders, while lying on her stomach."

The girl's face was suddenly radiant.

"It's gone!" she shouted. "I can't believe it."

The stretch had caused a pull in the small of her back, just a slight muscle nudge, and a pinched nerve had apparently been freed. "You never know what exercise will be most helpful in the beginning," Marcia observed, "so I mix them up."

I was hoping to get around to the Lotus pose before I wound up my course. "But even if you don't accomplish it in a few months," she encouraged, "you are gaining flexibility and control in the hip and pelvic area that you can get in no other way."

Gently, but persistently, we worked at stretching that would help attain this goal—and picked up a few incidental lessons on the way. Spreading my legs diagonally, from a sitting position, I reached for the toes of first the left leg, then the right. After weeks of stretching I was now almost able to lower my chest to the mat, but it was still difficult to keep the knees still and reach the toes. Holding the posture for a few seconds brought on a stress that was almost painful.

"Stop just this side of the pain threshold, and relax your whole body, including that knee," Marcia said.

"Impossible," I said.

Nevertheless, I tried to relax, concentrating furiously, and felt the pain recede.

"I find this exercise useful at the dentist's," Marcia said. That didn't seem to make sense.

She smiled. "No, I don't straddle the chair. It's a matter of letting the subconscious, schooled by these exercises, go to work for me. As the dentist reaches my threshold of pain, I send a message of relaxation to every muscle and nerve in the area of my mouth."

"Does it work?"

She shrugged. "It doesn't seem quite as bad."

In a month I had learned quite a bit about specific exercises. I had inadvertently wrenched a hip (not at Yoga), getting a sciatica-like stricture in the upper thigh. Pains shot up to the hip, and it was painful to move this area. Experimenting gingerly, I discovered that in doing the Swan, if I slid back on my heels—simulating the position of Chinese ancestor worship—the resulting stretch instantaneously eased the pain in my hip. The injured muscles stretched and relaxed. It felt so good that I repeated the exercise.

In two days I resumed a full schedule. The hip no longer bothered me.

That was part of Yoga, getting to know your body as you never had before. For instance, in trying to cross my legs in some approximation of the Lotus posture, I had discovered that though my legs were flexible, my ankles, pressing against the insides of the opposing thighs, developed cramps from the strain. I had sprained both ankles years before.

So we did an ankle-strengthening exercise. It was like visualizing skiing downhill. "Bring the feet together, point them diagonally, and twist the trunk in the opposite direction," Marcia commanded.

A few days of this, stretching the ligaments and cartilage, and I found my ankles toughening. I could now even sit back comfortably on my heels.

"You'll get to know about yourself increasingly as we go along, not only physically, but mentally and spiritually," Marcia said. "The most rewarding thing about Yoga, I sometimes think, is what it reveals of us to ourselves."

In the months that we worked together, I was as close to Marcia in some ways as I had ever been to another human being. At times, I found myself both admiring and resenting her. I did whatever she asked at times, and then found myself resisting whatever she asked.

She seemed to anticipate my moods, and surprised me one day as I sat grimly reflecting on the monotony of exercise and the dreariness of Concord.

"As I told you before," she said, smiling, "your subconscious wants your body to give up so that it can get on with its routine aging process. It groans every time you do anything to make yourself younger—stretching and invigorating your connective tissue, strengthening the back and abdomen, increasing the activity of blood, nerves, and glands."

All I knew was that I pined for my unwholesome routine in the big city.

But something about Marcia held me—that, and knowing she was right. I had been aging, and now I was getting younger. I felt it with every breath, every movement—and I was reacting as I had not reacted for years.

I began to take notice of the pretty girls on the streets of Concord—and Boston.

I got up early and went to bed late. My mind was active, groping for ideas. And I seemed more intuitive. Marcia, too, sensed this, as she sensed many things about me.

I had noticed a relation almost of analyst and patient forming between us. She had said that my progress would not hinge so much on her teaching prowess as on the rapport we developed. This seemed a commonplace, as every teacher had to reach his pupils. But I soon discovered what she meant by rapport.

One evening, three of us were driving to a movie in nearby Cambridge. We had worked out intensively during the day, and I had at times anticipated the exercises Marcia would suggest, though she frequently varied them to break the tedium.

We had not done the Twist for a week, but I suddenly *knew* she was about to propose it. It was too trivial an incident, of course, to classify as an example of extrasensory perception. It was not even enough to show minds functioning on the same frequency.

But driving along to Harvard Square, we were discuss-ing Ingmar Bergman movies, as they were having a Berg-man festival in Cambridge. I had found the melancholy Swede's pictures uniformly dreary, with but one exception. And I could not recall the picture.

"*The Storm*, or something like that," I said.

Marcia shook her head. "I don't recall that title, but I must agree that I find him a torment."

"That's it," I said. "*The Torment.*"

Had my subconscious reached out and nudged hers, or was it merely another of those remarkable coincidences that seemed so common at the Concord ashram?

One afternoon, jaded by a vegetarian diet that I had never really accepted, my thought turned to a nice crisp tuna-fish salad as I hiked through Thoreau's woods.

That evening, there was tuna fish on my platter, with lettuce, tomato, and onion. My vegetarian diet had ended without my saying a word.

This was not a big thing in itself, but I was beginning to wonder about Marcia's ESP.

On another occasion, I mislaid my wallet and was con-cerned by the loss of licenses, credit cards, and other papers.

"I better write away tomorrow for a new operator's license," I said, "along with my registration."

"You won't have to," Marcia said serenely. "The wallet will turn up."

That night, in the light of a full moon, I found the wallet in Boulder Grove.

Marcia's commentaries were often intriguing. I was bal-ancing on one leg, doing the Stork, when Marcia observed drily, "I saw an ad recently in which a girl was shown doing the Stork. It said that if the reader couldn't hold this posture for fifteen seconds, he needed one of their exercise machines. I would say that he needed to practice the Stork."

When I was discouraged at my slowness in mastering such demanding exercises as the Sun and the Peacock, she pointed out encouragingly that I could almost do the difficult Lotus posture by the fourth week. "Some people take as long as three years, some never do it." Some, of course, did it almost the first time they tried—particu-larly supple, agile, broad-hipped teen-aged girls and mothers who had recently delivered.

After some initial difficulty, I did well with the breath-ing exercises. Originally, I couldn't see the point to breathing in one nostril, and out the other, holding the breath for a fixed count in between. But Marcia stressed that alternate breathing, done rhythmically, together with the staccato breathing of the Recharge, were of paramount importance. "Breathing properly," she said, "is more important than any posture."

What she meant was that without proper breath control the dramatic effect of the exercises was lost. The alternate breathing and the Recharge flooded the body with vital pranic energy and helped mind and body jointly develop an easy rhythmical way of coping with emergencies, as I was to find out for myself.

I had flown to New York one morning to take care of business matters, and then had to hurry back for a lecture at the First Spiritual Church in Boston the same evening.

I was tired, and not in a good frame of mind for an inspirational, or even educational, discourse on psychic phenomena. On the way to the lecture, I half-thought of taking a couple of therapeutic doses of brandy to nerve me to the occasion, but dismissed the thought as being unworthy of a yogi, even a neophyte such as myself.

I then remembered what Marcia had said about breathing, generally. I started breathing rhythmically, pushing out my stomach as I breathed in deeply, contracting as I breathed out. I worked slowly, concentrating on each breath. This I did for about five minutes, sitting in the car, and for another five minutes, walking from the parking place to the hall at the Exeter Street Theatre off Boston's Commonwealth Avenue. By the time I arrived, my fatigue and nervousness had melted away. I was calm and optimistic, looking forward to my talk. As I surveyed the crowded auditorium, I was so completely detached that I could pick out faces I knew in the audience. I felt so relaxed that I knew my thoughts would tumble out without effort.

I had chosen a text from St. Paul—Corinthians. St. Paul declared that while great knowledge of the universe came to those with the gift of prophecy, and while faith could move mountains, none of this meant anything without love. Love, he said, did not vaunt itself, nor puff itself up, nor concern itself with self-interest; it devoted itself to others. And so, with St. Paul as my guide, I pointed to the failings of psychics who had used fame and publicity to aggrandize themselves at the risk of their spirituality, and who, with this loss, suffered a resulting decline in power.

I sensed the responsiveness of my listeners, and felt in rapport with an audience for the first time. Lecturing was a chore I ordinarily assumed only when I could not painlessly extricate myself. But now, remarkably, I found myself thrilling with a new sense of communication. In my fresh awareness, I noted every rustle and movement in the back rows, every look of interest or detachment.

I did not reflect once on the outcome, but lived the experience, yogi-style, and let the result speak for itself. It must have worked; I was kept two hours after the lecture answering questions—until I felt that no amount of rhythmic breathing would draw another breath from me.

I understood from Miss Viola Berlin, who sponsored the lectures, that many in the audience had also felt this rapport. "Come back and talk whenever you can," she said.

As I discussed the experience with Marcia, later, it occurred to me that the whole business of concentrating on breathing could have been nothing more than taking my mind off an anticipated ordeal, and that breathing itself might have had nothing to do with it.

She would not concede this for a moment.

"In only four weeks of Yoga," she pointed out, "you have already conditioned your body to respond to the suggestions of the mind, with the breathing supplying the pranic energy needed to translate this union into purposeful action." It sounded impressive—and it was. For never again did I feel nervousness facing an audience—a gift perhaps from my subconscious which had absorbed its lesson well.

I was beginning to appreciate the breathing exercises. Marcia had convinced me—with herself as a sublime example—that oxygen was the most vital food for not only the rarefied superconscious states, but for fueling body and mind for everyday functions. Because of the deep breathing, relaxing between exercises was doubly important. In the beginning, when Marcia had talked about breathing as I relaxed with her classes or alone, I had only half-listened. I found her voice soothing but the words didn't register. I hadn't advanced sufficiently to understand their significance.

Now I listened carefully, allowing her suggestions to become autosuggestive. As we stretched out in the Sponge, my favorite exercise, she said, "Feel the life force flowing from the heart center out to the extremities so that the limbs seem not so much attachments hinged to joints as vital extensions of this inner force. As you exhale, let the power flow out through the toes, fingertips, and head, radiating beyond the visible outer form. As you inhale, feel the healing energies of nature enter all parts of the body, circulating through the system."

It sounded like so much balderdash, but it worked, and with renewed force, as the student kept achieving a higher discipline of mind over body—or rather, a union of mind and body. For in Yoga, as I got to know, body and mind are essentially the same.

By the fourth week, I had upped the count of the alternate breathing from the original four, eight, eight. Now I breathed in through one nostril for four seconds, held for eight, then exhaled from the other nostril. I could almost feel the oxygen, carried by the blood, surging through my system to nerve centers—creatively visualized throughout my body. And this pranayama, or controlled breathing, the yogis say, also feeds seven psychic centers in the spinal cord known as chakras.

When the energy mustered through pranayama reaches the highest of these centers in the brain, the advanced yogi, so Marcia assured me, becomes detached from body and mind and his spirit is liberated from the confines of time and space.

"In this state," Marcia said, "many yogis become extremely clairvoyant, though this isn't the purpose of pranayama. Actually, they are striving for a plateau where they comprehend life as continuous existence and, being at one within themselves, are at one with God."

There was little danger I would approach this state. I was perfectly content to improve my general health and well-being, mental attitude, emotional reactions, and leave it at that.

Why was it essential to breathe through one nostril and then another, when we seem to use both nostrils naturally?

There were two reasons. "By breathing exclusively through the nose, the air is properly purified," Marcia said. "Mouth breathing is not only irritating to tissue but destroys the rhythm of pranic breathing."

Secondly, the individual does not ordinarily use his nostrils equally in breathing, and this may lead to nasal and sinus problems. "Invariably," Marcia pointed out, "students discover that their left passage is considerably more clogged than their right, so that it takes several rounds of breathing to clear the passage."

When a person breathes through only one nostril for

twenty-four hours or so, the yogis feel that it is a sign of approaching illness, and that the left and right nostrils set up a postive-negative charge, vitalizing the body.

Marcia was pleased that I had not only advanced the count for alternate breathing, but had increased the rounds from three to five. "Very few pupils progress this quickly," she said.

With the alternate breathing going well, we turned to the abdominal breathing or Recharge exercise. The Hindus call it Kapalabhati, the skull-shining exercise. "All the higher centers are affected," Marcia explained.

Some lower centers appeared to be involved too. "We often do this exercise in a Lotus or semi-Lotus position, the legs comfortably crossed," Marcia said, "to better control the abdominal muscles. Emphasize breathing out rhythmically, contracting the abdominal muscles and pushing them upward." By breathing in, pushing my abdomen out, and then contracting as I exhaled, I could build up a fairly rhythmical interchange. And then by gradually exaggerating the exhalation, I found myself breathing out with a staccato rhythm unique in Yoga. The breath was pushed up from the diaphragm and expelled through the nose, with a little extra thrust from the notch of the throat.

It took a week or so before I was breathing out with the desired rhythm. "This exercise should be practiced in the beginning only under the supervision of an experienced teacher, as the pupil might otherwise strain his breathing apparatus," Marcia stressed.

Alternate breathing following Kapalabhati and concluding the exercises, toned down the charged-up battery, preparing it for relaxation and meditation. The effect carried over for hours, and in time, Marcia promised, would become lasting.

"With all that oxygen churning around in you," she said, "you can't help but feel better."

Her own motor ran very well on oxygen, so much so that she could carry a heavy schedule, and still fast one day a week, drinking coffee, her only vice, and fruit juice. She didn't smoke, drink, or eat meat.

But smoking was the only habit she generally tried to get her students to give up. "I don't mind alcohol or meat for others in moderation," she said, "but smoking defeats what we are trying to accomplish with the breathing exercises. It constricts the blood vessels and makes it more difficult for oxygen to reach the cells; purification becomes impossible."

"With all the foul air we breathe in the big cities, maybe we should cut down on breathing altogether," I said.

She laughed. "That's one value of dissection classes for Yoga students. We visited the morgue at Bellevue Hospital in New York City recently and saw a typical pair of city lungs—instead of being naturally pink and white, they were black with soot, cigarette smoke, and other polluting factors."

"Then, the less of this air we breathe, the better."

"It doesn't work that way," she said. "By our deep, rhythmical breathing, we get more purifying oxygen to every cell and nerve center. But the soot content doesn't increase proportionately; we just make better use of the oxygen."

I had given up smoking years ago, long before it got credit for cancer, and this may have helped my progress. My mind and fingers seemed nimble, my concentration and retention good, this in a household where three growing youngsters often made concentration seem a major pursuit.

I stood straighter, sat straighter, and walked straighter. I was more aware of my body than I had been in twenty years, and I felt at times a new direction of the mind, which seemed to sweat forgotten ideas and experiences out of my subconscious. I was unduly cheerful and optimistic, though separated from home and family. I slept well, ate and digested well—when there was anything to eat—and I was even beginning to enjoy the meditations.

But with all this, I still couldn't do the headstand.

I had been working up to it one day, just before dinner, when an unexpected development occurred.

A slight, round-faced woman with fading red hair and melancholy eyes, Thelma Thoresen lived in nearby Maynard. She had come over for the day to help Marcia with the cleaning and the kitchen work. But she was no ordinary domestic.

When I first saw her, she was standing behind a chair, her hands resting gently on the head and forehead of Bill (the Scientist) Mercer, who was sitting quietly, eyes closed at her command.

"Think only pleasant thoughts," she was saying, "keep thinking pleasantly, and soon it will go away."

She was praying almost inaudibly as she stood over him, a look of concentration on her face.

"What's going on?" I whispered.

"He's getting a healing," somebody whispered back.

"What's the matter with him?"

"A migraine headache."

The whole procedure took about five minutes. "You are healed," Thelma said. "Think of yourself as healed."

Mercer got up and shook his head like a waking lion. His eyes were glazed, but in a moment they had cleared. His face seemed composed.

He shook his head again, and disbelief showed in his eyes. He put a hand to his head gingerly, and then surprise gave way to relief.

"It's gone," he said, "by gum, it's gone." He turned to the sad-eyed woman who was now watching him dispassionately. "How did you do it?" he said. "It's a miracle."

"I was only the instrument," she said modestly. "We all know who did it."

Marcia turned to me in an offhand way. "Thelma is a psychic healer. She lost her gift for a while—she had many problems—but it's coming back now."

"I am getting so healthy that I hardly need a healer," I said rather glibly.

Thelma fixed me with her spaniel-like eyes. "You can never tell about these things," she said glumly.

"She can see into the future, too," Marcia said, obviously trying to change the course of the conversation. "Tell me, Thelma," she said, "what do you see for our Yoga book?"

Thelma apparently didn't hear. She vanished into the kitchen, and when she came out she was wringing her hands.

"Yes, Thelma," I said, "what do you see for our book?"

Again she disappeared into the kitchen, but this time when she reappeared she was wearing a radiant smile. "When I think of your book," she said, "all I want to do is smile."

"Is that good?" I asked.

"Very good," she said.

And then her face resumed its dour expression. She looked at me as though I were Typhoid Mary. "But if I were you, I would be very careful."

"What do you mean by that?"

She frowned, standing in the doorway. "Well, I just wouldn't go doing any headstands—not at your time of life."

And so, it happened.

I had been doing a simple exercise known as the Fish. It generally followed the shoulder stand, stretching muscles which had just been contracted. Lying down, I simply arched my back and rested my weight on hips and head, with some support from my arms. "Now bring your hands forward and breathe in," Marcia ordered.

I felt a slight strain in the old whiplash area, as I withdrew the support from my neck and head.

"Everything all right?" Marcia asked.

Bravely, I nodded.

"Can you do one more?"

I grunted.

And then as I removed my hands once more, my full weight coming down on head and neck, I felt a sharp twinge. The right side of my neck, above the shoulder, began to throb.

"I guess old Thelma was right," I said. "You can't beat your destiny—and I didn't even do the headstand."

Marcia's face betrayed her chagrin. "I thought we were out of it," she said, frowning.

That night I noticed her studying my horoscope.

"I should have known better," she said cryptically.

She had warned me to be careful of my neck because of Mars squaring my Uranus, which was supposed to make me accident prone. But that danger period had apparently passed when Mars moved on a bit.

She was still studying my chart. "Many astrologers feel an equally dangerous period occurs when Mars squares the mid-point of Uranus and Jupiter—and I overlooked it." She looked up. "It's exactly today."

She looked as contrite as a tardy schoolgirl. "It's my fault," she said, "for being such a poor astrologer."

Ten days later, I resumed the exercises, after an adjustment from Broadway's favorite chiropractor.

"It's the rotator that turns the head," said Doc Ed Crozier. "What have you been doing?"

"Yoga," I said.

"Yoga?"

"Yoga. I was doing the Fish—they call it that because you can float in water doing it, if you don't drown."

He cracked me in place. "Your neck was probably out before," he said, "and the strain aggravated it."

I was as good as new, feeling suddenly easy and free from pain.

But I wondered about Thelma; had she really known anything?

She was inclined to be coy. "I just wanted you to be careful about your head," she said.

"Am I all right now?"

"Just be careful." Her voice sang out like a chant. "Just be careful."

I really had no idea how psychic Thelma was—and then one day a curious coincidence occurred.

Marcia had gone off to New York to appear on a television show, and she had asked Thelma to come in the following day and do a few chores.

Instead, Thelma jogged over the six miles from Maynard that very day, almost as Marcia's eleven-year-old son Jonnie was brought home with a bad concussion. He had had an accident with his bicycle.

"I just had a feeling something was wrong," Thelma explained.

She was a witch. But I had the magic of Yoga going for me.

After two months, I was beginning to feel like a veteran. I was getting so flexible that I could do things I hadn't done even as a young man. And I had passed successfully through several rather trying stages.

I had hurdled the first two or three weeks of aches and pains. Then I had encountered a period of discouragement, which attacks most beginners as they wonder how they can ever simulate the grace and effortless ease of their guru. That, too, had passed.

Even my old feeling of resistance began to leave me, as I found myself puffing with pride occasionally from doing a difficult exercise, such as the Crow. "You are beginning to reverse the aging process," Marcia advised, "and your body is adjusting. In time it will stop protesting completely, and just give in to youth."

I felt a new determination to master exercises which had eluded me in the beginning. During one session, I did little but practice the Sun exercise, Suryanamaskar. My neck felt good, I had new confidence, and my mind and body were beginning to let me know what I was ready for.

I kept rehearsing the twelve different stages of the Sun: the upward stretch, the downward bend, the knee to the ground, like a sprinter taking off; the Cobra-like movement, breathing in, rising out, descending. Before the session was over, I had old Suryanamaskar by the nape of its neck.

Marcia beamed approvingly.

"You have learned to visualize your exercises," she said, "and that's even more important than doing the exercise."

In three months, my progress continued apace. I could now do the shoulder stand as well as Marcia, holding the posture for as long as five minutes without discomfort. "You are as straight as a plummet," Marcia said, as I tucked in my buttocks and stretched my back upward from the base of the spine, not even using my hands for support.

"You couldn't even begin to do this properly at first," Marcia said, "because you didn't have the strength in your lower back then, nor the control of mind over body." She drew off and looked at me. "You are completely motionless from the tip of your toe to your head—and that is the test of self-control."

I could feel the added profit of performing an exercise exactly as diagramed by the old masters. I no longer had to push my chin down to meet the notch in my neck, and thus activate the old thyroid. "Because you are standing perfectly vertical, upside down," Marcia pointed out, "gravity pulls your chin down by itself."

The neck exercises had also done their work. The effects of the injury had quickly disappeared, my neck was strong and pliant, so flexible that I could easily rest my chin on my chest—something I had never been able to do before. All trace of the traumatic whiplash, which had bothered me for five years, was gone too.

I constantly surprised Marcia—and myself—with my new-found suppleness.

"Let's try a back bend today," Marcia suggested. I had successfully done the forward bend, touching my forehead to my outstretched knees, and shaming a lissom editorial assistant, who had been unable to to the same though she was some twenty years younger.

I remembered with an inward grimace that we had given up the back bend almost a month before because it had cramped my arms and legs as I tried to stretch backward with legs bent under and elbows back. But bending my knees and resting on my heels, I dutifully attempted the exercise.

I leaned back on one elbow and tried to juggle back on the other, meanwhile noticing with some surprise that sitting on my heels didn't seem to bother my ankles.

I still didn't think I could make it, but suddenly I was there, lying back almost parallel to the ground and feeling not the slightest strain. I could hardly believe I was doing it properly; it seemed so simple.

Marcia was even more delighted than I. "All the stiffness is leaving your body," she said, "and soon you will be as flexible as a child—a flexible child."

"I suppose my arms are getting stronger."

She shook her head. "Your ankles are strengthening, and your back is more supple—that's why you can now do it so easily."

I remembered what she had said about people's temperament reflecting itself in the rounding of their shoulders and the stiffness of their spines.

"I suppose I will be getting more flexible mentally," I said half-seriously.

"It works both ways. As your body grows more elastic, it conveys a sense of its own pliancy to the mind." She paused. "Yes, I think you are becoming more adaptable, mentally as well as physically. It cannot be otherwise."

Still, I wondered whether I was acquiring an equivalent control of mind. It seemed to me that it was hard to be detached and yet participate fully in life.

"How can a man be in love and still be detached?" I asked one day.

Marcia answered, "He can be in love, and yet be aware of the pitfalls. In this awareness comes independence and detachment."

"You mean he becomes a spectator at his own romance?"

"Just as he has taken apart his own body, gotten to know each part, and then put it back together in new perspective, so does he examine his ladylove."

I couldn't help but laugh. "Very few would stay together."

She shrugged. "Then maybe it's just as well—there's plenty of fish in the sea."

I still hadn't tried the headstand; Marcia was taking no chances on my neck. But I had not given up.

Visiting the great Yogi Vithaldas in New York one day, I had been signally impressed by his faith in the inverted exercises as rejuvenators. He had quoted liberally from his book, *The Yoga System of Health and Relief from Tension:*

"As to standing on the head, what at first sight would seem to be a childish exercise is really an obvious method of countering an inadequate blood supply to the brain. Such an inadequate supply results in degeneration of the brain tissues, and in a loss to the mentality of the alertness necessary to cope with the trying conditions of modern society."

In maintaining the shoulder stand for three or four minutes, I was apparently getting all the blood I needed in my brain for whatever I needed it. The headstand was sugar coating.

But why hadn't a beneficent nature, which seemed to consider about everything, arranged for the requisite flow of blood to the head?

Evidently, as Marcia had touched upon, it had something to do with an evolutionary lag.

"In the dim past," stated Yogi Vithaldas, "when the progenitor of man trotted about using his hands as supports, much as the apes do, his head was lower than his heart and gravity sent the blood rushing to the brain with comfortable ease, and kept it healthy and responsive during the process of evolution. Walking upright as we do now, gravity does not send this blood to the brain, and the heart pumps up a reduced quantity through the carotid arteries."

It was all part of developing an inner unity. "As mind and body work together," he told me, "we get rid of the tension and strain responsible for so many of today's emotional disorders."

His face lit up with the magnetic smile of a man whose muscles, nerves, and arteries were twenty years younger than his fifty-six years. "Without all the inner conflict modern living seems to breed, we wouldn't be having all these mental health programs, and that's what Yoga aims to eliminate—conflict."

I had discovered a growing interest in Yoga by people wanting to stay young, vital, and calm—mostly calm.

During a weekend in New York, as I practiced my Yoga in a midtown gymnasium, several people doing calisthenics trooped over to watch curiously.

"You're looking amazingly good," observed Arthur Levitt, comptroller of the state of New York.

"Yoga," I said. "It certainly couldn't be anything else."

Levitt brightened. "My son is studying Yoga, but he's having his difficulties."

"Like what?" I asked, trying to slip my legs into the Lotus.

"Sitting cross-legged, for instance; he can't bend over and touch his forehead to the floor in front of him—and it's maddening because his wife does it with ease."

Though Arthur, Jr., was years younger, I bent forward easily and brushed the mat with my forehead. There was no great effort, even though I had never attempted the exercise before. The flexibility induced by other exercises affecting the hips and lower back had made the posture a simple one.

As I continued my exercises, the gallery grew.

"What are you doing for yourself?" asked advertising executive John Duffy, who had known me for fifteen years. "This is the best I've ever seen you look."

He examined me closely. "It isn't only your body; you got a new look about you, like a young man."

Whiskey baron Phil Meyers gave me a glance with the shrewdness and penetration that had helped make him a millionaire. "Whatever you're doing," he said, "I wish you'd tell me. You've lost the tire around the waist, and you're moving like a kid."

In the hot room—the sauna—Paul May, an insurance tycoon whom I had not seen for months, eyed me appraisingly.

"You look ten years younger," he said. "Have you been on some diet or rest cure?"

"I weigh nearly the same—one hundred and sixty-six pounds." I had dropped five pounds.

"You don't have an ounce of fat, and your shoulders are built-up, like a fighter's."

I took the compliment as a tribute to my guru.

"I've been doing Yoga," I explained for the *nth* time.

Paul looked mystified. "Aren't those the fellows that sit for hours admiring their navels?"

"These may be extreme cases of mind over matter," I said, "but I'm interested in a moderate Western Yoga—mind and body working together to produce some useful result."

He was still perplexed.

I thought of how the simple exercise I had performed for Arthur Levitt might explain Yoga practice and philosophy.

"In Yoga," I said, "the important thing is concentrating

so that the mind will send a signal to the area you are trying to influence. In time, a regular pattern between mind
and body develops. Since I have strengthened this link
daily for three months, it was rather elementary to tell my
mind to tell my body what to do; it obeyed automatically."

"Interesting," Paul said vaguely, "but how do you get
to looking younger?"

"You become more aware, more alert, body and mind
blend in a perfect union; there is more inner relaxation,
less conflict, just as you have isolated a limb or a body
muscle, so you detach parts of yourself at will."

"But in a few weeks you have become a new person."
He shook his head. "I don't quite see how."

I remembered what Marcia had told me, about as being
as young as one's connective tissue, and drew again on my
own experience.

"Glands, blood, and nerves are all recharged, calcium
deposits are washed or worn away—all brought about by
the mind's power over the body. The aging process is re-
tarded, for stiffening in the joints, poor circulation, poor
elimination, are all part of getting old." I laughed. "You
couldn't have bad elimination if you wanted to, doing
Yoga, and that's part of the purifying process that makes
the Yoga student look as if he just had a Simoniz job."

"You do seem more relaxed," he conceded.

"The body also influences the mind," I said. "As it
learns to relax, it sends its sympathetic messages to the
mind, to tone it down, or quicken its pace, as the situation
indicates."

He looked doubtful. "How could that happen?"

"As you isolate and relax each part of the body, resting
between exercises, you are setting up a conditioned response in your own mind, telling it to relax at the same
time. Mind and body become one."

Paul smiled agreeably. "Obviously," he said, "it worked
for you."

Looking myself over, I could not see where my appearance had changed so drastically that friends should
consider me a new personality.

Yet this reaction was commonplace.

I was chatting on a terrace in Rumson, New Jersey,
with Joan and John Rendon of nearby Monmouth Beach,
when I noticed Mrs. Rendon scrutinizing me curiously.

"You've changed," she said at last. "I don't know what
it is but you look different somehow."

She kept searching my face. "I don't know whether I

should say this, but even though you were always on the slim side, you had a double chin, and now that's gone. You look lean and youthful." She took a sip of her gin and tonic. "What in the world ever happened to you?"

"Yoga," I said.

"Yoga?" Her face screwed up into a frown. "You mean those Indian exercises?"

"They originated in India, but we're Americanizing them, trying to relate them to everyday living."

Joan Rendon was in her early forties, and looked remarkably fit, having the French joie de vivre.

"Can you show me a few exercises?" she asked.

"The breathing," I said, "is important, and control is all-important; otherwise, you might as well be doing calisthenics. Immobility, holding a posture, is a reflection of this control."

So I stretched out flat and began my demonstration. First, one or two limbering exercises, the good old Suryanamaskar—the salute to the sun—and then into the shoulder stand, the Plough, the Cobra, the Locust, and the Bow. I wound up with forward and backward bends; then I demonstrated the deep breathing, pushing the diaphragm out on the intake, contracting the abdominal muscles as I expelled the air.

"The alternate breathing," I said, with all the authority of a practiced guru, "will settle you down, and prepare you for the Sponge."

"Sponge—what is that?"

"Lying down, letting the oxygen in through your pores and the poisonous carbon dioxide out. Visualize yourself as open and absorbent as a sponge."

Mrs. Rendon laughed. "That exercise I can do—just lying down makes the whole business attractive." She looked at me doubtfully. "But doesn't it take a lot of time?"

"What I showed you would take less than a half hour a day, and can be done at home."

The Rendons had to be off for a dinner date. They were dining with a Park Avenue psychiatrist at his summer place in neighboring Sea Bright.

As she took my hand, Joan said, "If it can do this for you in twelve weeks, I'm for Yoga." She looked at her husband. "Maybe John will get interested, too."

Her stockbroker husband wagged his head good-naturedly. "I get all the Yoga I want concentrating on the Big Board."

The next morning, Joan telephoned. Her voice sounded the least bit troubled. "I have something to tell you," she began. "I discussed the Yoga with the psychiatrist last night, and he says it can be dangerous."

"I imagine he's talking about the advanced Yoga, as they do in the East, but what I'm doing is no more hazardous than calisthenics."

"Anyway," she said, "he would like to talk to you."

I knew the doctor as an earnest, open-minded investigator into many areas of the mind, and I looked forward to the discussion.

One weekend, while Marcia was visiting at Rumson, we all joined on the Rendon veranda, within the smell of the ocean. I had seen the doctor last three months before in the Virgin Islands. He eyed me closely. "Well, you're certainly looking fit."

I introduced Marcia.

"You have an attractive guru," he said.

I mentioned that Marcia had suggested Yoga might change my way of life.

The psychiatrist smiled. "And has it?"

"Considering the short time I've been at it, it has apparently worked wonders."

He regarded me evenly. "In what way?"

"Aside from the physical improvements, I've discovered myself becoming more detached, worrying less, thinking more introspectively."

"You realize of course that Yoga is very powerful medicine, and not everybody can take it."

"You are probably referring to the advanced Yoga, where the students concentrate on the nerve and psychic centers, to awaken the superconscious."

He nodded. "That's part of it. But over-all, we must remember that the East Indian is a different person than the American, and is geared to different disciplines. His climate, food, thinking, and philosophy are all different, and so he reacts differently to Yoga."

He turned to Marcia. "You know I have many schizoid patients who were Yoga students."

Marcia replied, "I don't doubt it. But they were schizophrenic, I'm sure, before they took Yoga. As a matter of fact, I've had little luck with students who were highly neurotic or psychotic. Yoga helps people who are nervous and have problems, but essentially they must be people with well-integrated personalities."

She mentioned a young Oriental, a student at Cornell,

who was considered a brain. "After three or four lessons, he just gave up; he couldn't concentrate enough—and he was too neurotic, anyway, to want to be pulled together." Another dropout was a Harvard student of seventeen, a mathematical genius. "He just collapsed when I tried to get him into the shoulder stand," she said. "He was an intellect, but virtually inert from the neck down."

The psychiatrist nodded gravely. "You realize, of course, that Yoga is comparable to hypnosis, with all the attending hazards in untrained hands."

"We're dealing with the subconscious as the hypnotist does," Marcia conceded, "but what we try to do is toughen body and mind so that it can control subconscious forces developed through the meditations."

As we talked, I recalled a recent conversation with Mrs. Marguerite Haymes, mother of singer Dick Haymes. The celebrated singer had been a disciple of Paramahansa Yogananda, who trooped the U.S.A. gaining converts for Yoga. "The exercises are great," she had said, "but when these young enthusiastic Americans, like Dick and Herb Jeffries (another well-known singer) got involved in meditating on all those chakras and bandhas, that was something else again."

From what she said, I gathered that the control gained in the exercises had been lost in random experimentation.

The doctor nodded comprehendingly, but Marcia cut in. "The problem, of course, is advancing in easy stages. I read somewhere, for instance, that three minutes is the minimum for the headstand or shoulder stand, and anything less is a waste of time. That is absurd. We have to keep the student at the one-minute stage for a while, then two minutes, and three; and some students, I would say, get as much out of two minutes as others do out of ten, depending on the effort involved."

She looked squarely at the doctor. "Now, the Indian yogis hold their postures, ideally, for as much as ten minutes, but as you pointed out, our temperament and aims are different—we are trying to achieve changes in ourself with the Yoga, not make it a way of life. It is detachment for participation, not withdrawal."

She paused. "And we do not get people meditating, or visualizing or deep breathing, until they have shown some measure of mind control in the Yoga exercises."

I had deliberately avoided the muscular locks—or bandhas—that advanced yogis applied to the throat, solar plexus, and base of the spine. With deep breathing, these supposedly generated powerful electrical currents, heightening metaphysical powers. But they were the kind of thing Mrs. Haymes and Marcia had warned against unless there was a good deal of preparation.

"I'm not sure I could handle them now, and anyway I'm getting all I want out of Hatha Yoga and the meditations," I pointed out. "You don't really think that anybody became schizophrenic because of Yoga?" I had seen no evidence of it.

"I have evidence that a good many Yoga students are schizophrenic." The doctor was persistent.

Marcia held up a protesting hand. "As I said before, I think you will discover that they were already schizoid before they took up Yoga, and when that failed, they turned to psychiatry."

"How do you account for the order of therapy?" I asked.

Marcia said, "Yoga is cheaper. I only charge students two dollars in class; that's better than they can do with a psychiatrist. Actually, we get many people who haven't been helped by psychiatrists."

She contemplated the doctor with a serene smile. "One of our students had been going to a psychiatrist for three years with severe migraine headaches. She still had them when she came to us. I had her standing on her head and shoulders in three or four weeks, sending new blood up through the shoulders, neck and head, relieving congestion—and the headaches disappeared."

"Was that all there was to it?" I asked.

"She was very nervous, so we also took her off coffee and tea, and this may have helped ease the tension causing the headaches."

The doctor didn't seem terribly impressed.

"Most of my schizoids are rigid in the neck, lower spine, and the ankles, as though enveloped in a cast—and that cast is a protection. Break it off suddenly, and the patient is in trouble; it must be gradually removed."

"But ordinary gym exercises would get rid of this rigidity," I observed, "and the individual could be perfectly normal mentally. Nearly everybody after forty begins to ossify at the joints."

He shook his head. "Calisthenics are purely mechanical exercises. The moment you stop them, the whole rhythm of bodily change ends, but in Yoga, an interchange has been set up between mind and body—and the involvement may be more than the unstable mind can handle."

Marcia's face lit up. "I agree, Doctor, I don't think Yoga is for the unstable, only for those who have an idea of what they want and how to accomplish it. But we have a built-in safety device; the unstable can't continue with Yoga because they are unstable."

We seemed to agree that Yoga was a discipline for those who could react favorably to discipline, which meant nearly all grownups in the normally functioning world.

Joan Rendon smiled brightly. "I guess," she said, "I'll try the exercises for a while." Obviously, there were no hazards for the average person, neurotic or otherwise.

For myself I felt a new confidence. Despite the neck incident, which had resulted from my own vanity, I no longer had any fear of getting hurt. And I felt a new authoritative control of my body—and mind.

But I still had much ground to cover.

In many different ways I now realized the importance of concentrated breathing. I was nearing the end of a session one day, doing the Kapalbhati, or Recharge, when Marcia said, "Hold your breath as long as you can, visualizing the areas you want to recharge with a jolt of energy."

I felt a little arm-and-leg weary that day, and I decided I would try to vitalize my flagging limbs. I closed my eyes, inhaled, holding my breath, and relaxed my muscles; deep breathing and relaxation, following stress, appeared the key to every Yoga exercise.

As I held my breath, picturing a river of energy coursing to my limbs, I experienced a feeling of lightness throughout my head and body; the heaviness in my arms and legs left me.

I was determined to hold my breath as long as I could comfortably; thirty seconds had been my limit the first week of exercise. But my capacity had mounted and multiplied.

"One minute," Marcia called out.

My eyes were closed, and I felt far away, yet full of unaccustomed power; it was an intoxicating experience.

"A minute and a half . . . two minutes."

There was a trace of concern in my guru's voice.

"I think that's enough," she said.

I waited five seconds and exhaled.

I felt elated with my new power. "I could have held another thirty seconds."

"Not one person in a hundred could hold that long," she said.

I regarded her fondly. "I owe you an apology," I said.

She looked up questioningly.

"When you first stressed the breathing exercises, I thought it an exaggeration intended to get me to pay some attention to breathing. Now it leaves me completely recharged and refreshed. It seems almost incredible."

She looked at me curiously.

"Did you feel anything else?"

"Just a little lightheaded."

She nodded, satisfied. "That's the first step in psychic development. Many yogis become clairvoyant through concentrating on the Recharge."

She paused. "Now we'll simmer you down a bit with the alternate breathing."

I felt a certain sense of accomplishment, but I still couldn't do the headstand.

"Go out and meditate," Marcia said.

"On what?" I said.

"Meditate for about a half hour, meditate on the nature of yourself."

I looked at her doubtfully.

"It will do you good to sit in the sun and breathe the fresh air, if nothing else. You will be surprised at what you will get."

Rather grumpily, I sat out on a mat, picked up a copy of the Bhagavad-Gita, thumbed through its pages listlessly. My mind was restless. It wandered from unfinished business in New York, to what my publisher was doing about my most recent book, and then it latched on to a visit the day before to a highly successful Concordian. He had reached his three score and ten without systematic exercise of any form, and was rather vehement in his repudiation of Hatha Yoga. "We pay altogether too much attention to the physical, to diet and exercise," he had said. "The body takes what it needs, does what it needs to keep fit. It is only a vehicle for the ride through life."

I saw Marcia inwardly squirming.

"But Raja Yoga, the mental Yoga," he had gone on surprisingly, "is something else again. I ask myself, What is the nature of my being? Is it my physical self?" He had shaken his head. "That is only the vehicle, as I pointed out. Is it my emotional being, my mind, my spirit?"

Over a remarkably productive life, in which he had achieved a good deal of inner contentment, he had never made a major decision without taking pause to analyze the nature of his reactions to specific situations.

"I ask myself, am I being influenced by my emotions, are my prejudices affecting my decision, or am I detached and impersonal in giving the situation the judgment it warrants?"

As I thought of this fortunate man, rooted in generations of New England forebears, who practiced one form of Yoga while eschewing another, my thoughts suddenly flashed to the nature of myself—my own Raja Yoga.

Were the things I had been thinking about, the mundane, the material, all part of my nature of self? Surely, everything that happened to me, or that I made happen, was part of my nature. I was my motivations. A wise friend had said, "I judge a man not by what he says, nor by what he does, but by what he wants."

Try as I would, I could not keep my mind to any subject. One moment I was a reporter, talking to General Eisenhower, another a small boy, looking to my grandmother for guidance.

I saw her now as she was just before death, a smile in her eyes, despite the labored breathing that came in heartrending gasps. She had asked that the oxygen tent be removed, so she could say what she had to say before she died. She was a courageous woman. I hoped that some of this courage had rubbed off on me.

My grandmother had always preached that we boys could do anything. All we had to do was want it and make the effort. Was her faith now part of my nature? Did it influence my thinking even today? I thought of the kind and unkind, the worthy and unworthy things I had done, the bursts of temper and the marks of patience. Did one balance out the other, the good compensating for the bad?

I thought of wife and children, my broken marriage. Had the nature of myself made the break inevitable? And even analyzing my nature, could I have altered my course?

My mind turned back to the Concordian philosopher who had dismissed Hatha Yoga. His mind was so disciplined, so in tune with the rest of him, and the Universe, that he already had the bodily control which in its turn influenced the mind. "Through meditation," Marcia had observed, "he had made his personality immune to the inner conflicts and confusions which cause so many ills today. All his life he has meditated like an Indian holy man."

Obviously, in the discipline of the mind lay success; and if, in disciplining the body, one inevitably had to school the mind, was this not a justification of Hatha Yoga? For, essentially, the exercises were designed to build up the breathing power and vital currents—pranayama—supplying fuel for a mind, body, and spirit functioning in unison.

It was not easy to meditate in a connected way. I remembered about the mind being the raft to carry the yogi from the banks of the conscious to the superconscious. But no raft could get anywhere taking the zigzag course of mine. My thinking was inconclusive, amorphous, nebulous at this point.

But there was a stirring back of my mind. I didn't know how much it had to do with the meditation, or what it foretold. I was vaguely conscious of God, and creation being God's universality. Was God then the great Universal Mind, as the mystic Edgar Cayce had recognized in trance? The fulfillment of Cayce's predictions—volcanic eruptions, floods, and quakes—had impressed me. For if these events were not in the order of things, how could they then be so clearly foreseen?

Or were we all the victims of one great hoax? There was no God, no creation, no plan, and we lived then only in aimless relation to each other. I couldn't believe this for a moment.

For there must be a plan, or how could the future be known to some gifted psychics, as even great scientists had acknowledged. There was too much evidence to be discounted. Just before leaving for Concord, I had met with an actor friend, John Conte, who had flown in from Beverly Hills, California, to appear in an off-Broadway production. This was an apparent letdown for a performer who had scaled the heights in radio, television, and Broadway itself.

"Why did you take the job?" I asked.

"I haven't worked regularly since I hosted the Matinee Theatre on NBC six years ago, and I would have taken anything." For an actor, John was terribly frank.

The show had a burlesque format, and Conte had the lead. It didn't seem like his cup of tea.

"I don't think the show will go," I said.

He replied good-naturedly, "I think you're probably right."

"It doesn't seem to worry you."

"I'll be all right."

"Do you have an oil well?"

He laughed, and it was the happy radiant Conte I knew from better days.

"You know," he said, "even though I come from California, I never really bought clairvoyance. But last April, I went to a psychic named Lucille Joy in Hollywood, and now I'm a believer."

She had been very specific. "She told me," John said, with a musing eye, "that in two weeks I would get an offer for an off-Broadway show; the show would be unsuccessful, closing within two weeks, but it would lead to other things, and touch off the thirteen best years of my career."

As he looked at Mrs. Joy, John had laughed. "I don't know how anybody off-Broadway would ever hear of me."

"They will phone you," she had said. "Now, when you

get there, watch your lines closely, for they will want you to do things that could hurt your career."

"What then?" John had said, with a polite smile.

"In the middle of June," she had said, "you will be offered a contract for another show, and that will be the beginning."

She had looked at him kindly. "Now, another thing: when you leave California for New York you will be offered six hundred dollars; take it, you will need it until things straighten out."

She had told him he would fly to New York in May, and here he was, ready to go into rehearsal.

"How did you get the part?" I asked.

"That's the funny thing," he said. "It was an accident. Do you remember Jean Martin?"

I nodded; she was the former wife of Chock Full o' Nuts mogul Bill Black, and John had once tutored her with her coffee commercials.

"She recommended me. She knew the producer."

"When did all this happen?"

"About a week after I saw Lucille Joy."

"How are you fixed for money?" I asked, knowing that rehearsal pay was small.

He laughed. "I have six hundred dollars."

I looked up questioningly.

"My wife scraped up a hundred dollars, and that was about all the cash we could spare." But as the actor was leaving for the airport, his elderly mother arrived. "John," she said, "take this, please, and remember that my heart goes with it." She stuffed something into his hand, and he started to give it back, but then he looked again, and his eyes popped. She had given him five hundred dollars.

As John finished his story, we regarded each other rather blankly. "So," he said, "remembering Lucille Joy, I kissed Mom, took it, and ran."

Meditating, I had made a mental note to check out the rest of the prediction when I next saw Conte. Meanwhile, I was trying to meditate on the Master Planner, to whom nothing was a surprise. "We have no news for God," a wise man had once said.

I began to visualize God. He came to me in the image of man, as I would expect from a boyhood with the Bible. I saw Him with a beard, and a benevolent, all-wise look, and then I realized the face was that of Leonardo da Vinci, inventor, artist, engineer, poet, philosopher, a godlike man if there ever was one.

The vision of Jesus next appeared. Was Christ really the son of God, had He been sent by the Creator? And if God was the Creator, who had created Him?

"There are three ways of examining the reality of God," a guru had told Marcia. "If you don't believe in God, and then die and discover there is no God, you will have a double disappointment. If you believe, then discover in death there is no God, at least you will have felt good on this earth, believing. But if you believe, and then dying, discover there is a God, then you will be doubly rewarded. So what can one lose by believing?"

I was to know more about meditation later, but during my first sessions, I was aware only that an attitude of skepticism was still very much part of my nature. And I would not have had it different.

Marcia was not concerned by my first abortive experiences. "Everything in Yoga," she said, "proceeds by stages. When you have completed one stage you will find yourself progressing naturally into another." Actually, hurrying things, physically or meditatively, could be damaging. And the mind is more vulnerable than the body.

"Meditation will come naturally after a while," Marcia said, "particularly as pranayama—breath control—develops. But meditation can be dangerous for the beginner if not supervised." She recalled an example of unwise meditation, ascribing almost incredible powers to the subconscious processes. The incident had occurred in class. "One woman in her middle years had been interested in rejuvenation. Her menstrual periods had stopped, signaling the change in life, and she was obsessed by the melancholy feeling that her productive life had ended. She began to experiment. Without supervision, she concentrated on the sacral area, in the pelvic region. She did this after extensive pranayama. As she lost herself in concentration, opening her subconscious, the menstrual cycle resumed. But she could not control it. She was taken to a hospital, and later a hysterectomy was performed to relieve her new problem."

The story startled me. "Perhaps," I said, "I am not ready for meditation."

"She was undisciplined, and sought a result she had not prepared herself for," Marcia replied. "The nature of your work obviously compels disciplined thinking. Because of this habit pattern, you should be able to control any resulting energy force."

Hatha Yoga and meditation run hand and hand. For it is necessary to fortify the container that is to house this vital electrical current, this kundalini, that uncoiled through the system like a serpent, awakening long-dormant glands and nerves and spiritual centers.

In meditation it was obviously helpful for a seed thought to be planted. My mind could not even begin to concentrate without a focal point. Some teachers would place a lighted candle before the neophyte, to rivet his attention, and in time establish a conditioned thought reflex. Others had their pupils visualize a point of the body, either the solar plexus below the navel or the pineal center between the eyes.

I had concentrated briefly on the solar plexus, described as the sun or center of the chakra group. Nothing happened.

"It takes time," Marcia assured me. "Yet in only a few years, from the power produced by concentration I can manipulate my subconscious and get it to perform helpfully for me. For instance, getting ready to lecture, I may feel my energies flagging after a day with classes and children. So I tell my subconscious that if it will provide the energy I require for a successful talk, I will reward my conscious later with a good meal and a warm bath."

Was she jesting?

"No," she said, "it really works."

"Just the thought of that bath makes you feel better," I suggested.

She smiled placidly. "It has all been pragmatically, if not scientifically, established," she said. She turned to the pages of *Beyond Telepathy* by Dr. Andrija Puharich, a physician and inventor, who had long labored in the extrasensory field. The practiced meditator, Puharich, explained, had a built-in world of his own. "He is not aware of, or bothered by, the noises of the body. These have been brought under harmonious control. His mind, as a result of the concentration exercises, is not disordered, and therefore he can allow a single hallucination to appear in his mind and manipulate and control it as though it were a puppet. He controls it; it does not possess him."

Apparently, this was Marcia's way.

I had a new seed thought. It was peace. I stood in the center of this peace, the source from which it emanated— a strange thought considering that I was not at peace and my mind was ever grappling, Western-style, with personal problems. Nevertheless I intoned after Marcia: "At the center of all peace I stand and nought can harm me there."

It was a comforting thought, but I still had to cope with the stress created in my own life by others. How could I attain harmony all by myself? There was a way.

"If it had not been for Yoga," Marcia said, "I don't see how I could have gone through my own breakup and divorce."

"Did you just blot it out?" I asked.

She shook her head. "That would be complete withdrawal. The yogi withdraws into his own mind, soul, spirit, only to look at himself with detachment and then act in a way to assure inner harmony."

It still seemed a bit vague.

She explained, "I was at my lowest point, bogged down with failure, not knowing how I was to carry on for myself and my three children, when suddenly, one day, I heard a voice. It was gentle, yet insistent; it said, 'The hierarchy shall not let you down.'"

"Hierarchy?"

Marcia's face lit up. "Yes, hierarchy, the order of things, headed up by God, a God who becomes very personal during meditation. As I heard this voice, I felt a general irradiation, like the feeling I often had during meditation, and I realized then that deep in my subconscious I had a storehouse of power, which my subconscious had summoned in my need."

"And that was all?" I felt let down.

She gave me an almost beatific smile. "My whole life was changed, and you ask was that all. Some people talk of a magic moment of illumination, in which they suddenly are face to face with God. But from my own experience, I would say that we do not find Him all at once. But we never know when those first glimpses of a universal harmony that we get in meditation will crystallize into a self-revealing irradiation."

So I thought of myself as the center of all peace. I saw myself between two huge columns. Behind me was a bearded Jehovah, the highly personal God of the Jews: then came a sublime Jesus. He considered me with serene detachment. I held this image for a while; it was succeeded by the image of Abraham Lincoln. But it was not Lincoln himself that I visualized but a statue of the Great Emancipator, sitting in bronze majesty on a bench, compassion stirring in its suffering eyes. As I concentrated on this image, a thrill ran through me. The image of Lincoln was so vivid that I opened my eyes to see if it still held. With this, it passed, but closing my eyes brought it back.

I told Marcia about it later.

"Ever so slightly," she said, "you are beginning to manipulate your subconscious."

The next morning we did our Hatha Yoga, but did not meditate. We were to meditate in the evening at the home of Anne Harkless in nearby Belmont. Anne was a divorcée, and, like Marcia, a Radcliffe graduate and a teacher of Yoga. She had two children, who were in their beds when we arrived. They were not old enough to meditate. Anne, barefooted and wearing a long flowing dress that resembled a sarong, greeted us with a smile. She was a slim thirty-three, with impassive good looks, and like Marcia, of solid New England stock. She introduced us to a young friend, a Harvard student. He was only nineteen, but, as Marcia said, more of a man than most.

As I shook his hand, the thought struck me that there must be something about Yoga that leveled all age barriers between the sexes. Or perhaps sex had little to do with it. I wasn't quite sure.

Ours was a group meditation. With three others, we sat down cross-legged in a rather bleak living room for our communication with the higher forces. Another guest was a young East Indian, a graduate student in nuclear physics at Harvard, whose father was the Swami Bhola Nath, a truly wondrous holy man back in India, according to the son. The other two were Americans, novices like myself.

We sat around in a circle, our spines straight, masking our thoughts behind a façade of polite inquiry.

As I sat, eyes closed, I waited for the seed thought to be planted. But none was given. Apparently there were seasoned meditators, who needed no spur to jog them into the road to sublimity. But it was different for me. My mind rattled restlessly all over creation. In fact, I was thinking about how I should be home, working, when I was startled by a sudden sibilance. I looked up, and saw the barely perceptible movement of Anne's lips. There was another, equally musical sound, and I saw her young friend's lips moving slightly. The sound was like a chant, a long drawn-out *om* or *aum*. *Om* was the sound of nature, God, creation; and repetition supposedly worked like prayer, helping to get one in tune with the Maker, setting the mood of peace and harmony in meditation.

It was a pleasant sound, and the meditation ended in

fifteen minutes on the same note. We opened our eyes and exchanged experiences. Imbued with the traditional truthfulness of Yoga, I observed that minutes had passed before I even realized we were in meditation.

The East Indian, Priya Mehta, nodded understandingly. "The mind is as restless as the sea," he said solemnly, "it takes much practice to harness it." He spoke well, with a bright animation and a barely perceptible accent. "A mullah [Moslem priest] was sitting outside a mosque meditating, when a woman apparently immersed in her own thoughts walked by so closely that her dress brushed against the mullah. He looked up, annoyed. 'Can't you see, woman, that I am deep in holy meditation and you have disturbed me?' The woman replied, 'I was also meditating, but I was thinking of my household chores, and I did not even know you were there. Were you as concerned with your God as I with my household, you would not have noticed me.'"

We all laughed, though I noticed that our Indian friend had made the priest a Moslem, not a Hindu like himself. I suppose this was allowable in the circumstances.

From what Marcia had said, I had gathered that Yoga was not a ruling passion of India, and wondered why, considering its traditional association.

"Everybody in India knows about Yoga, but few live by it," Priya acknowledged.

"Why is that?" I asked.

"It may be the influence of Buddhism, which is basically agnostic, and sees only the eternal now."

But Buddhism had begun with the Gautama, some six hundred years before Christ, whereas Raja Yoga, the Yoga of spiritual introspection, had been formally systematized by the Hindu Pantajali some two hundred years before Christ, though it went back, loosely, another three thousand years.

Frankly, I didn't see the connection. Was it true, perhaps that India was not as spiritual as its boosters would like the West to believe?

Priya Mehta conceded that true Yoga made certain demands. "Nehru practiced Yoga faithfully," he observed, "but only the Hatha Yoga, the physical. He never believed in God." He added reflectively, "But lately, I do not know, there were signs before death that his eyes were opened."

He looked around with a gleam in his eyes. "If you believe in death, you have to accept God. For without death there is no life." And without life, to be sure, there was no death. He obviously believed in reincarnation.

He smiled enigmatically and his dark liquid eyes seemed to travel back to his home in the Himalayas, where his father was a high and noble sage. He recalled what his father had said before he came to this country for his doctorate. They had been talking about finding God.

"How long," the father asked, "have you studied in the colleges?"

"Four years," the son replied.

"And now you must leave your family and journey to a far country, and when you are through, all you will have is a diploma. Is that not right?"

The son nodded.

"And yet," the Swami said, "people who take years to acquire a scrap of paper expect to find God in a moment of prayer."

Marcia, too, had a story, more American than Hindu, about God and his relation to man. "There were once two neighbors," she began. "One caroused, went out with women, drank, coveted his neighbor's wife, apparently broke all the commandments, and yet prospered. Meanwhile, his neighbor prayed to God every day, sometimes several times a day when things went wrong. Yet his fortunes lagged as the other's rose. In desperation, he finally appealed to the Lord: 'Why is it, Lord, that you do so well by this sinner who never thinks of you, and so badly by me, who constantly turns to you?'

"The Lord thought a moment and replied, 'Because he isn't always pestering me—that's why.' "

There was an obvious moral. "Egotism," said Marcia, quoting from the Swami Pavitrananda, "divides man from man and separates him from God." She elaborated: "In other words, man finds salvation not in thinking about himself, but in working for others."

With meditation—or what passed for it with me—my powers of analysis appeared sharpened. I dug deeper for reasons and the reasons behind reasons. I became keenly aware of the relationship of apparently isolated events to the whole of the great human drama. Nothing could be judged in itself or by itself. A young woman I knew, defending an extramarital peccadillo, had protested that "a beautiful relationship justified itself."

She was trying to convince herself, of course, and it was not for me to awaken another's pangs of guilt. But what was this beauty she talked about? That was the root of the equation. Could there be beauty without truth and integrity? In the very proportion a relationship departed from truth, so was it lacking in beauty. Beauty was truth, and truth lay within the self. Could we find the truth without first knowing ourself? And so as Yoga sought to provide this knowledge of self, so Yoga became an instrument of truth and beauty.

To attain truth, the individual had first to rid himself of a blinding vanity. "As a first step to finding ouselves—and truth—we must eliminate the rot and excrement of false ego," Mrs. DeVries had said. "As we purge ourselves, a vacuum forms within, and since Nature abhors a vacuum, truth will be ready to enter."

It was ridiculous, Mrs. DeVries had said, for anybody to think they could just sit down and begin meditating. However, my own work habits, plus my application to Hatha Yoga, had enabled me to develop sufficiently for the concentration and contemplation that preceded the highest meditation.

I never reached Samadhi, the most exalted level, where the individual spirit supposedly merges with the infinite of the universe, but I did quiet myself inside and think things out, and I did manage some peace of mind in difficult circumstances. New ideas and concepts ran through my mind. At times, I felt as much a part of the universe as anything in it, and this gave me a strong feeling of being protected, but not at all times.

My reaction was not unusual, I discovered on discussing it with Mrs. DeVries. "That is what Yoga is supposed to do for you," she said, "make you free through better understanding of yourself and the world around you."

But in order to profit from Yoga, either the physical or the meditations or both, the individual had to understand what he was looking for and what Yoga had to offer. Nobody, she felt, had said it better than the great teacher Prasad Shastri. And in her musical voice, as we sat looking out on the majestic Hudson as it rolled past Nyack, Mrs. DeVries read aloud to me from *Yoga,* Shastri's great work:

"All wish to live free, free from the tyranny of the mind and the senses, and also from the fear of adverse circumstances. Restriction is always painful, and man will never be satisfied while he is subject to it. His search after pleasure, power, wealth and knowledge is the outer sign of his need and instinctive longing for expansion and freedom. After making countless experiments which lead nowhere, at last he turns his attention in on himself, and seeks truth there and not in outer experience. Then Yoga having revealed the goal and the significance of his search to him, proceeds to give the method whereby it may be realized. This method cannot be practised successfully where there is prejudice or enmity toward others, or where it is employed to run away from life and its responsibilities. The chief aim of the Yoga"—Mrs. DeVries held up a delicately modeled hand for emphasis—"is to give the aspirant first an intellectual idea and then a direct vision of truth and his identity with it. Through this progressive awareness of his true nature, the Yoga teaches him how to live as a master of circumstance and at home in any walk of life."

This seemed to sum up the total purpose of Yoga pretty well. But I knew the burden of meditating would bother others more than the Hatha Yoga itself, just as it had bothered me.

When did we stop thinking and start meditating? Actually, there was no clear cut line of division, but there were several stages to meditating properly. Hatha Yoga played an important preliminary role. It developed pranayama—the breath control that built up the pranic energy bestirring the subconscious—and it advanced a certain mental discipline which was valuable in controlling the conscious thinking sufficiently to keep it concentrated on the seed thought. As our thoughts stir restlessly, Shastri had said, we learn one of the laws of yogic control. "No thought can remain long in the mind unless we actively support it with our vital energy."

To help meditators, he had drawn a little analogy. "We must not argue with the thoughts or elaborate on them. They are like pigeons whom we have fed every day. Now they come as usual for their food, and if we do not give it, they make a clamor. They fly around in agitation and try to attract our attention. If we shout at them, they become encouraged, feeling that they have at least secured that. But we must leave the window closed and all silent within. If we do it day after day, they become discouraged and go to seek for food elsewhere."

Actually, as I remembered my grandmother once saying, most of living was in the mind. It was what we thought of things—not what they were intrinsically—that determined our state of mind, our happiness or sadness, our feeling of success of failure. That was what was meant by free will: our response to an event, rather than control of the event itself. "To be able to think what we like," Shastri said, "instead of being prey of any wandering thought and the hypnotized victim of any orator who wishes to exploit us is true freedom."

In the first stages, as he seeks control, the meditator sits in the cross-legged meditative posture, or on a chair if he prefers, and tries to calm the mind and nerves with a little pranayama, breathing in and out rhythmically and crystallizing his thoughts in images—creative visualization. This was the beginning of the concentration stage, and Shastri had his hints on this, too, for the disheartened beginner. "For some time," he said, "when we present the object of meditation to the mind, we have the experience that it soon fades away. If it is a test, the words seem to be of little meaning; if we meditate on a form, it becomes vague. At other times, the meditation is disturbed by restlessness, by wondering how we are getting on, by doubts as to the validity of the process, and so on. . . .

"While we are practising concentration we should be very patient. Again and again the text of meditation is dropped by our wavering mind, and again and again we pick it up and revive it without fuss or disturbance. Slowly a current of interest is created and now the concentration becomes easier and more natural."

After concentration, which is relaxing if nothing else, comes contemplation. In this stage, which I eventually reached, the pieces of events or situations examined in concentration are seen clearly in a unified, integrated whole. And the false ego, which Mrs. DeVries had been so critical of, began to lose itself in an awareness of the greater grandeur of the individual's relation to the universe. Here he should really get to know himself better. I could visualize Mrs. DeVries' musical voice reading from Shastri: "All the limitations of the ego as well as of the object begin to be transcended . . . the separate ego, identified with body and mind, annihilates itself before the grand vision of unity, the Consciousness which contains the whole universe. Then that Consciousness is found in the individual also, where it had been merely concealed by the false ego, as the sun by a thick cloud."

The ultimate goal was Samadhi, a superexalted state, in which the "last veils are dissolved that separate the Consciousness encased in the limited body and mind and the consciousness that underlies the whole universe."

I had no intention of worrying about Samadhi. Only the saints approached this state. The higher Samadhi supposedly reveals the truth about man's spiritual relationship with the universe, but there is also a lower Samadhi, Shastri said, in which the truth of certain cosmic laws was revealed when the object of the meditation itself was something finite. "Professor Yukawa, the Japanese physicist who won the Nobel prize for physics for his prediction of the particle called the meson, said that the new idea came to him when he was alone, late at night, and he had passed into a state of meditation on the problem. Newton, too, passed into meditation states in which he was totally insensible to the world around him, and many artists speak of such experiences as the source of their inspiration."

To provide meditation with a sort of running start, there were six broadly different types of seed thoughts which the sage Patanjali had classified in his survey of Yoga long before Christ. The first of these was meditation on peace of mind, one of my own first seed thoughts, with a stress on feelings of sympathy and compassion for the unrighteous and the unhappy.

Then came meditating on the true self, shining and beyond limitations. Two startling thoughts: "Before Abraham was, I am," and "I and the Father are one."

"These meditations," said Shastri, "are like reviving the memory in a man who has lost it. He is given his real name by the doctor and repeats it with conviction. He is shown pictures of his house and relatives and friends and tries to remember them. His mind says: 'I do not know these people,' but through repetition with conviction his memory comes back, first in flashes and fragments, and then completely. The memory is not just the idea, 'Well, I do know them after all,' but a living experience which brings with it all the associated memories of incidents in childhood."

As a third seed thought, the lives of the great sages— Socrates, Confucius, Mohammed—might be taken, and I had done this with Lincoln. Or it might be a great incarnation. The Hindus felt that Christ, Krishna, and Buddha were all incarnations of God; another was Kalki, the Messiah of the East who is yet to come. One specific seed thought: Visualize Christ leading his disciples and yourself sitting in peace and reverence among them.

Meditating on dreams was another focal point. "In the dream our hopes of wealth and fears of destruction will never be realized because they are unreal. By deep meditation we should understand this is true of the waking world also."

As for the fifth starter: Calm the mind (with pranayama), shut the eyes, and think of a line of light down the center of the body. Press forefinger between the forehead, down the middle of the navel, using the pressure of the sensation as an aid to begin.

And, lastly, the *om,* the supreme word of God, signifying all of nature and the universe—the sacred word by which the meditation had taken off in Anne Harkless' home in Belmont without my even being aware of it.

Like the rest of Yoga, meditation was a highly personal experience. Only the subject could tell what he was getting out of it, and, to even make a start, he had to have a rough idea of what he wanted out of it. Otherwise, it was so much wasted time and energy. As the Bhagavad-Gita had said, "A man must raise himself by his own efforts, and must not allow himself to be dragged down. He alone is his own friend, and he alone is his own enemy."

Just as meditation had different seed thoughts, so it had many different stresses in achieving detachment and freedom within certain channels. These were meditations stressing either Karma Yoga, Bhakti Yoga, Jnana Yoga, or Raja Yoga. All meditations overlapped, but Karma Yoga was easier for the Westerner because it was meditation on work, and work was something tangible. Actually, the teachings of Karma Yoga were little different than those preached by the great leaders of the West. It was not result but the striving that counted. The Swami Pavitrananda had said, "It is very doubtful if you can improve the world, but you can certainly improve yourself by means of unselfish work. Work at full speed with the energy of your whole being, but do not think of the result in terms of success or failure. One who can be indifferent to success or failure is usually calm and serene; and it is obvious that such a person will work better—especially during a crisis—than one who is always in feverish anxiety about the result."

I meditated about the nature of work. I saw visual pictures of the great chiefs of our time, Franklin Roosevelt, Winston Churchill, Charles de Gaulle. A dying FDR sighed that few leaders lived to finish the work they were in. A penetrating Churchill stressed that a man should strive only for the right, since human affairs were so precarious at best, that he could at least have the consolation of having acted with integrity if events took a bad turn.

As I meditated, I began to realize I could work best with detachment. When friends asked how this book would do, I found myself shrugging. Not wanting to appear sanctimonious, I did not mention I wanted to produce only the best of which I was capable. How else could I work, when the only fruits I could be sure of were those of inner self-satisfaction!

From Karma Yoga we passed into Bhakti Yoga, the meditation aimed at achieving union with God through devotions. There was a tie-up between Karma Yoga and Bhakti Yoga. The Swami Pavitrananda had said, "If the Karma yogi performs his daily task in a sincere spirit of Bhakti, then he must begin to feel that his personal will is gradually giving way to the Divine Will. When this feeling at last ripens into actual experience, he enjoys a calm which nothing in the world can disturb."

Whether it was the exercise, or the meditations, or both, I had felt gradually more at peace in the first weeks of my regimen—I did not realize how much calmer until my temporary layoff due to the old neck injury.

I found my new hard-won tolerance leaving me, and had to check a critical attitude that had been briefly dormant in Concord. I tried meditating, but could not concentrate as well, when I was not doing my exercises daily. Marcia did not find this surprising. "The concentration required by the exercises helped with the meditation, but you weren't at it long enough to make it part of your habit pattern."

As I returned to Hatha Yoga and the meditations, Marcia stressed that even for a beginner they were not idle, unrewarding meanderings. "Many people may never meditate properly, but will settle for the peace and relaxation inherent in concentrating on sitting still. But in properly meditating, one inevitably gets a glimpse of truth, and with it some application to everyday affairs."

Meditating on the great sages was indeed helpful, for the clarity of their thinking was often revealing in current contexts. Ramakrishna, perhaps the greatest of the Indian holy men, meditating, saw clearly through the sham that masked so much human activity, even in the field of philanthropy, and his thinking, opening my eyes, started me off on similar lines. So much of this charitable effort, he found, reflected personal vanity, a secret wish for glory, the desire to alleviate a guilt complex, relief of boredom feeding on shallowness.

This was a most potent seed thought. I turned to the do-gooders: the rich New Yorkers who preached integration, and gave liberally to the Urban League and the NAACP while living in the pristine lily whiteness of the Silk Stocking District, home of the liberal-talking Rockefellers, Javitses, Nixons, and Wagners, while city blocks away in ugly squalor seethed the most segregated of all-black ghettos —Harlem.

And how many of these great talkers sent their children to the public schools for which they advocated integration for others? The answer would not be charitable.

In Concord, the charitable had issued a Declaration of Welcome to all creeds and colors. But how many Negroes could buy the large-zoned plots in this cradle of the free and the brave? "It would only be twenty or twenty-five thousand dollars for the land, and another thirty or forty thousand for the house," I recalled a Concord philosopher telling me with a glint of gray humor.

At this point, I thought it charitable to pass on to a new meditation for another week or so.

In Jnana Yoga, which most students never reach, the meditator lays stress on the individual's place in the universal scheme. Jnana Yoga was often known as the Science of Wisdom. It was advanced stuff, and I only piddled at it at best. "Through Jnana," Marcia pointed out, "the yogi sees that life and death are all the same, a merging of the personality with the universe, and so the prospect of death does not faze him. He sees life nakedly, in its bright and dark aspects, and learns to separate the tinsel from the tree. In this Yoga we get the full realization of spiritual detachment from the body. There is complete control of the mind, marked by the ability to withdraw at will from any situation or circumstance."

The Vedas—Hindu scripture—suggested that only those who had mastered the previous disciplines should approach Jnana—and I was inclined to agree. I was a long way off but I was trying.

It was Raja Yoga, the ruling Yoga, that intrigued me. It combined different elements from the other meditations and sought to weave them into a pattern by which a man could run his life.

It comprised eight stages, including the Asana or posture stage, and the pranayama, the breathing exercises designed to promote concentration and kindle the electrical currents which supposedly induced clairvoyance and raised the level of consciousness.

"By means of concentration," Swami Pavitrananda had said, "the mind may become such a fine instrument that its possessor may at times develop certain supernormal powers like that of seeing into the future, or reading another's thoughts."

Yet the psychic was not in itself spiritual, as I had discovered from observing many clairvoyants in action. Many exploited their strange powers to their own advantage—

and to the disadvantage of the gullible. Through Raja
Yoga, I considered many subtle uses of the psychic, my
mind dwelling first on the familiar.

Could the psychic force ever be developed and channeled
to meet the needs of a challenging space age? It was a
prospect, as one Air Force researcher had told me, with
the U.S. hopeful of being able to land spacemen on the
moon and other planets, then communicate back and forth
via telepathy. "We haven't yet found how to cultivate this
power," an Air Force major reported, "but we hope to find
a common denominator in the psychic personality that we
can isolate and develop—once we know what it's all about."

At any rate, there was no doubt in Marcia's mind as to
how to develop the paranormal or psychic.

"Concentrate on the third eye as you deep breathe,"
Marcia directed, "and you will find the electrical energy
mustered in breathing rushing to this center after a while.
In time, as you concentrate, you will notice a tingling sensation, indicating pulsating energy and budding psychic
power."

After weeks of concentration I noted a slight buzz between my eyes, then a whirring sound. Psychic after psychic, meanwhile, reading me clairvoyantly, was telling me
that I had become as psychic as they. I began to get pre-
monitions, and looking at a couple who seemed perfectly
happy, I found myself thinking, "They will be divorced
within two years." It was not altogether pleasant, particularly when the prediction materialized.

At her best, Marcia represented the new Western school
of Yoga, which frowned at an East caught up in the ancient
stereotypes of holy men who tried to move mountains before they moved themselves.

"In this country," Marcia related, "the pupil is all-important, not the guru, though the student is often only a
reflection of the guru's teaching. We try to show the student how he can improve mind and body with Yoga, while
in India many holy men see Yoga as a prop for their own
holiness. Such nondetachment contradicts the very detachment that Yoga fosters."

We all wondered what kind of a holy man Priya's father,
the Swami Bhola Nath, would be. He had spent a year in
England, mostly London, before acceding to his son's re-
quests that he come to the United States and illuminate
the West with his wisdom.

Not long after, the phone rang at Concord ashram, and
Priya Mehta announced that the personage had arrived.

There were a number of arrangements to be made for the twelve-mile jaunt from Cambridge. "Do you have camera and film to take pictures of my father?" Priya asked.

There was a dearth of film, but Priya suggested that his hosts would have ample time to acquire some before his father arrived.

"Perhaps," Marcia said, "you could pick up the film on the way out." They were being driven by American friends.

"It is enough," Priya said, "that I am bringing my father; you do not seem to realize the importance of this visit."

Louis volunteered to get the film and take the pictures, easing the crisis.

In the afternoon, after the last Hatha Yoga student had lifted his weary muscles from Boulder Grove, the Indian mission arrived. The Swami, a dark man of serene mien, could be identified at a distance by his bright orange turban. He was a picture of Hindu trimness, in a black button-down coat below the knees, and narrow, puttee-like trousers. He reminded me of scenes from the old movie *Gunga Din,* which I had so much enjoyed once, and I half-expected to see a passel of Khyber Rifles at his heels. But there was only the thin, brooding, hawklike face of son Priya, who appeared inordinately nervous for so auspicious an occasion.

There were a couple of dozen Yoga aficionados on hand to meet the Swami. As big as life, he perched himself at one end of the large room, and we formed a wide arc about him, eager to hear what a distinguished spiritual leader had to say. But there was to be a formal introduction first.

Priya's introduction followed an interlude during which he played a sacred Indian hymn on a stringlike instrument indigenous to his native land. "In India," Priya began after the last note had faded away, "my father is known as a very holy man. In the streets, hundreds, thousands of people adore him wherever he goes. He is known for his wisdom and for the help he has given so many."

Deferentially, he turned the floor over to the Swami. The holy man sat as he addressed the group. His English was good, though marked by a curious sibilance. He proposed to lead us in an old-fashioned meditation, but first he had a personal message.

"Do not think of me as Indian and yourself as Americans," he said. "We are all the same. You do not know me, but in India I am well-known, even famous. Thousands follow me in the streets, the President of India sends people to me for guidance. And now I have journeyed nine

thousand miles to do what I can to help you. Believe me
when I tell you that I am your servant; no, your slave."

As he spoke, Louis' camera busily mirrored each noble
expression and gesture. "Thank you," the Swami said with
each flash, "your picture is in my heart."

As the picture-taking continued, often interrupting the
Swami's flow of words, Marcia observed almost testily,
"Louis, don't you think we have quite enough pictures?"

"I'll run out of film soon," Louis rejoined, taking a shot
while perched in the frame of a window.

"Thank you," the holy man said, placing a hand on his
chest, "your picture is in my heart."

The Swami had a couple of basic thoughts. "To know
what Yoga is like, you must experience it yourself." This
had a familiar ring. He nodded toward a nearby listener.
"This gentleman," he went on sonorously, "asked me what
Yoga was, and I pointed to this cup of tea"—he bent forward and touched the cup—"and told him that the tea
must be tasted to be described; it must be experienced. To
tell somebody that it is good or bad is meaningless, or even
that it is bitter or sweet. They must find out for themselves.

He spoke of detachment; there must be separation, self-
analysis, before there could be union, or rather, reunion,
of the personality. He was there, he assured us, to help us
understand such intricacies. "I came from a noble family,"
he said, "and could have remained in that atmosphere, but
I chose to serve. And now"—he smiled—"tell me how I
can serve you. That is all I ask."

A smile wreathed his dark, expressive face. "One minute
at the feet of a guru," he said, "is worth a thousand hours
of meditation."

It was a startling thought, considering the emphasis some
placed on meditation.

But we were to meditate, too. "Think yourselves in the
august presence of God," the holy man said.

We closed our eyes and meditated.

The next fifteen minutes seemed interminable.

Then the holy man spoke, ending the meditation, and
son Priya rose and announced that his father had come a
long way, the journey was expensive, and there would be
a free-will offering to help defray expenses of the holy
man's passage. Marcia brought out a basket for donations,
and shortly thereafter the distinguished visitor took his
leave.

The holy man was no surprise to Marcia. She had seen
his like in India. He was a kind, sincere man of the old

school, seasonably imbued with a sense of mission. "In
India," she said, "it is traditional for the holy man to feel
at one with the divine." She smiled drily. "But so often,
standing so close to God, he can not distinguish the difference."

"I get by very nicely on eight hundred calories a day."

It seemed incredible.

She was on the go from six in the morning, getting her children off to school, making three different meals each meal—vegetarian, meat, and modified vegetarian (for me). She did virtually all her own cleaning in a ten-room house, except for a cleaning woman who came in once a week. At midnight, she was revising and typing husband Louis' term papers. And she was busy with two outside Yoga classes at the Boston YMCA and a Lexington church, her own home groups, and private lessons.

Also she wrote poetry, studied astrology, gave astrological readings, and found time for conversations with children and friends. Yet she never seemed tired.

But still, eight hundred calories were about twelve hundred less than the basic minimum to maintain weight and health. With only eight hundred calories, it hardly seemed likely that she could assimilate enough fats and carbohydrates, not to mention the vital proteins needed to produce the energy she was burning during a nonstop eighteen-hour day.

It could be, of course, that her calorie count was off. That was scientist Bill Mercer's suggestion.

"Nobody," he said, "could be doing what you do every day and get by on eight hundred calories. That's a starvation-type diet. You must be nibbling on things through the day: walnuts, a handful of sunflower seeds, a cookie now and then."

"I have that included," Marcia said.

"But you're not even getting the meat and fish we need for high-type protein," I protested. "There must be something wrong."

"I take eggs, which some vegetarians don't," Marcia said, "milk, and soybeans in various forms—that takes care of the protein intake."

Marcia was five feet three and weighed one hundred and five pounds. There wasn't an extra ounce on her slim, sinuous frame. Yet, she was gracefully molded, curving in and out in the various approved places. In fact, she was so symmetrical, so perfectly proportioned, that I could think of no more suitable model to pose for the Yoga postures in this book.

Yet, having experienced the rumblings of hunger from my brief vegetarianism, I could hardly credit the accuracy of the calorie count.

"How do you do it?"

"Deep breathing," she said, "and meditation. Getting off by myself and withdrawing for a half hour, slowing down mind and body. So many people eat just out of nervous habit. And food is just something to carry around long enough to get rid of; it does no good in excess."

Through improved metabolism, Marcia was making better use of the food she did eat. There was less wastage, and fatigue-producing carbon dioxide was being constantly replaced by the high oxygen intake of deep breathing and pranayama. "As I keep saying," Marcia observed, "oxygen is the most vital of foods, and it is completely calorie-free. When you are really tired, it is sleep, enabling the body to replenish its oxygen reserves, which refreshes you, proof again of the fallacy of eating just to reduce fatigue or heighten energy."

"I still don't see how you do it on eight hundred calories," scientist Bill said, "when nine hundred calories is the most drastic reducing diet short of hunger."

"I can keep count of everything I eat and write it down," she said helpfully.

"That would never do," Bill said. "How would you measure the calories in an apple, or a watermelon, or a portion of asparagus, with any precision? You're bound to be a few calories off."

"I could weigh them," she said.

"You're not going to be weighing three or four grapes, a couple of crackers, a few walnuts, or anything else you nibble during the day. It's not practical."

"I could do it with Metrecal. I can try four cans of soup, 225 calories each, four times a day, and see how that works out." She laughed. "With that extra hundred calories, I might even gain weight."

"That's settled then," Bill said. "A scientific experiment it shall be."

Louis and I had been following the discussion with interest. "I don't think that's at all necessary," he said. "Marcia has nothing to prove."

"That's all right, Louis dear," Marcia assured her husband, "I would just like to prove it to myself."

The experiment began without fanfare, the very day that protein in the form of fish was added to my diet.

I had gone along with vegetarianism grudgingly, and

had admittedly felt lighter, almost floating at times. But since none of the meat or fish substitutes appealed to me, and I was allergic to most vitamins, Marcia had suggested adding fish to my diet. "If you liked soybeans, it would be different. But you have too many new things to contend with at once, what with going through Yoga and trying to absorb everything, including the meditations, at the same time."

But she still maintained her prejudice against red-blooded meat—stale flesh, she called it.

"You can have eggs too, if you like," said Marcia. "I don't insist that the children keep our diets. We have meat for them regularly, and eggs in the morning."

I felt like a villain for the next few days, digging into a swordfish steak or a halibut, while Marcia sipped at her Metrecal soup.

"What flavor is it?" I asked.

"Vanilla," she said, "and not bad at all."

"Don't you miss solid food?"

She shook her head. "It has all the vitamins and minerals I need, and I will continue just long enough to see whether I can maintain my energy level and weight with this nine-hundred-calorie intake."

In the week that followed, Marcia did every exercise that she showed me, others with her classes, and ran her household with unremitting vigor. I watched her closely. She rested for an hour or so during the afternoons, but she was up before seven in the morning and didn't turn in until midnight.

I saw no sign of a slackening pace, nor of weakening.

Day after day, she took her soup, mixing it with water and heating it to the temperature she preferred. She used four cans for the first few days, and one day she only used three; it was all she wanted. She was down to less than seven hundred calories that day.

"I'll make up for it later," she disclosed. "I'll have three or four grapes."

She took coffee every morning—her gravest fault as a food purist. "It's a ritual," she said, "and it has no calories." She took it black, without sweetening.

At the end of the week, she was ready for the weigh-in. We brought out the scales without ceremony. The hand stopped at 105½. She had, inexplicably, gained a half pound on a near-starvation diet.

What she had done, she did not recommend for others, unless they did Yoga and had the same attitude about food.

"Actually," she said, "I don't believe in dieting. With Yoga, I think we make the revealing self-discovery that food is generally an indulgence, and we quite often eat food that we don't even enjoy, and certainly don't require.

"Nearly everybody eats too much as they get older. Show me a person with excess meat on them, and I'll show you a person headed for trouble." She frowned. "Calories really don't mean much, because the required intake varies with the individual, in size, metabolism, and activity."

One day in class, she singled out a slim, alert-looking woman in slacks, who was standing on her head with the greatest of ease. She appeared in perfect health.

"I have never discussed diet with her," Marcia said, "but I am willing to wager that she doesn't consume a thousand calories a day, and I'm equally certain that she doesn't require the normal amount of sleep."

Shirley Clark was a housewife and mother, and a full-time bookkeeper, living in suburban Weston. In fifteen year her weight hadn't varied five pounds. She was five feet four, 110 pounds, age forty-one.

"Sleep?" she said. "Five or six hours is all anybody needs."

"Calories?"

She never counted them. "But it must be seven or eight hundred a day."

"How do you get by on so little?"

She smiled. "I have to work at it to get up that high. All those calorie tables don't mean a thing; it depends on what you're doing, will power, and what you want for yourself."

She regarded her slim hips critically. "Even with my so-called low-calorie intake, if I didn't do the headstand and other exercises regularly, my hips would bulge into a middle-age spread."

"Are you a vegetarian?"

"I don't believe in fads. I eat whatever I like, when I like, but with the exercise I find my appetite diminishing. Obviously, through exercise my body makes better use of the food I do eat, assimilating whatever minerals and vitamins it needs."

Her meals were not exactly Lucullan. She had coffee and a slice of toast in the morning, an apple or an orange for lunch, but might indulge in a steak or roast for dinner, the one meal she enjoyed with her family.

She was seldom hungry.

"Through controlled exercises I have managed to know

my body and its needs pretty well, and I can almost tell how much food I need any specified day."

Like Marcia she felt that excessive eating was a nervous habit, and the more relaxed the person, the less compulsive eating there was.

"There is no reason in the world," Shirley pointed out, "why a person who has attained his growth has to sit down to three squares a day. It's a plot against the house-wives of America."

Calories do count, but counting calories isn't enough. "The main advantage of calorie counters and charts," Marcia stressed, "is that it proves that most people habit-ually overeat. But still, many obese people have woefully inaccurate ideas about how much they consume and how much food is required to fuel the human machine. They are full of fears. They are afraid they will become weak if they miss a meal or two, just because their stomach grumbles a bit; they are afraid they will run short of needed vitamins, not realizing that a healthy body can muster what vitamins it needs on demand. But they're obviously not afraid of pandering to an infantile appetite, proving that chronic obesity is a form of immaturity."

Emotional frustration, of course, had a lot to do with overeating, that and the unadulterated monotony of dull, unimaginative living. Some food problems were to such a degree psychological in origin that Marcia often found herself wishing that she were a psychiatrist—except for the fact that many of her problem people had already gone that route.

One was a red-haired mother of four small boys, who had recently separated from her husband. She was tall, with classical features, marred by a double chin and a slack jaw. She was thirty years old and forty pounds overweight. On her third trip to the psychiatrist, he had said casually, "You know, you'd be a beautiful woman if you'd take some of that weight off." She never went back.

When she turned up for Marcia's class, she mentioned that she wanted to feel fit.

"And how about your weight?" Marcia said. "Don't you think some might come off?"

She nodded. "That's part of why I'm here."

She was an extremely well-coordinated woman, and seemed to do the exercises well. "She was one of the few fat women," Marcia recalled, "who I eventually allowed to do the headstand."

Long practice preceded the headstand, as Marcia worked

at toughening her student's neck so that it could bear the weight of her body. "She did neck exercises until her neck was as flexible as her waist, and she became adept at the shoulder stand, a natural preparation for the headstand because it strengthens the back and gets one used to the idea of being upside down."

She thought the headstand would give her student a psychological lift, since she had expressed interest in achieving the posture. But even so, the results were disappointing.

She came to the Yoga sessions faithfully once a week, but unlike most obese students she never dropped a pound. As diplomatically as possible, Marcia began asking about her diet. As she suspected, the woman was sampling about everything she made for her four hungry boys, from pecan pie to peanut butter sandwiches. But Marcia didn't have to be a psychiatrist to know that this compulsive eating was only a symptom, not a cause.

She thought perhaps the woman was frustrated because of the estrangement from her husband.

"You know," she said one day, "you'd be a beauty if you'd take some weight off."

The woman grimaced. "That's what the psychiatrist said." And she walked away.

Obviously, she wasn't profiting from Yoga. "It didn't matter whether it was her fault or mine," Marcia observed, "the guru is always responsible for a pupil's failure." And so she was determined to bring the matter to a head.

After the next class, they sat down together for a heart-to-heart talk. "I don't feel you're getting what you should out of the classes," Marcia said.

"I'm getting what I want," the woman replied.

"But these aren't just simple exercise sessions, the discipline you pick up here is supposed to extend to other areas of your life."

"I don't know what you mean." She sat stiffly upright in her chair.

Marcia smiled to take the sting from her words. "I mean that you're not a very good advertisement for Yoga."

"Why should that matter?"

Marcia tried another tack. "I'd like to see you do something more with yourself. With your natural beauty you could have any man you wanted if you would only slim down."

The woman laughed mirthlessly. "That's just what I don't want." She grimaced. "If I lose weight, my husband might come back."

That was the last Marcia saw of the lady who didn't want to be beautiful. But women overeating to confound their husbands were by no means rare. One woman of twenty-eight, sixty pounds overweight, had actually been sent to class by her husband. She had picked up the excess poundage in twelve months. He couldn't understand it, but it took Marcia only one session. "She couldn't have children of her own, and wanted to adopt one," Marcia said, "but the husband was against it."

It was a case of revenge, pure if not simple. "She had let herself get fat, eating everything in sight, so that her husband would find her unattractive and be accordingly frustrated."

From her experience as a teacher, Marcia was astounded by the number of women who overate through indifference to their husbands, and yet were too conventional, or bored, to attract anyone else.

"Yoga can't help anybody do anything they don't want to do," she stressed, "whether taking off weight or calming nerves."

But she might have accomplished more with the overweight mother of four in a private class.

"In a group session, it is obviously difficult to discuss personal problems in relation to the exercises." She sighed. "So many of these fat women are half-starved without knowing what they're starved for."

In three months of Yoga, I had slimmed down a bit and found myself younger-looking, stronger, and far more energetic with an ever diminishing appetite. I enjoyed my food, but I had stopped thinking in terms of three meals a day. I discovered that I could get by comfortably with one solid meal a day, with fish or meat, and a light snack for breakfast and lunch.

If I had a hearty dinner at night, I could work easily two or three hours the next morning before breakfast, disproving in my own case at least that a good breakfast was essential to a productive day.

Though I was eating less, I had an idea that my body was doing more with the food. I did not even mind getting up a little hungry from my one substantial meal after Marcia pointed out that "many people gorge themselves simply because of the time delay required for the stomach to signal the brain that it is satisfied."

I could now remember many times in the past leaving the table hungry, and feeling full an hour later.

Autosuggestion was of paramount importance in dieting

and for that reason Yoga was normally almost a specific for losing excess weight. I remembered accountant Charlie Weiser losing twenty pounds with Yoga, and I had not quite understood how it was done until I had a few weeks of Yoga myself. It was as easy to detach myself from food as from my problems—easier, since I fed on problems.

Yoga had changed my thinking about many things. I would have laughed three or four months before at Marcia's self-hypnotic tips for would-be dieters.

"Train the body to let go at a moment's notice," she said, "even when not tired. Just stretch out on a rug or any firm surface, lying on the back, and deliberately relax each part in turn, working from the toes up to the head and including also the inner organs, cells, nerves, muscle. Let the mind also relax and create soothing images of beautiful scenes, sunshine, and healing radiance, refreshing and vitalizing the whole body."

Dieting, like Hatha Yoga, has to begin in the mind.

"Many people eat to reduce tension, not realizing their power to accomplish the same end through direct suggestion."

On the honesty—and purpose—of the goal hinged success.

"Construct a vivid mental picture of the way you would like to be, not just physically but inwardly as well. The image should be realistic in that it represents the essence of all the finer qualities latent in your nature and which you are to some extent capable of activating. Feel that the object of your striving is not so much an outer change as a release of the true form within, even as a sculptor might be said to liberate his statue from encasing rock."

The dieting individual should let his figure speak for itself. "For your own sake as well as for the sake of your family and friends (who probably wouldn't believe you anyway) let them discover for themselves the amazing fact that you mean business. Otherwise, hard resolve may be frittered away in aimless conversation. Talking out something often precludes doing it."

There were a few specific prohibitions, of course. Whiskey, beer, and alcoholic beverages of any kind were out, as were barbiturates, tranquilizers, marijuana, tobacco, and drugs of any sort. Pupils on barbiturates and drugs couldn't summon the energy to persist with any serious discipline, were generally on edge.

I recalled Harold J. Reilly of the Rockefeller Center Health Service once telling me that sleeping-pill addicts had so little marginal emotional reserve that even the slightest upset might trigger suicide.

"When people habitually turn outside themselves for support," Marcia commented, "they are not conditioned to developing inner forces to withstand sudden crisis, whereas Yoga sets up a disciplined response almost as a reflex action."

As a vegetarian, Marcia's food pointers were rather routine. "Natural foods are better than those unduly bleached, processed, and preserved. Honey and molasses make satisfying substitutes for the empty calories of white sugar; and in the hands of a sympathetic cook, lentils, cabbage, and carrots prove surprisingly tasty. Much meat is unnecessary (vegetarians are rarely fat and generally endure to a healthy old age). Fresh vegetables, cereals, nuts, fruit, and dairy products are plentiful and important, but the main thing is to be as unfanatical as possible about food, serving what seems natural with the least fuss and nuisance. Herbs and spices can enhance the appeal of the simplest foods."

Marcia's own shopping habits were elementary. She never made out a grocery list. "I just pick out what looks freshest."

Dieting should be treated incidentally, even if it isn't incidental.

"The trouble with most diets is that one spends so much time debating what is to be on the day's menu that eating suddenly becomes of supreme importance. It's thinking about it that makes dieting hard. Normally, I take what food I want when I want it."

"But with all the things you're doing," I said, "you should require more energy than the average housewife or schoolteacher, for you combine the activities of both."

"It's not that difficult. Actually, the movements we do in Yoga diminish the appetite rather than increase it. Every last cell in the body is bathed with blood, more oxygen is assimilated, and the metabolism changes, with the glandular system stimulated to a point where excess tissue is more likely to be burned off."

I had watched Marcia now for weeks. Her normal diet was relatively simple. "I'm not a faddist," she said, "and I wouldn't remain a vegetarian for a minute if I thought it was detrimental. But I know from experience that meat often makes people logy. Fighters given big steaks a few hours before a fight have acted in the ring as though they were drugged."

Louis wouldn't so much as look cross-eyed at an egg,

but Marcia was not as fussy. "In India," she said, "they had a furious debate as to whether eggs belonged in a vegetarian diet. Some decided that unfertilized eggs were meatless, but others thought this unfair to the cock, which normally fertilized the hen—and so they took eggs off the vegetarian menu. But I'm not as meticulous."

Fish was a fresh food, even though classified with meat, and could be served on a Concord table the day after it was caught, or even the same day. "Fish is a vegetable," young Chris quipped one evening, "it grows in the ocean."

Marcia advocated vitamin supplements, particularly wheat germ oil, especially beneficial for improving the endurance and heart responses.

"It not only stimulates vital hormones but helps one to bear stress and hard labor," Marcia said. "In a test at the University of Illinois Physical Fitness Laboratory, sedentary middle-aged men, taking a teaspoon of wheat germ oil daily for twelve weeks, stepped up their endurance 50 per cent while exercising. A similar group, taking the same exercises, without the wheat germ, increased their endurance just under 20 per cent.

The Moore-Acker table was well-stocked with fruits, vegetables, cheeses of all types, milk, rice, and the inevitable soybeans. There were cereals, cold and hot, and meat for the children. "To be a vegetarian, a person must be imbued with the feeling that they are accomplishing something for themselves, and that's asking too much, philosophically, of the children," Marcia explained.

Honey and molasses were available, potatoes baked in their skins were plentiful. When I wanted bread and butter I generally had to ask for it. Milk, despite the attacks of health faddists, was regarded as a good protein source.

The ancient yogis counseled different foods for different temperaments. The Bhagavad-Gita of India—and Bronson Alcott—listed three varieties: the pure, stimulating, and impure or rotting. The vegetarian foods were naturally the pure, and presumably brought pureness and tranquillity to the mind while soothing the body.

There were many famous vegetarians in the Western world, notably George Bernard Shaw and Adolf Hitler. Hitler, known for his tantrums, would not have struck the most ardent Nazi as a calm type. Shaw was provocatively elfish, but may have been calm inwardly.

The stimulating foods were mainly meats, fish, eggs, spices. Theoretically they stirred the passions, and who knows but what Hitler might have been sneaking them in, just as he quietly kept Eva Braun as his mistress, while correspondents were writing from Germany that a eunuch-like Fuehrer didn't have time for women.

These highly-flavored foods, the vegetarians insisted, also induced hardening of the arteries, high blood pressure, and uremic disorders.

And the impure foods?

"Mostly meats or fish that aren't served fresh but are processed, and contaminate with time." This was Marcia's definition of the Hindu's tamasic foods.

Traditionally, Hindus didn't eat of the sacred cow. And in a Bengal famine during the early stages of the war some three million peasants and workers died of hunger without a single cow being killed.

But this attitude was not universal. I vividly recall one high-caste Indian in this country saying, as he downed a thick steak, "These taboos are for the peasants. Centuries ago, when there was a milk shortage in the land, the rulers enlisted the support of the priesthood to keep cows alive and producing, and so the cow became sacred."

With a cynical smile, the Anglicized Brahmin reached for the steak sauce.

I experimented, indifferently, with total vegetarianism and then a fish supplement for a month, before adding meat again, with Marcia's blessing.

"I agree," I said, "that we shouldn't make issues about food, and so I'm going to eat what comes naturally."

She had no objection. "You know what it's like now, and the evaluation is up to you."

I remember Mrs. DeVries saying, in Nyack, as we dined on chicken and ham, that moderation in all things was part of Western Yoga. Vegetarianism, she pointed out, was particularly prevalent in southern India, where temperatures held at 110 degrees in the shade. But in the moderate temperate zones even the yogis engaged in moderate consumption of heat-giving meat. "You could hardly expect Eskimos to be vegetarians," one pliable yogi pointed out. And the Tibetans living in the Himalayas, though Buddhists, were meat-eaters, while Buddhists in the warmer climates were often vegetarians. "They modified their religious tradition," Marcia observed, "to suit a harsh terrain that could feed animals but not men."

In an America that worshiped youth, it was remarkable how many people carried surplus poundage that made them look, feel, and act older.

Was the desire to be youthful vain, and therefore an undesirable aim?

"Hardly," Marcia said, "when you consider that productivity and youthfulness go hand in glove." She mused a moment. "People who stay young relish living more; their marriages are better, they make better parents, and being more at ease, they avoid dis-ease."

Perhaps because she was twelve years older than her husband, she had given the subject of youthfulness so much attention. "People not only look younger when they lose weight," she observed, "but some of their new youthfulness stems from the fact that they thought young enough to lose weight. Youth is even more psychological than it is physical. I have walked down Newbury Street in Boston and Fifth Avenue in New York, admiring the exquisite styles and new hats in the windows, but the very people who pay hundreds of dollars for new clothes, and preen themselves on how they look, disregard the fat that makes it impossible for any dress to look good.

"Beauty is the greatest lack today. I can't understand why people will be so selective about a dress, or any article of attire, and neglect the figure which they are supposedly adorning.

"I see their heavy, drooping faces in the subways and buses; at thirty and thirty-five the men are already aging, showing signs of decay. Their faces are beginning to sag, their cheeks losing their firm line, their waists thicken; their eye has lost the alertness of youth. The women do a little better, but their posture is bad; they have lost their springiness of stride, they seem harried and worn, and wrinkles show in telltale lines around their eyes and mouth."

It was almost a diatribe.

"I get somewhat explosive about it because it is so completely unnecessary. But just dieting itself, or calisthenics, won't restore youth. People have to learn how to ease their pressures and take a clear look at themselves. And Yoga is the only exercise that joins mind with body in relieving tension and providing a fresh perspective."

I had remarked that Bill Mercer, Bill the Scientist, looked years younger than when I had first met him a year and a half before. He had seemed in his mid-forties then, with an air of stolid middle age. He now looked under forty, the chief difference, outwardly, being the loss of weight under the chin and jaw line, with a new clean-cut definition of the lower face.

"Nothing," Marcia said, "makes a person look his age

more than fleshiness in this area. But more important, before this flesh forms outside, think of the excess forming inside, as fat is first deposited internally."

Although nearly all Yoga postures were good for firming, the neck-stretching exercises had been especially helpful in causing Mercer to lose his jowls.

The Locust, the Cobra, the Bow, and the Swan, given in the same sequence, served not only to strengthen the back, but tightened the muscles from the shoulder to the jaw. And the revolving head exercise, devised chiefly to keep the neck supple and strong, also nipped at any suggestion of a double chin.

Perhaps because of its harmonizing effect on the glands Yoga was the great equalizer for those concerned with diet. Many underweight students had picked up fifteen or twenty pounds in six months; others, overweight, had lost as much.

One student, a twenty-two-year-old secretary, was a classic example of weight equalization. In two years of intermittent Yoga she had run the gamut from thin to slim to fat to slim. She was curvaceously slim when I met her, and walked with the easy grace of a goddess.

"When I started the Yoga classes," she recalled, "I was underweight, but in a few weeks I had gained ten pounds and didn't have an ounce on me. But then I got too busy for class, and I kept gaining weight, and in two or three months I had picked up an extra fifteen pounds. So I went back to Yoga, and in three months more, watching my diet, I was back to my previous weight."

By diet, she meant she was back to being a vegetarian —a habit begun with Yoga and lapsed as she drifted away. How had vegetarianism helped?

"It just makes me feel lighter, cleaner, and I don't need as much food. I also think it results in de-emphasizing the importance of food generally, as you just can't get as excited visually about a plate of spinach and beans as you can about a good thick steak sizzling in fried onions."

As we were discussing keeping young, and its corollary, keeping slim, Bill the Scientist dropped by. He was a fund of information.

"It's all in the glands and the connective tissue and cartilege," he said. "And because Yoga is stretching and squeezing people all the time, it keeps the glands churning and the skeletal structure elastic."

He turned to me, and I noticed again his clean-cut lower jaw and his clear eye. "Haven't you noticed," he said, "how people grow old? Their glands dry up from inactivity, and the cartilage around their joints contracts. When this happens, they're aging, no matter what age they are."

Marcia was living proof that the reverse was also true. "It's my thirty-sixth birthday today," she said, "but I must be getting younger, because I was five feet two five years ago, and today I am exactly five feet three and a quarter. I've gained more than an inch in height since I was thirty and took seriously to Yoga.

"It's all in the stretching you've been doing with Yoga," Bill said. "You may even," he added with a smile, "get to be as tall as Louis before you're through."

He again turned to me. "Have you noticed any great difference in yourself?"

"I feel better," I said, "and I do the exercises with greater facility."

"Is that all?" he said, winking broadly at Marcia, who didn't appear to notice.

"I'm more vigorous, I suppose."

I had read somewhere that one of the dangers of Yoga was that it stimulated the sexual force, sometimes beyond the individual's control.

"I feel that I have a greater creative faculty, and am writing easier," I said.

Marcia thought it time to intercede. "Actually," she said, "though many people get a rush of sexual energy from the stimulation in the lower areas, together with the concentration on the pelvic region, there is little danger of uncontrollable sexual outbursts. I have heard of unprincipled Yoga instructors who have emphasized exercises singling out the sexual areas, but normally, by the very discipline it stresses, Yoga avoids any such immoderateness. The meditations spread the sexual force through the body, making the mind more creative and the superconscious more spiritual."

She smiled. "Don't forget that one of the principal aims of Yoga is detachment, in order to gain independence, and nobody enslaved by sex can be either detached or independent."

I looked her curiously. "Does that mean that Yoga counsels sexual abstinence?"

"Not at all," she said, "just moderation, as it does with food, work, recreation, and even Yoga itself."

"Sex?"

A look almost of distaste came over Marcia's placid features.

"Of course, people get sexually stimulated from Yoga, but this is not one of the higher activities." She frowned. "I just don't want to see people getting into Yoga for the wrong thing."

Offhand, it was difficult to think of a more proper activity than procreation.

"It's a matter of purpose," she said. "So many of the sex-minded are looking only for sensual indulgence, while we're working toward self-control, detachment, and moderation."

I had done the exercises long enough to know they were stimulating, even for one who had no wish to be stimulated, nor leisure in which to express this stimulation.

"We try to sublimate," she said, "divert our excess sexual energy into creative efforts—writing a book, meditating, building a bridge, advancing any work that man does."

She thought for a moment, seeking a way to illustrate her point. "The shoulder stand is considered stimulating, particularly with the chin pressed down into the notch of the throat, activating the thyroid. But we try to transfer this energy to the heart and head by visualizing these areas during the controlled breathing exercises."

She looked up. "This is advocated only in a problem of sexual control. Then the student can concentrate on drawing the libidinal forces up the spine, first into the solar plexus which is the great clearinghouse for all the energies below the diaphragm, and then elevating this energy, literally and figuratively."

"But how about all this pranic energy built up with the deep breathing?" It seemed to me there was a danger in building up a head of steam and not siphoning it off.

"When sexually aroused," my guru acknowledged, "one can feel the invisible electrical forces working through the lower centers. Prana then becomes a real thing and not just a figure of speech. But through advanced pranayama —concentrated breath-control—we become similarly aware of this creative force operating through the higher centers and opening up expanded states of consciousness."

Surprisingly, even the meditations were not entirely free

of a sexual taint; many students complained that their meditations often led to sexual stimulation instead of pious
thoughts. As an exercise in free association, meditation
could apparently stir up the skeletons in the subconscious
before the student learned how to pinpoint this new power.

Although a bit of a puritan, Marcia admitted that disconcerting sexual images had marked her early work in
meditations. It was a remarkable confession.

I wondered what form these images took.

She made a face.

"If it's that personal, forget it," I said.

She laughed self-consciously. "I don't know why I
shouldn't talk about it; it happens to almost everybody beginning meditation." She looked off thoughtfully for a moment, and frowned. "Generally, I would see myself together
with somebody else, a male."

"Was it somebody you knew?"

"Nearly always, though it would sometimes be somebody
I hadn't given much conscious thought to."

"How did you think about them?"

She cleared her throat. "Now this was before I married
again, I will have you know. Many people have similar
experiences without it being indicative of any lack of love
for their husband."

But couldn't it reflect some hidden frustration?

She shrugged.

"I would find myself thinking of somebody attractive,
and a warm, sensuous feeling would steal over me. But
that was as far as it went."

I smiled. "This happens to many healthy young people
without meditation."

"They're consciously fantasying. In meditation it becomes a dredging-up process. And once these erotic thoughts
come to the surface, the subconscious is purified and made
ready for more positive thinking."

The adult class at the Concord ashram followed our
discussions with knowledgeable interest. Many admitted
with pride that the exercises had given them a new lease
on life, so to speak. "There is no question," said one forty-
five-year-old disciple, "that my home life has become vastly
more rewarding during six months of Yoga."

"Just feeling better, generally, relaxing easily, will often
do that for you," Marcia said. In this regard, if no other,
she was careful not to give Yoga too much credit.

"Didn't you mention once," another student said, "that

the immobility and control one gains through Yoga could lead to much greater enjoyment of sex?"

Marcia blushed. "I was speaking in theoretical terms. But obviously, because of Yoga's emphasis on holding back or retention, there is a build-up of the sex potential."

Passion was apparently more pleasurable when it was less passionate. In her sacred, would-be adopted land of India, there were numerous temple carvings and paintings of deities clasped in carnal embraces so complex that they defied the Western imagination. But even this exotic demonstration of human ingenuity was a reflection of yogi-like control, Marcia insisted. "These unusual postures were not displayed to incite desire but rather to show the variety of ways in which people can remain immobilized together for their common good. It is the very antithesis of that lack of control, that frenetic activity, which characterizes the contemporary, let's-get-drunk-and-let-go school."

"Anybody showing postures like that in this country would probably get arrested," a student observed.

"That's the curious ambivalence about India," Marcia stated. "They talk a good game of sex, but it ends there."

Americans, of course, were a different breed entirely. "We preach puritanism," one student said, "but just as overtly we worship virility, while secretly fancying ourselves in all sorts of orgies."

Yoga students, even while continent, generally appeared ready to discuss sex frankly. "You get to working and thinking with your body so much that it seems only natural to think of yourself in terms of all your potentials," a middle-aged student observed.

Many of her male students of various ages had reported a rise in sexual energies within a few weeks. "At fifty-five," one man said, "I had been thinking of settling down to graze, and suddenly I discovered my body beginning to think young."

This was not uncommon. A middle-aged student, with teen-age children of his own, started to show interest in shapely teen-agers, and began to wonder if he was in his second childhood. However, it wasn't at all one-sided, as he told it. "Amazingly, they showed an interest in me."

He took up motorcycling, and the teen-age set seemed to regard him as another Marlon Brando. "Every time I idled the machine near a cluster of pretty teen-agers, two or three would look me over, and ask if they could ride on back."

He gave them a lift two or three times, and then quit.

"After we traveled three or four miles, they'd throw questions at me: Was I married; did I love my wife, what did I do for entertainment?" It was frightening for one of his years.

One girl asked, "What would you do, if you had your wife on back with you?"

Understandably, the middle-aged cyclist was puzzled.

The girl motioned to a glade that looked like a lover's lane. "Wouldn't that be romantic?" she said. That was the last of the lifts. "Yoga," he confessed, "hadn't done quite that much for me."

He was a well-muscled, active man with an alert eye and a bouncy step, and he looked a dozen years younger than his forty-seven years. After doing the exercises a year, he had come to a revealing conclusion. "In order to keep their home life well-balanced, a middle-aged man's wife should do these exercises with him." He smiled. "Otherwise, he should have a young wife."

Romantically speaking, age differences were no barriers between Yoga students. A retired planter of seventy bounced into class holding hands with an attractive young woman forty years his junior, and after doing their shoulder stands and Ploughs together, along with the rest of the routine, they loped off, arm in arm, immersed only in each other. This particular couple was a class inspiration. "Think of what I have to look forward to for another ten years, anyway," said a youngster of sixty.

All this enthusiasm was not lost on Marcia. And she was by no means prudish. "As a wife and mother, I recognize the importance and the pleasures of sex, but sex is truly important only as an expression of love and affection—and creativity. I don't want to encourage sex for sex's sake."

But from its earliest beginnings Yoga concerned itself with sex. Numerous exercises were almost specifics for relieving congestion leading to sexual apathy—or for stimulating the reproductive areas—and were devised originally for married people desiring children.

"Unfortunately," Marcia said wryly, "unmarried people can follow these exercises, too."

Traditionally, in India, she pointed out, chaste girls and widows were forbidden one of the bandhas, the contracting and locking of the sphincter muscle.

While my anatomy wasn't the best, I didn't see how such a taboo could be enforced.

"Through the sense of shame, instilled in the women of India, through centuries of tradition," Marcia replied. "The greatest untouchable in India is not some lowly porter or peasant, but intelligent discussion of sex among women."

"It seems almost taboo in a certain Concord ashram," I suggested.

"Not really; I just don't like an improper emphasis." She shrugged. "And I do know of cases where harm has resulted."

"In what way?"

"Not under supervision, mind you." She mused a moment. "I had a young actor in my Boston classes. He was not very stable, and I noticed he was concerning himself with the exercises generally associated with sexual stimulation: the shoulder stand, the Plough, the Stomach Lift—contraction of the abdominal muscles, while half-squatting with the breath expelled, and the bandhas.

One day the actor mentioned casually that he was passing on these routines to a young lady in his apartment building. Marcia was horrified. "I pointed out that only those interested in self-improvement should delve into any aspect of Yoga."

About a week later, the actor turned up with an apology. "You were right," he said. "Gloria was so stimulated from the exercises one evening that she dashed into the street looking for a man."

I expressed a sneaking suspicion that Gloria might have done so anyway.

"Perhaps," Marcia said, "but unstable people can mess up the best programs."

Marcia leaned heavily for some opinions on Dr. R. S. Mishra, an Indian psychiatrist and surgeon, who was rated one of the world's foremost Yoga teachers. His New York ashram was a sparsely furnished apartment on the fashionable East Side. There were no chairs, and when I interviewed him, at Marcia's suggestion, he was typing on the floor in a Lotus-like posture. He also maintained a modern ashram in Monroe, New York.

He was supposedly a celibate, sublimating his sexual energies. Yet he was only in his early forties, and looked years younger. He had dark, handsome features and looked most virile. He was rather amused at the thought that Yoga might be erroneously stressed as a sex stimulator.

He shrugged. "Yes, there is some effect, but it can be controlled by keeping busy all the time, using up the excess energy that Yoga has built up. In my own family, after a man has all the children he wants, he no longer has anything to do with sex."

And was the good doctor married?

His brooding face lit up in a smile. "I have a wife and two children back in India."

"And you practice celibacy?"

"It is very simple."

With a wife in India, this seemed self-evident. "Are you also a celibate here?"

"But of course—if I abstain from my wife." He smiled. "I am always busy with something."

I mentioned the widespread interest in the sex impact of Yoga, and wondered if absorption in sex was only an American phenomenon. He shook his head. "Obviously, they are more interested in sex in India."

I gave him a look of surprise.

He grinned. "We have five hundred million people in India, and you have less than two hundred million. Obviously, the only country more concerned with sex is China. They have seven hundred million." Equally obviously, the good doctor was putting me on.

But his friend, countryman, and peer in Yoga did not agree. "All India," Yogi Vithaldas said, "is confused about sex, and so, for that matter, is this country."

Yogi Vithaldas did not have the scruples of Marcia about sex, nor did he share Dr. Mishra's views on celibacy.

"What is wrong," he said, "with a man having six girls, if he has the capabilities. The Mormons did it, and they had a productive society in every respect."

The powerfully built Yogi strode around his studio, or ashram, high above Manhattan's streets, with the pent-up power of a caged lion. "That's what gets me worked up," he said, "the way that the holier than thou's—particularly the weak and impotent—are always knocking sex. That was true in India, and it is true here."

He looked out of a window, his dark flashing eyes dramatically taking in the city below. "All of nature is part of the sex process, and we try to make something evil out of that which is divine."

He smiled mirthlessly. "Don't they realize that if it were not for sex none of us would be here today, including them?" He waved a brawny arm toward the great outdoors. "The heat comes, and when this is vaporized, the rain falls. It falls into the hungry womb of the earth, and this rainfall makes Mother Earth pregnant with vegetation and flowers."

He sat down and poured me a cup of herb tea. "And

that," he said, "is what happens with man, the same process —heat, rain, and fertility."

Yogi's views were not hard to follow. He made them most clear. He considered sex a reflection of love, affection, and nature's manifestation of vitality; it was wicked only when seen through nasty eyes, and it became a problem only because of the hypocrisy surrounding it.

"They make me laugh even more in India than here with their ridiculous attitudes," he said. "The men have get-togethers at which they read all this poetry about love and sex." He laughed, and it was a laugh heavy with mockery. "They have one attitude about sex in books, another in practice. They will get up and recite how if all the ocean was ink it would not be enough to write how much they love their lady fair." He grinned, simulating a certain effeteness in the rendition of the poem. "Or they will sit around and clap with delight as one reads a poem how he tenderly pulls aside the blouse of his lady love and kisses her gently, then ardently, from top to bottom." His tone was derisive. "And then they go home, and don't even look at their women. It's all talk."

His voice again rose in a falsettto to mimic the poetry. "And yet among themselves, they spout things like, 'When my sweetheart is near me, how can I sleep?'"

He studied me gravely. "Once we realize that man is incomplete without woman, everything else falls into place. The ancient Vedas said that a man had to be married at twenty-five. And they weren't thinking that he should marry and meditate, but he should complete himself with that woman—and complete her. All this concentrating on higher thoughts to sublimate sex is contrary to the purpose of nature, and anything contrary to nature is wrong, and contrary to Yoga.

"We should rather concentrate on sex to make it more rewarding, creative, and enjoyable—not push it away because of fear. We have enough fears as it is. And it is because of fear, breeding tension, that the hormones dry up and the natural sex impulse is lost."

He pointed a finger of emphasis at me. "There is no reason for man to be impotent. For once impotent, he is half-dead. Five thousand years ago, the ancient yogis said that sex was life, and now the hypocrites and the blind are trying to change it.

"But if a man continues with his Yoga, if he learns to ease his tensions and yet remain strong, he will be capable of sex if he lives to be one hundred years old. He will never dry up, because nature intended sex and life to be compatible, one to flow out of the other."

Through Yoga, the glands were awakened and nourished, the nerves stimulated, and the blood ran warm. "The entire lower area gets a constant internal massage, but even more critically affected are the thyroid and the pituitary which control the sexual energies. The pituitary is the king of the glands"—he pointed to his head—"but without the thyroid"—he touched his throat—"there could be no productive sexual activity."

The shoulder stand and the Plough stimulated the thyroid and kept it healthy and alert, and all inverted exercises enriched the pituitary. The Stomach Lift relieved congestion in the pelvic area and helped the flow of sexual energy. But, generally speaking, all the exercises combined to provide the stimulation and control required in the consummate act of sex.

All this was rather tangible, and understandable. But what role could anything as nebulous as meditation play in liberating the sex force?

Yogi Vithaldas smiled. "That's elementary; that's what I've been driving at. You don't get rid of sex by burying it; it's always there whether it's sublimated or suppressed, and when you meditate you bring it up from the subconscious, where it has been lurking, causing all kinds of conscious and unconscious conflicts." He looked up with a shrug. "With all these hidden, furtive desires in the subconscious, how can anything healthy emerge?"

He thought a moment. "After all, sex, like nearly everything else, starts with the mind, though a body strengthened by Yoga often conveys its own signals to the mind." He shrugged again. "What is being in love but a state of mind? Another face may be fairer, another form lovelier, another mind nobler, but it is the eyes—or the mind—of the beholder that find a special beauty in his ladylove. And so, merely touching her, he thrills." He threw up his arms. "And so what is so base and wicked about this?" He shook his head. "It makes no sense, no sense at all."

Yogi was convinced that sexual frustration is a fundamental national problem. And it leads to corollary problems. "In not encouraging sexual honesty, we are encouraging homosexuality. To protect their adolescent daughters, rich Americans send them to Europe's fancy schools, and there they find lesbians and male homosexuals for teachers. Other girls, made fearful of sex, gravitate to men who don't make overtures, and soon they may be marrying homo-sexuals."

He looked up with a dour eye. "Isn't sexuality preferable to homosexuality? Fears of sex, implanted at an early age, turn many women to each other. Similar fears, leading to lack of confidence and impotence, make men homosexuals."

But sex was not a wild rampant force for Yogi Vithaldas. Like Yoga itself, it was controlled and disciplined, and it was most beautiful, most productive, when mind, body, and spirit were in harmony. "Then," said Yogi Vithaldas, "we have love."

But even with love, there must be planning for the harvest to be properly reaped. There must be consideration for the female partner, and knowledge of how to implement that consideration. "The great problem of sex," said Yogi from a personal awareness of students' plights, "is that man's problem is soon solved, while woman's problem is never solved." He sighed. "There can be no lasting love if woman is not completed, and once she completes herself regularly and rhythmically" he kissed the tips of his fingers—"she is man's forever."

The setting for love, as Yogi Vithaldas saw it, should be in tune with the beauty of the act itself. And between married couples, regardless of age, it should be performed at least once or twice a week, to maintain the closeness and empathy of the union. "Too often," Yogi observed, "the man seeks out a younger girl friend, because his wife feels with middle age or maternity that sex is no longer important. But it becomes even more important then if she wants to keep the marriage. Without sex, life must certainly be dull. For sex inspires poetry, the theater, art, fashions, all forms of beauty. In our expression of it, we separate ourselves from the animals. That is why it must be kept beautiful and be kept up."

For a moment his eyes were lost in meditation. He seemed miles away. Then, suddenly, he brought himself up with a start. "Everything about love must be beautiful," he said. "The room should be a harmonious color, the furnishings comfortable and soothing. There should be a faint aroma of perfume, the music soft, and the lights low."

But the principals themselves, their state of being, was of prime importance. Participation in sex demands the man's exclusive energies. There should be at least a three-hour interval after a meal, as the blood should have left the digestive areas and been free to roam elsewhere.

"Everything about sex should be leisurely. It should begin

with a kiss, bringing blood to the lips, and the technique should be one of yogic control. The breathing is as important in love as it is in Yoga. As in Yoga, the air should be inhaled and exhaled through the nose rhythmically slowly, and with complete control."

Yogi Vithaldas put his hand to his lips and began to simulate a pant. "As they get excited, and breathe in and out of the mouth, the couple loses not only control of their breathing but of the very act of sex itself. When the man practices diaphragmatic breathing while making love, he has more energy, doesn't become fatigued, and through this practice of detached control slows up his automatic responses.

"As I said before, one of the great problems in America today is that man solves his own problem, but not the woman's. This leads to more separations and divorces than most realize, for different reasons are generally given, arising out of the frustrations and unhappiness of sexual incompletion."

Yogi Vithaldas got up and began demonstrating the breathing of love. "When I breath in and out slowly through the nose, keeping my mouth shut, pushing the air in and out from my diaghragm, I have complete control of every nerve and muscle of my body. My mind becomes detached to a certain extent, too—interested detachment, I would call it—and with this complete control comes attunement with the woman. The man should know exactly when the woman is ready, and be ready for her."

With consummation, the act of sex is not completed. In the intimacy of a true marriage, consideration of the other person keeps the flame of love hard and true. "The man should gently massage the thighs of his wife for a minute or two; it will relax and restore her, giving her a feeling of replenishment. To restore himself, he should drink a glass of milk, with a dash of powdered almonds, saffron, or nutmeg in it."

A smile came to Yogi's lips. "The man who has been doing his Yoga exercises faithfully should be able to run around the block ten times after sex."

At this time, he should not drink water, or alcohol, for the depleted glands are thirsting for food. "The glands are ready to receive food after sex, and water will only disappoint them. But the milk will do much to replace what has been lost."

In the aesthetics of sex, cigarettes and liquor are taboos. "Alcohol inflames the imagination, but douses the libido."

And since all the preliminaries should be sweet, and without a false breath, the odor of cigarettes on milady's lips, or the scent of a martini, would be enough to remove the aura of beauty from romance. Women should smell of their natural fragrance.

Many people came to Yogi Vithaldas with their sexual problems. Generally, they were prematurely aged men with younger wives. "They're afraid they're going to lose their wives to younger men," Yogi said. "They made the mistake of letting their bodies age before their minds."

Yogi counsels not only Yoga exercises—beginning slowly where the physical condition is poor—but changes in diet. "Some must eliminate meat because it creates acids which work against potency." Some teachers recommend fish, rich in iodine and phosphorus and other potent minerals.

Usually, the middle-aged with a sex problem are noticeably overweight. On a simple vegetarian diet, supplemented with fish, they could not only regain their vitality but lose a pound a day, Yogi advises. "Cereal in the morning, perhaps fish for lunch, and a serving of eggplant, broccoli, and a baked potato at night." The various vegetables, cereals, and fish can be varied to the individual's taste.

"Hot dogs, pizzas, all these things that Americans like to indulge in, weaken sexual potency in the long run because they clog up the system without giving it sustenance. Sex can never be effective or rewarding unless the inner body is purified; good elimination is a requisite for sex, otherwise the mind is sluggish and the body toxic, without the keen edge desirable at any age."

Along with the middle-aged male, unhappy women of nearly every age seek out Yogi Vithaldas in his ashram overlooking the East River. Many fashion models, lean as a lathe, have come to him for counsel. "From dieting to wear the clothes designed by homosexuals," he observed, "they have breasts like dried raisins, and vinegar runs through their veins. They have hardly the vitality to drag themselves around, not to mention making love. And how they trigger any response in the warm-blooded male, attracted by the booby traps of a provident nature, is more than I can say." He has given the flat-chested exercises to develop the bust. The Cobra, the shoulder stand, the Locust, and the Blade, knifing the shoulder blades together without moving the arms—all do much to develop the pectorals. And Yogi adds the advice (to only the married, of course): "If you think of love, not modeling, as your goal, you will soon find yourself blooming with femininity."

Many of Yogi's students have had mingled feelings about sex. "They have been held back by fear, tension, and the habit of repression carried over from childhood. Consciously or unconsciously, sex is not to be enjoyed; it is a necessary evil in the marital relationship." Many of the women had never experienced consummation; some did not even know what it was. "And yet a woman who has not had an orgasm develops the temperament of an ungrateful snake, she strikes out irritably at every little thing; she is an unpleasant, unpredictable, unrewarding companion in any pursuit."

The best testimonial to the beliefs of Yogi Vithaldas were his students. Often marriages had been on the verge of break-up. But the right experiences and advice, bringing renewed vitality, yet detachment and control, rhythmical breathing, and a new mental attitude, all combined to introduce a sexual balance that satisfied the two partners instead of frustrating them.

Sex became a new unifying influence to some. Despairingly, a thirty-five-year-old housewife had come to Yogi with a familiar plaint. All her life she had regarded sex as an animal act—it had been dinned into her at home, in her church, by her spinster friends and relatives. "Yet," Yogi pointed out, "sex was always on her mind, and she was nervous, irritable, suffering from high blood pressure."

She studied with him for three months, once or twice a week, meanwhile practicing her exercises daily by herself for a half hour or so. Then, with her mission accomplished, she went back to her home in a small Midwestern city.

Whatever she learned had apparently been put to good use. Yogi brought out a letter he had just received from the once-frustrated housewife. It was brimming with happiness.

"Your suggestion made last September has been followed and worked out very well," it stated. "Here I am living the life of a goddess, with an unfailing devotee in my husband, and we are both happy in this new life. I want to thank you because you were the one who counseled me and gave me the courage to proceed."

Her first sentence seemed particularly provocative.

"What was your suggestion?" I asked.

Yogi Vithaldas laughed. "I told her to get her husband to breathe through the nose."

The men called her their beautiful guru, and many kept turning out, because the teacher was so attractive, the epitome of the slim beauty and patient detachment she was seeking to instill in others. And there were ladies, too, all seeking to emulate her.

They were psychiatrists, lawyers, professors, truck drivers, day laborers, students, clerks, secretaries, housewives. They were young, middle-aged, old—the youngest, sixteen; the oldest, a retired millionaire over seventy. They were Protestants, Catholics, Jews, even Buddhists, Hindus, and Vedantists, and they were all seeking to improve themselves.

Some came because they wanted to lose weight, others for the exercise and circulation, some for relaxation, and others to find the inner peace so essential for creative living.

A few had suffered disabling injuries, and thought Yoga might help. They understood it was slow and easy, and they were too old, they felt, too weak and brittle, to plunge into strenuous calisthenics that might pull muscles or tendons unused to exercise.

Marcia gave classes in three communities, and I participated in all, getting to know the students, their motivations, the impact of Yoga on their lives. Generally, they came for more than exercise. One young man told me, "It is as if every breath fills me with new vitality and vigor. When I stand on my head, I feel, oddly, as if I am seeing the world right side up for the first time."

Two down-to-earth brothers, Don and Jim McGrath, never missed a Sunday at the Concord ashram. "I can't afford to," Jim said. "While relaxing, I feel myself getting stronger and full of ambition." He was past forty. "At my age calisthenics would tire me, without any corresponding benefits."

Another student, in her early thirties, had been distraught because doctors told her that her husband had an incurable disease. "My Yoga hasn't helped my husband's condition," she observed, "but it has helped me to think clearly and remain calm, while doing what I can for him and contemplating the future."

There were almost as many reasons for "conversion" to Yoga as there were students. But no conversion was more striking than that of Linda Hodgens, a radiant, twenty-one-year-old beauty who reminded me of Mrs. DeVries' observation about neophytes who came for lunch and stayed for life. Linda apparently had come for life.

I met her at Marcia's mixed classes for men and women at the Boston YMCA on Huntington Avenue. She was a lissom, seductive figure in black, skintight leotard. But she performed her exercises, including the difficult headstand, with serene unconcern, though her elfish features occasionally broke into a sunny smile as Marcia explained the significance of the exercises with a parable out of India or Concord.

With Bob Kennedy, a well-known Boston radio personality, I partook of some of the exercises, every other one as it was still early in my development, meanwhile appraising the class out of a corner of my eye.

Besides Linda, there were two secretary types in their early twenties; a slim girl with the heavy calves of a dancer; a middle-aged blonde with bleached hair; and five or six men, their ages ranging from the mid-twenties to the mid-fifties. All had ordinary jobs.

During an exercise break, I had an opportunity to learn what had driven this motley group together. The oldest, a Boston Irishman with a bluff, hearty face and grizzled gray hair, was a driver for the MTA, Boston's transport system. His name was William Hennessey.

He was fifty-three years old, a Catholic, a husband and father, and here it was ten at night, and he had to be up at four the next morning to work. He had been at it for five weeks, attending class once a week, but practicing at home daily.

Before signing up, he had read a few books on Yoga and became interested in its philosophy as well as the exercises. "At my age," he said, "I didn't want to risk calisthenics, but I liked what I read of the slow, relaxing action of Yoga."

The results were better than he had hoped for. "I'm not only getting in shape, but I'm relaxing better, and fall asleep the moment I hit the bed." He had had some difficulty sleeping before.

He did not feel his Catholicism was affected. "It's a way of doing things, of thinking, and it's not at all contradictory to what my faith holds for me."

The two secretaries sitting next to him had both come for the exercise. It was enough for them; they had no other problems but smoothing out their contours.

Of all the pupils, Linda was clearly outstanding. She did the exercises with professional éclat—the headstand, the Peacock, the Tortoise, the Crow, the Lotus, all advanced postures.

"Linda," Marcia said proudly, "can do the exercises as well as I can, and she can hold the postures as well as any Hindu teacher."

In her zeal for Yoga, she had embraced vegetarianism, a difficult deviation for a working girl taking midday meals in restaurants, and she practiced deep meditation. She seemed wholly committed to Yoga, and was a graceful, sylphlike testimonial to its possibilities.

I wondered if she minded discussing her Yoga in front of the class.

"Ask me anything you like," she said with composure.

"How long have you been at it?" I asked.

She shrugged. "Eighteen months, I guess."

"Has it had much influence on your life?"

Her deep-set eyes seemed suddenly afire. "It's not only changed my whole life," she said with a surge of enthusiasm, "but it is my life."

"How did you become interested?" I asked.

She eyed me speculatively. "I became interested in the philosophy first, and then the exercises."

The class was closely following the conversation, and I hesitated at asking anything personal. But Linda said, "Ask me anything."

"I'd like to know how it changed your life."

"Became my life," she corrected. She moistened her lips, tossing her head a little. "It's made all the difference, not only exercisewise, but in my attitude toward people."

She smiled enigmatically. "You wouldn't believe it, but I used to wilt if anybody said hello to me. But you can't come to class in a leotard,"—she gestured toward her shapely limbs—"and be shy very long."

Looking at this lovely girl, with the face of a gamin and the body of of a courtesan, I wondered about the nature of this new attitude.

She smiled and threw out her arms gracefully. "I've lost all my hostilities," she said. "I love everybody."

"That can be dangerous," I said drily.

She laughed. "In a nice way that makes me want to be friendly, and help anybody that needs help."

She looked as though she might be Irish and in Boston that likely meant she was a Catholic.

"I'm a Hindu," she said.

"A Hindu?" I tried again. "I know that's probably what you feel like when doing Yoga, but what's your real faith?"

"Hindu," she repeated. "I know it sounds kooky, and my family thinks I'm a kook, but that's what I am—a Hindu."

"What were you before you were a Hindu?" I asked.

"Nothing."

"Before you were nothing?" I was determined to get at the bottom of it.

"Catholic," she said, "but it was too restrictive."

The rest of the students were mostly Catholic, and they now looked up in amusement.

"I just couldn't accept a lot of things," she said, "like Hell and Heaven, death and damnation. Here we are just litle specks living on specks, and why should anybody take enough notice of us to wish us in Hell? It just doesn't make sense."

"As a Hindu," I said, "do you believe in reincarnation?"

"Of course," she replied. "Wouldn't it be horrible if this was all there was to it?"

"This is it on this earth, and this is all the world we're living in."

"I'm making the most of it," she said, "and I'm doing my best to help others enjoy themselves, including my family, who think I'm some sort of a nut."

In other respects, Linda's life was quite ordinary. She was a secretary at the Massachusetts Institute of Technology in Cambridge, working for four professors who seemed tolerant of her Yoga, if not interested. One had come to a class, performed the exercises, and never came back. The prospect of becoming tranquil had apparently frightened him.

The turn in Linda's life had come when she was nineteen. She was in conflict over leaving her Church, and felt a void. She was searching for something, but didn't know what. One day, walking in downtown Boston, she noticed a large, green-jacketed book in a bookstore window. The book was about Yoga, by the Swami Vishnudevananda. She had heard only vaguely of Yoga before, but somehow she felt impelled to buy the book. "It was almost as though I was guided."

She was intrigued by the philosophy, the introspection, the meditations, the detachment. "It was all so simple, there was nobody confusing you, telling you that you couldn't do this or that. It wasn't negative, and it preached selflessness, serving others."

I remarked that other religions—Christianity, for instance—seemed to convey a similar message.

"You can do this yourself," Linda said. "You don't need anybody confusing your thinking for you."

She sat down and wrote a letter to the Swami at his Yoga Center in Montreal, asking where she could learn more about Yoga. He wrote back, suggesting that she consult Marcia, a former pupil. And so she began taking lessons and changing her outlooks.

But even with her zest for Yoga, I did not understand why she found it necessary to accept Yoga as a faith, when her teacher thought of it as a science or philosophy. "As a philosophy," I pointed out, "Yoga rejects nothing, embracing parts of Catholicism and other religions." I observed that a Belgian priest, J. M. Dechanet, had stressed in his book, *Christian Yoga,* that Yoga might even fortify one's Catholicism.

Elder William Hennessey nodded comprehendingly. "It certainly hasn't affected my Catholicism and I don't see the conflict."

Marcia then broke in. "Yoga is not a religion," she said. "Anyone can retain his own faith and still benefit from Yoga. I am a Unitarian, some of my students are Jewish, others are Catholic and Protestant and some"—with a smile for Linda—"have been Hindu, born to that faith." She turned to me. "Actually, you know, a person has to be racially a Hindu to be of the Hindu faith. Actually, Linda is a Vedantist, subscribing to the Vedas, the teachings on which much of Hinduism is based."

Linda appeared unruffled. 'I should know what I am," she said. "I'm a Hindu."

Linda's Hinduism intrigued me. But the reasons for her conversion were still not quite clear. But, later, after the rest of the students had left, she tried to explain. "It was hard to talk frankly with the others around," she said, "but I might be able to clarify things without a large audience."

We agreed to another meeting, and said good-bye till then.

Marcia's classes fanned out from Boston: Cambridge, Brookline, Lexington, Concord. They kept her on the move, but she always appeared calm and humble. She told advanced students, who were considering forming class groups of their own, "Always realize that Nature, not you, is taking over and that where you may feel personally inadequate, Nature's abundance is ever at your disposal." It was admittedly autosuggestive, but nonetheless effective.

Even the most sophisticated took their Yoga seriously. One class, at Lexington's Follen Community Center, consisted of upper middle-class housewives with three or four children each—"Three point six is the average," as one Wellesley-type put it.

There were a dozen in the class, and they moved with slow, easy, confident movements, reflecting their social assurance. As I looked around, I was particularly struck by an alert, smiling lady in a leotard, wonderfully flexible, who went from shoulder stands to headstands, to the Crow, Bow, Wheel, and Bridge with the greatest of ease. As she gracefully performed the Wheel, arching her back so it was parallel to the floor, head hanging back and palms dropping to the floor, I wondered at the suppleness in a woman I assumed to be thirty or thirty-two. She was fresh-faced and eager, but it was her girlish pliancy and clean limbs that caught my eye. She moved like a girl.

After the workout, I questioned a few of the students. The lady in the leotard was first on my list. She wore a pleasant, relaxed smile, mirroring the well-bred detachment of the proper Bostonian.

Mrs. Kay Davis had a successful husband and three children, and they all lived in a big comfortable house in Lexington. She also held an administrative post at Boston's Simmons College. She was a busy woman.

"How," I asked, without any great imagination, "did you become interested in Yoga?"

She was friendly and articulate. "I have always been interested in Oriental philosophies, so I decided to go through the exercises and see if they heightened my understanding of what I had been examining from the sidelines."

Soon she had discovered herself becoming more vitalized and energetic, more than compensating for the ninety minutes she spent at class once a week, and the few minutes a day at home practicing. It had gotten so that her children were now doing headstands in emulation of their mom.

I wondered how small children could muster the required interest and discipline.

"Oh, teen-agers have many drives." She seemed amused.

"Teen-agers? And how old are you?"

She laughed. "I'm forty-one, but I certainly don't feel any different than I did fifteen or twenty years ago."

She couldn't have looked any better, for at forty-one

her figure was that of a girl of eighteen, and a shapely eighteen at that.

She had been attending the classes for six or seven months, but had been in reasonably good condition before, having taken dancing lessons in keeping with the sound body, sound mind principle.

In this class, there had been some initial resistance to an unfamiliar discipline. Originally, Mrs. Davis had rejected the concept of body control by an apparently separate mind. She already thought there was too much mind control in her social category where the women managed homes, children, and outside interests with a hard, well-bred detachment. "Our type of person," she informed Marcia, not entirely patronizingly, because Marcia was of the same stratum, "is already too controlled and rigid. We need to develop ease and spontaneity so that we can relax and forget ourselves."

Marcia nodded. "I couldn't agree with you more." Yet Yoga itself, as she pointed out, was essentially a technique of discipline and control to achieve freedom through freeing the mind.

Mrs. Davis was not readily convinced. "I feel you are setting up an arbitrary division, one which doesn't exist naturally, and which impairs body and mind working together in natural self-expression."

As a yogi should, Marcia appealed to the mind. "The exercises are the channel by which the individual gets to isolate different parts of himself at will, and then puts himself together in a meaningful manner." She looked up with a smile. "There is a difference," she said, "between being repressed and being controlled, because natural expression can only come out of a controlled detachment which has risen above fear."

Mrs. Davis still wasn't impressed. But, as Marcia observed, the mechanics of Yoga could not be easily grasped intellectually. "To understand the process one must feel it taking place in body and mind. In bringing the mind to sharp focus to achieve a precise perfection of movement, we are developing a form of autosuggestion to which the body will eventually react without conscious direction."

In an emergency, physical or emotional, the mind and body, in smooth interplay, would respond calmly and effectively. "And the body, toughened by the exercises, would throw off adverse reactions in supreme emergencies, which might give the tense and rigid a heart attack or stroke."

Watching Mrs. Davis, noting the remarkable control of

every part of her body at will, I was inclined to believe that Marcia had gained a convert, whether that convert knew it or not.

Marcia agreed with a smile. "Actually, the discipline that marks the bringing up of the Boston Brahmin makes it easier for her to become adept at Yoga, even though the aims of the two disciplines—social and yogic—are completely different. We want to liberate people, not put them in a social strait jacket."

Even in a class as intellectually superior as the Lexington group, there was an occasional student with a health or emotional problem. In other classes, indispositions were more common. And many came individually with problems.

Nevertheless, Marcia didn't regard herself as a therapist, nor Yoga as medical therapy. Yet she had seen some dramatic restorations to full-blown health in her classes. "The exercises are usually effective with people with nervous, respiratory, and psychosomatic ailments," she observed. "We've had good experience relieving backaches, shortness of breath, palpitations, and what I euphemistically call female trouble. We can't always help people with slipped discs, but we can toughen them up so they don't get them. We can't help too much after a hysterectomy, but our students usually don't need them."

One of the Lexington pupils was a blonde with tremors. She had consulted many doctors, without being helped. Her hands shook so that she couldn't hold a cup of coffee without spilling most of it. She was rather desperate when she arrived for her first class, referred by a friend who had mentioned the tranquilizing nature of Yoga.

She was given the same limbering exercises as the other women. She balanced on one leg, then closed her eyes. "If there is any hardening of the arteries in the head," Marcia pointed out, "the person will find it virtually impossible to balance on one leg with the eyes closed."

She was not given the shoulder stands, headstands, or any of the inverted exercises, which might bring a sudden surge of blood to the brain, straining vessels that might have already lost their elasticity.

She passed this test, and the additional table test, so-called from the rectangle formed from squaring off on hands and knees, with the stomach parallel to the floor. The individual then breathes in deeply and lowers upper chest and neck to the floor; the degree of ease with which this is accomplished reflects the person's condition. "Obstetricians advise this exercise, without realizing its Yoga origin," Marcia observed, "in order to recondition a woman's pelvic area after delivery, since it releases pressure on the ovaries and helps tip them back after any downward pull."

Although she had a little trouble with this exercise, the blonde with the trembling hands passed the tests. However, she tired easily and had little strength. Nevertheless, she was a zealous student, not missing a class, and took pride in beginning to do things that she could not do before. She began to forget her shaking hands in her concentrated drive to do as well as the women twisting and bending on all sides of her.

Her progress was gradual at first. But as she gained confidence, she started to try the postures done by the most advanced students. By the second month, Marcia knew her difficult pupil was going to make it. "One day as she was doing a deep-breathing exercise, there was a beatific expression on her face; she appeared to be almost in ecstasy. The exercises, and the little discussions we had together, had begun to have some effect. She was with it."

Ironically, the girl with the greatest problem had made the greatest progress. "She had gone into it with the hope of getting the most out of it, and so had put the most into it," Marcia said.

By contrast, there was another Brahmin housewife in the class, the only one with superfluous flesh on her aristocratic frame. She was an attractive blonde who might have been radiantly lovely had it not been for the droop of her mouth and the discontent in her eyes.

She was the only one who seemed to mind being questioned, and the only one who indicated she had no interest in the Yoga philosophy. "I'm interested in exercise, period," she said rather abruptly.

"But why not calisthenics then?" I asked. She could not have been more than thirty, and looked robust enough to stand a little depletion.

"Because I don't want to," she said shortly. She studied me with a frosty eye. "Why are you interested—because you're getting a book out of it?"

"I'm trying to cultivate detachment," I said.

She turned away.

It didn't appear to me that Yoga was making much headway with at least one member of this class. I observed later that she seemed to have difficulty with most of the exercises, and didn't attempt half of them. "She didn't even do the deep breathing properly, pushing her bust in and out instead of her diaphragm," I mentioned to Marcia.

Marcia seemed unconcerned. "When people don't catch on right away, I feel that if I can keep them coming, some of the philosophy may eventually rub off."

"With all this resistance, what is she coming for?" I asked. "She's vastly overweight, and yet if she took off twenty or twenty-five pounds, she'd be the prettiest girl in the class." She had a peaches-and-cream complexion, deep-set blue eyes, soft golden hair—and she was fat, disgruntled, and unhappy.

"I think she would like to do something about herself, but hasn't decided how far she wants to commit herself to a strange discipline." But once she did make up her mind, Marcia was confident the excess weight would melt away and she would radiate. "I find it significant," she said, "that the one woman taking the course exclusively for exercise has profited least from that exercise."

What one put into life, one got out, and so it went with Yoga. As I continued my own exercises, working with other students, I noticed that individuals who had the greatest trouble with the exercises seemed to get the most out of them eventually. The reason was self-evident.

"They have to concentrate more," Marcia observed, "exerting more of their inner will, and so they sharpen the connection between mind and body, in time setting up an almost automatic current."

One Sunday, as I groaned and strained, I almost gave up as I noted the performance of a lovely blonde teen-ager next to me. She looked twenty or twenty-one from every aspect, but was only sixteen—and it was all so terribly easy.

The class looked on in wonder. She had never been to a Yoga class before. Yet she stood on her head perfectly at the first try, straight as a die. She went into the Lotus posture on the first effort, crossing her legs with the ankles nestling comfortably on the opposite thigh—a feat that had taken the greatest yogis weeks or months. She managed the Tortoise easily, spreading her legs, sliding them under her extended arms, and then lowering face and chest to the mat in one graceful swoop. Only the most advanced could do the Tortoise.

Even Marcia was struck with amazement. "I've never seen anything like it," she exclaimed. "Have you studied acrobatic dancing?"

The girl shook her head. "I went to regular dancing school two or three times."

"Actually," Marcia agreed, "aside from maintaining flexibility, the ordinary dance class is no help in Yoga, since the turns are all out, for the most part, whereas Yoga turns one in, physically as well as introspectively."

I examined the girl with interest. She was obviously pleased by the attention. She did not seem to take the class seriously. She had come with a young man, and they had giggled together through the exercises. Many of the envious senior citizens in the class, myself included, had found this a discordant note as we strained to stretch our aching joints.

Marcia had sharply reprimanded them and they had subsided for a few minutes. But after a while, as the flexible blonde was doing a difficult back bend, similar to the Wheel, the young man nudged her in the ribs. She collapsed in a convulsion of giggles.

Marcia showed her first glimmer of impatience, and the session drew to a close sooner than it might normally have.

"We will now lie out in the Sponge, relaxing for ten minutes, and then anyone who likes can remain for the meditation," Marcia said.

Again I overheard the blonde and her young man giggling together. He was nudging her again, and she snuggled up to him and murmured softly, "Let's go for a walk in the woods."

Alternately holding hands and poking at each other, they made off for the forest primeval of Emerson and Thoreau.

I never saw them again, though I was in Concord for months.

"Too bad that girl didn't come back," I said to Marcia one day. "She would have made a wonderful yogi."

Marcia smiled. "I'm afraid not," she said. "It came too easy, there was no discipline involved, and she might as well have been doing calisthenics as Yoga. She didn't have the slightest idea of what she was trying to do. She was really a fluke; she had a back as flexible as a kitten's and she was performing like a kitten. She was obviously insensitive to discipline, and I could have predicted that she wouldn't come back."

"Are you suggesting," I said, "that a person can gain nothing from Yoga unless they sweat and strain?"

"I am saying that unless they are sufficiently disciplined to establish a meaningful rapport betwen mind and body, they might as well do calisthenics or acrobatics."

"But suppose the exercises are so easy that they don't have to think about them?"

She laughed. "In her case, I would string out the headstand to ten minutes, gradually, and this would require all the attention she could muster and more—as controlled immobility requires more concentration the longer it is held." She sighed. "But once it became difficult, she would get bored and quit."

"How can you be so sure?"

"If you can't stop giggling or petting in a period devoted to silence and self-appraisal, how can you stand quietly on your head for ten minutes?"

One didn't have to be over thirty-five to appreciate Yoga, but it did seem to help.

Marcia's guru, the Swami Vishnudevananda, had cautioned Marcia on the young. "Do not count on the college students," he said. "They are not mature enough to invoke the needed discipline."

It was remarkable what some oldsters could do. I also worked out next to sixty-five-year-old Frank Vogel of Newton Upper Falls, a bank employee and book connoisseur, who advised me in a whisper that my shoulder stand was not as good as it should be. "You should be as straight as a plummet," he said from a position practically on his head.

Vogel had been doing Yoga for fifteen years. A nervous type, he had originally been interested only in relaxing. He had suffered from constant headaches, but they had disappeared. "I can't remember when I had my last headache." Twice in recent years he felt a headache forming and he went into his shoulder stand for five minutes. "By the time I got to my feet, the symptoms were gone."

He had also had a chronic constipation problem, was sluggish, lacked appetite. He was now regular, vigorous, and required little sleep. "But above all," he said, "I've given up worrying. Relaxation becomes a habit after a while, and the mind learns to throw off things that it can use constructively."

But Yoga was not by any means a cure-all or help-all. "I rarely stress its therapeutic nature," Marcia said. "My feeling is that if it helps prostate, circulatory, and respiratory conditions, it's chiefly because any improvement of the whole helps the parts.

Almost anybody could do what Frank Vogel had done. Besides the Sunday class at Concord, he worked out at home a few minutes every morning. His exercises took but ten minutes, and he meditated a few minutes more. "All I do is the shoulder stand, the Cobra, and the forward bend, standing up, as a sort of warm-up. And then I relax and commune with Nature a bit."

It seemed so little to keep well with, and yet it had changed Vogel's whole outlook. "The exercises," he explained, "quiet my mind and body, making it easier for the subconscious to take over, and work on my problems. On this level, we often see ourselves clearly in relation to the universe, people, and events, and some things just don't seem as threatening as they did."

At Concord the meditations were an adjunct to Hatha Yoga—the physical Yoga—a self-revealing sequel to the exercises, particularly when the student meditated after tuning in mind and body.

The reactions to the meditations were varied. As the class relaxed, Marcia spoke of inner peace and harmony, and planted the seed thought for the meditation: "At the center of peace I stand, and nought can harm me there."

For fifteen minutes silence prevailed, and then, at a signal from Marcia, the meditators sat up and rubbed their eyes. I had a suspicion that most had taken the opportunity of basking in the warm sun to take a snooze.

But they appeared ready, even anxious to discuss their experience.

"How can we have peace anywhere," one middle-aged man said reflectively, "when people can't find peace within themselves? Certainly one hundred million people not at harmony within themselves will not long be at harmony with another hundred million who have no inner harmony."

"Wars," another chimed in, "don't come so much from inequities, as the reaction to these inequities—resentment, anger, hate."

The rapt concentration and contemplation of early meditation often touched off a chain of introspection completely new to the student. "Many of us," said a graying woman who had performed the exercises with remarkable precision, "think only of self, and become so self-willed that we don't acknowledge a higher power. So when we eventually louse up, as most people do at some time, we have nothing to turn to but ourselves. If we could achieve selflessness, we might find it easier to get with God when we need Him."

Marcia nodded thoughtfully. "That is the hard core of Yoga: selflessness."

The discussion was rather spirited, as there was some disagreement. "If you make yourself completely selfless, you also make yourself small," a younger student observed with a frown.

"Not small," the rebuttal came, "just humble enough to listen for the voice of God."

In the class, but sitting silently, was my young Hindu friend, Linda. She wore an expression of beatific serenity. I had learned that she was seriously dating a young student from Israel. They were planning to marry and live one day in Israel, an intriguing prospect for an Irish-Scottish-English-Swedish Hindu.

I found it odd that Linda had no comment; she had normally been so articulate, but she made up for it later as we sat down privately to discuss her self-styled conversion to Hinduism. She was a profound meditator herself and had experienced a sort of soul-universe communion which was difficult to put into words. "It is like a moment of revelation when you see yourself in perspective to every living thing in the universe, including the God force."

In these higher moments she usually saw lights, purple lights, and felt a great sense of tranquillity. "Until I took up Yoga," she said, "I never knew what it meant to be at harmony with myself."

Her conversion, if it was that, was still unclear to me. "I know many Catholics," I said, "who are in harmony with their faith and themselves. Why couldn't you have found this peace meditating in your own Church, or by concentrating on the God of your fathers?"

"Because Yoga—and Hinduism—isn't against anything. The Vedantic teachings, which are the basis of Hinduism, preach that God is in everybody, so how can you help but love everybody, since God is love." She regarded me gravely. "I just don't want to be told that there is anybody I must resent or dislike because he or she is different from me."

She nodded. "Some people are hard to like, but I don't go by first impressions any more." She had plenty of friends now, of both sexes, whereas she was once afraid of people. "I was shy to the point of being neurotic, and hated people because just meeting them was a problem." Linda was the product of a mixed marriage. Her father was Catholic, her mother Episcopalian. Her mother had self-effacingly taught Linda her Catholic prayers as a child, and sent her off to church and parochial schools, without becoming a Catholic herself.

"When I was very young," Linda said, "I wanted to be

a nun, and I loved the thought of Jesus and Mary. They seemed so full of love for me and the whole world. But as I grew older, I felt there was not so much love as there was fear and restraint, and restrictions of all sorts. It was wrong to do this and to do that."

"Wrong to do what, for instance?"

"Wrong to wear slacks, for instance . . ." There was a trace of belligerence in her voice.

This didn't seem a terrible deprivation to me.

"It was all part of a bigger thing—this emphasis on negativism instead of being positive."

As a youngster, she had had an unhappy experience in connection with the ritual of the Rosary consecrating Russia to the Immaculate Heart, asking the Holy Mother for the conversion of Russia and peace. Trying to make an analogy which would forcibly bring home the urgency of the prayer, a teacher had said, "Visualize Mary as holding an enormous bulldog—Russia—at one end of a chain, and each link in the chain as a rosary. Whenever the bulldog takes a big leap, links may snap or be weakened, so that each time you say the Rosary you strengthen a link."

Then came the part that had particularly bothered Linda. "If the chain runs out of links, or snaps because enough prayers haven't been said, then the Russian bulldog will get loose and kill us all with the atom bomb."

This little analogy had affected Linda's little sister even more than Linda. "Every time anyone mentioned anything about the bomb, she'd start bawling," Linda recalled.

While the phraseology may have been unfortunate, it seemed to me that one's faith should have firm enough footing not to be dislodged by the ill-considered remarks of an unsophisticated nun.

"Did you talk to anybody about it?" I asked.

"I spoke to my cousin, a Jesuit priest, and he pointed out that in any large organization anybody could err."

There had been another unhappy incident. She had come home from school one day and announced to her mother that her class had prayed for the Episcopalians that day. Her Episcopalian mother had bridled. "That's mighty nice of them," she said drily.

It occurred to me that Linda was going through a phase. A Monsignor friend, now dead, had once told me that Catholic children of mixed marriages were apt to feel ambivalent about Catholicism if the non-Catholic parent did not convert.

Linda took issue. "My mother did everything she could to bring me up as a Catholic, and even went to church with us occasionally."

She was determined to be a Hindu, and felt that it had broadened her sufficiently to permit her to marry outside her own faith.

"Is it possible," I asked, "for a Hindu to marry a Jew?"

"Oh the Hindus accept something of every religion—Christ, Mary, Moses, the whole story of the resurrection."

"But how about the religious ceremony?"

"There will be two ceremonies. We are going to be married first by a rabbi in an orthodox Jewish wedding."

"And then the Hindu ceremony?"

She shrugged. "Then we'll have a civil wedding."

"Why not a Hindu ceremony, if you're a Hindu?"

"It wouldn't be binding, for one thing."

"And for another," I pointed out, "the Hindus only admit members of their own race into the sacraments of their own faith in their temples. You have to be one of the four castes; they don't have a place for even their own outcasts."

Linda wasn't impressed. "Regardless of anything," she said, "I know my whole life changed with the Vedantic teachings."

"How," I asked, "do your parents feel about your proposed marriage?"

"They're quite understanding," she said. "They tell me it's my life, and my right to do what I want with it."

"They're quite broad for a couple of non-Hindus," I pointed out.

"Oh, they've been wonderful parents," she said. "Without their moral teachings I would not have known right from wrong as I do."

"And what teachings were they?"

She seemed puzzled.

"Weren't they Catholic teachings?"

She nodded. "But of course." She smiled. "But I'm still a Hindu—and I wouldn't be able to keep that Irish temper of mine if I weren't."

"That was our main reason for marrying," Marcia said fondly.

"What was that?" I asked.

"Our astrology charts; they matched perfectly. My moon and Pluto were conjunct to Louis' Venus and Mars, and this of course accounts for our mutual attraction."

Louis nodded happily. "Besides that, Marcia's Venus was on my Uranus and was also trine—at a 120-degree angle—to my Neptune. That made it pretty definite."

He caught me blinking. "Here, let me get the charts; that might clear it up."

His head bobbed as he compared the two charts. "You see, our Mercurys are conjunct, and so are our ascendants, and that's most unusual."

"What do you mean by ascendants conjunct?"

"We were born within three degrees of each other in the zodiac in relation to the Eastern horizon."

That didn't seem to make the marital cloth any more binding.

"Oh, there's lots more to it than that," Marcia said. "There was hardly an aspect that wasn't favorable for marriage."

Even their meeting appeared to have come about through the stars. They had met in December, 1961, at an astrology conference. Marcia was the speaker and Louis was in the audience. But Louis had Leo ascending and Leo liked to occupy the center of the stage. "I got up and asked a question," Louis recalled, "and then I made a point of my own for ten minutes. I was most rude."

But Marcia didn't mind. Just meeting Louis, she had a premonition which astrology was to startlingly confirm. They were meant for each other, despite all the apparent differences and obstacles. The first question they asked each other when they were alone was about their respective birthdays. It was as Marcia had suspected; they were both in Gemini. Marcia was born on the cusp, May 22, making her a perfect Gemini. Louis was born on June 2, with strong Taurean aspects.

"Louis can be quite obstinate at times," Marcia observed, "and that's a Taurus sign." She smiled. "But we call it will power."

They didn't waste any time dancing, spooning, or strolling

in the moonlight. They got right down to business, mapping each other's natal charts.

"As we studied our guiding planets," Marcia said, "we realized that our marriage was inevitable. Our charts looked almost as though they were the same person's, there were so many points of identification."

Louis took off his shell glasses, rubbed his eyes drowsily, and poked his glasses at the charts. "If it hadn't been for the charts," he drawled, "we would hardly have dared to go ahead. There was so much against our marriage on the surface. Marcia was twelve years older than I with a growing family; I was only a college sophomore, without a job or prospects of one. It looked pretty bleak." He wagged his head slowly. "I just don't see how we could have managed without those horoscopes."

"Well, you loved each other?" I suggested.

"Sure," Louis said, with a wisdom far beyond one of his years, "but love alone doesn't make a marriage. Nearly everybody thinks they're in love when they marry, and look at all the divorces."

"Were all the aspects favorable?" I asked.

"Oh, no." Louis shook his head. "They never are."

He looked over at Marcia affectionately. "Wouldn't you say that most of our problems come because of my Neptune squaring both our Mercurys and your Saturn?"

He laughed the least uncertainly. "Planets squared suggest a stressful situation; they come together at right angles, and they can collide like two cars at an intersection."

"Saturn," Marcia pointed out, "is a sort of cosmic taskmaster, while Neptune is often vague, illusory, and foggy. That's what makes Louis so absent-minded at times."

Louis smiled like a small boy. "That accounts for a sort of disciplinary relationship between us. Marcia's logical, precise mind, governed by Saturn, is always picking up my bad spelling and writing."

"And jogging your memory," I suggested, "when you forget your own astronomy classes and mowing the lawn."

"Marcia's Mercury opposed to Saturn gives her an unusually controlled and disciplined mind." Louis spoke with the detachment of authority.

Marcia gave her husband an enigmatic glance. "It can also lead to mental tension," she said shortly.

"And to a certain restrictiveness," Louis said. He smiled quizzically. "Like my college term papers, for instance, Marcia gets to edit things to death. By the third or fourth version, there's very little left of what I wanted to say."

I thought Marcia was about to say, "Well, you could type your own papers," but Saturn exerted its discipline.

"Actually," Marcia said, "whatever difficulties we do have come from the unusual degree of identification in our charts. There's no demarcation of spheres of interest, so it leads to competition. We're both teaching Yoga and astrology, and we're both interested in the psychic."

"You get to cook alone," I said.

"Yes," she said with a smile, "nobody tries to take that from me."

"What would be the best charts for people thinking of marrying?" I asked.

"Oh, ours is very good, I would say."

"But what would be the best for the long haul, for people not young or strong enough to stand up to conflicts of interest?"

Marcia spoke with professional crispness. "It depends on the purpose the marriage is meant to serve. I would say that in most cases it is helpful when planets tend to complement rather than duplicate each other."

"Then an inevitable marriage is not necessarily a good one?"

"No, but it may be necessary for the soul's evolution."

They were married in June, six months after their first meeting, at a time considered astrologically fortuitous. And now, married two years, they were still confident that the stars were as good a reason as any for getting married.

"They tell you so much about yourself and your partner," Louis said, "that it's not hard to see how you can go wrong."

Louis was still analyzing his own chart. "From this, I would say I'm full of inspiration, but I diffuse myself too much. I've got to tighten up my writing style—that leads to difficulties and conflict."

"With all these squares and oppositions," I said, "without knowing the first thing about astrology, I don't see where this is the ideal marriage—chartwise, of course."

"Every human relationship has its favorable or unfavorable aspects," Marcia said. "It's knowing about them and being prepared that counts."

I was not to be put off. "But I thought that your charts matched perfectly."

"I could see the marriage plainly in our charts," she said.

"Will the marriage continue, can you see that?"

"I do not see myself ending the marriage," she said cryptically.

"Why are the stars so hazy about the duration of the marriage, when they were so clear about its inception?"

"They indicated that we should be married," Marcia said.

"Then why don't they indicate whether you should remain married?"

"We'll cross that bridge in time," Marcia said.

My hosts seemed suddenly much more concerned about the aspects of my marriage than their own.

"Your marriage doesn't necessarily have to break up," Louis said. "If you can ease past the stress points during the next two years, you should have it made."

The rest of my horoscope was a bit more optimistic. There was material success, particularly for a book I was now working on, though it took no astrologer to determine what that book was. My health would be good if I didn't overwork.

It was not at all explicit.

"Why are you so much more explicit about the universe in your predictions about earthquakes, business, depressions, and comparable catastrophes than you are about individuals?"

"Because people can overcome some of their stress points and make things work out differently," Louis said. "They have a choice."

"What choice do they have when the earthquake comes?" I asked.

"They have freedom of movement. If it's going to hit California, they can move to New York, and if it's hitting New York, they can go to Timbuctoo, or anywhere it isn't."

"Well, where is it going to hit?"

He scratched his head. "I can't say for sure. But one psychic who predicted the Alaskan quake for 1964 also predicted severe quakes in Italy and California in '65 and '66."

The spring of 1965 was going to be a particular time of trial. At this period there would be a triple conjunction of Mars, Uranus, and Pluto, the three most violent planets, astrologically, and they would be opposed—another bad sign—by the unhappy planet Saturn, from which our word saturnine is aptly derived.

"This will be the most likely period for earthquakes, and for riots, wars, depression, and earth-shaking changes in the social order," Louis said. "The last time Uranus and Pluto squared off, we had the Great Depression and Adolf Hitler; so with four of these planets lining up, look for a serious decline in the market and racial upheavals."

As these lugubrious, slow-moving planets continue in conjunction, financial conditions will reach a crisis in February, 1966, as will other human affairs, and not till late '67 and '68 will things begin to iron out. "By '69 and '70, we should be back to normal."

It was certainly a gloomy picture, but Louis had it straight from the stars and terrific tornadoes in the U.S. and severe quakes in Greece, Chile, and the Aleutians in the spring of '65 made him all the more sure of himself. He had charted individual horoscopes and the horoscope for the United States of America, born July 4, 1776, at 2:12 A.M., in Philadelphia. Now all one had to do was profit by the foreknowledge.

"You see now how it works," he said solemnly. "You have been told now, astrologically, when the market slump is coming, but it's up to you to get in or out of the market. If you get out, you can come back late in '66, buy low, and make a killing in '68."

"I got killed in May, 1962, and marketwise I'm very dead."

"Oh, I remember that from your psychic book," Louis said. "Four astrologers and psychics told you to get out of the market before May, but you didn't listen."

"I guess it was my destiny."

"Astrologically, I can't accept that," Louis said. "All you had to do was act intelligently, and you would have been helped, but you didn't put any stock in astrology."

"Not," I said, "when an astrologer can predict precisely for a country and a condition, but not for the individual."

"What do you mean?"

"Well, you've been concerned about your own predictions of earthquakes, not even knowing whether you're going to be safe here in Massachusetts."

"I don't follow you."

"You asked about Edgar Cayce's prediction about destruction in Manhattan and parts of California, Los Angeles, and San Francisco, and wanted to know when he foresaw it, and if the destruction would extend through New England."

"That's right," Louis said. "After all, Cayce did predict the Alaska quake; he saw new land rising in the Atlantic and the Pacific, and this had happened off Iceland and Ecuador. So why wouldn't I be interested in what he foresaw and when?"

Many astrologers checked their forecasts with the amazing trance readings of the late sage of Virginia Beach.

Cayce, closing his eyes, had been able to diagnose ailments of people he had never seen and prescribe cures that he had never consciously heard of. Now those familiar with his predictions were wondering when the ultimate disaster foreseen by Cayce would occur. He had said that certain things would happen first—land rises, volcanic eruptions in Italy and Hawaii, sinking of the water level in the Mediterranean, drastic changes in climate, and the complete disillusionment of man.

"Nobody knows precisely when from his predictions," I said, "because he was asked a question in trance, and said only that these various earth changes and upheavals would take place between 1958 and 1998. Some have already occurred, like the prediction in 1926 that there would be terrible race riots before the death of the second President in office, and we had them before President Kennedy's assassination; Franklin Roosevelt was the first to die after the Cayce forecast. And we have seen recent volcanic eruptions in Italy, a lowering of the Mediterranean basin, and those recent land rises that you mentioned."

"But why didn't Cayce more accurately fix the time and the place?" Louis said.

"He wasn't asked for the precise time, but he did say the destruction was going to extend to Connecticut."

Louis grimaced. "You don't think it'll get up this far, do you?"

"Why not consult your stars?" I said.

"But they only say when; you have to be psychic to get where, too."

"So, astrologically," I said, "you can see all kinds of upheavals, but not how they will affect you."

"That isn't quite right," he said. "I know where the earth faults are, and I could put two and two together, with the vote going to California. Or else I could really get down to earth, so to speak, and map the horoscopes for cities in the major fault areas, like San Francisco or Los Angeles. But I would need the exact moment of the city's beginning, and it is not always clear which date should be taken—the first settling of a community or its incorporation."

Many of Marcia's friends did not take Louis' dire forecasts seriously, but one person believed in them implicitly. That was Louis. He considered another recession inevitable, and was already making plans for the hard days ahead.

One day we all drove out to a Yoga retreat at Wingaersheek near the Boston Shore. It was rather a bleak, ascetic establishment, with the daylight visible through the loose boardings, and the fare was simple—baked potatoes roasted over hot coals in a towering fireplace.

Louis sampled a potato, and a faraway look came into his eyes. "I understand," he said, "that potatoes are un-usually rich in nutrition."

"They're rich in iron, for one thing, particularly with the peels," Marcia agreed.

"With a slump coming up," Louis said, "why wouldn't it be a good idea to put in a patch of these potatoes back of the house?" His face lighted up. "We might even have a sort of Victory Garden."

Bill the Scientist, munching on a potato of his own, said with a snicker, "If things get that bad, the bank may take away your house, and the potato patch with it."

Louis smiled. "I don't see a depression lasting that long."

Louis regarded everybody astrologically. As some people said hello on being introduced, Louis would ask, "When were you born?" And then he might do their chart. It gave him a clue, he felt, to the individual's temperament and thinking.

One day, being interviewed by a lady producer for an appearance on a television show, he offered to do her horoscope. She looked only mildly interested, but the next day he was back with the charts.

She regarded him stolidly.

"For one thing," he announced cheerfully, "you have stomach trouble."

The producer nodded, unimpressed.

"In fact, you just had appendicitis."

Now she looked startled. "How did you know that?"

"Your Mercury is in the last part of Virgo," Louis explained.

"Now about people close to you." He cocked an eye at the chart. "Your children are very mercurial (a tactful way of saying they were emotional), read a lot, and are highly intelligent."

The producer beamed as any fond mother would.

"And you"—here he hesitated—"are having financial difficulties."

"Well, who isn't?"

"But your difficulties," he said, "are caused by your husband."

The producer looked a trifle embarrassed.

"You've been talking to somebody," she said.

"Not at all," Louis said. "Certain planets in your eighth house, ruling a partner's finances, are afflicted by Saturn."

As it happened, the husband hadn't worked for months.

One of Louis' most remarkable predictions concerned President Kennedy. But, as he pointed out, practically every astrologer he know had foreseen the President's death in office.

It had been a badly kept secret in astrology circles.

"How does it happen," I asked, "that practically every astrologer I met before the Kennedy assassination predicted his death?"

"That was quite obvious," Louis responded. "Because it concerned the United States chart as much as it did Kennedy's. He just happened to be President. It would have happened to anybody that was President. We were all sure it was going to happen because of the twenty-year planetary cycle disastrously affecting American presidents for more than a hundred years."

Kennedy, I understood, was told of the tradition as he was campaigning for the Presidency, and reportedly replied with a lighthearted laugh, "I'm the one who's going to beat the jinx."

Even as the youthful, vital Kennedy was striving for high office, many astrologers, including David Williams, president of the Astrologers Guild, and Olive Pryor, a New York stargazer, had publicly foreseen that he would be elected and not finish his term.

"For that matter," said Marcia, "Isabel Hickey, a Boston astrologer, told her classes before election that she was more concerned with the Vice-President, as he would eventually become President."

Williams, a former executive with the Consolidated Edison Company of New York, had sat in my living room three weeks before the assassination and predicted the President's death. And in August, 1960, soon after Kennedy's nomination at Los Angeles, Williams had forecast the President would die in office and be succeeded by Lyndon Johnson. At the prodding of seven scoffing business associates, the prediction was written down, and then lightly signed by the seven. When I spoke to several shortly after the assassination, they were confused, unbelieving still, but no longer scoffing. "There may be more to life," conceded an engineer, "than you can get the square root of."

I turned to Louis. "On what," I asked, "did Williams base his predictions?"

"I would think he probably took the U.S. chart as well as the President's, because Kennedy's chart would have only shown bad aspects, not death necessarily, and bad aspects were predicted, by the way, for that particular November."

Williams' reasoning was, fortuitously, at hand. Marcia dug up a current issue of the magazine *Horoscope* and turned to "JFK: Our Martyred President," by David Williams. Kennedy's birth was fixed at 3 P.M., E.S.T., May 29, 1917, at Brookline, Massachusetts, and Williams had sought to show how Kennedy's rise—and fall—was ordained by his stars. He quoted astrologer R. C. Davidson's *The Technique of Prediction:* "The cardinal principle of prediction and the golden rule which should be remembered, first, last, and always is this: Nothing will come to pass that is not promised by the nativity"—the natal chart.

"One of the most striking features of Kennedy's chart," Williams pointed out, "is the stellium (group) of five planets—Mars, Mercury, Jupiter, the Sun, and Venus—in the eighth house. The Sun in this sector brought him financial benefits from a trust fund established by his father, gain by marriage, death through self-sacrifice, and fame as a result of his tragic death."

Williams' summation could of course have been put down to hindsight, had his foresight not already been established.

Marcia, reading on, exclaimed, "Ah, here it is—the prediction of four years ago."

Here it was, as Williams had analyzed it: "Kennedy's eighth-house Sun signified that about his forty-fifth year would be a critical period for him. The agency that was to bring this about was the Jupiter-Saturn conjunction at twenty-five degrees Capricorn on February 19, 1961, in opposition to Kennedy's tenth-house Saturn at twenty-seven degrees Cancer."

It sounded like so much Greek—or calculus—to me, but Louis nodded understandingly and Marcia's eyes gleamed with comprehension. "Transiting Saturn's opposition to its natal place normally marks a turning point in everyone's career," she continued, "but in Kennedy's case, that particularly transit was associated with Jupiter, an aspect which foreshadowed his death in office.

"It was from a consideration of the interrelationship of Kennedy's tenth-house Saturn in Cancer and the Jupiter-Saturn conjunction in Capricorn that the writer made his August 4, 1960, prediction that Kennedy would be elected president, would die in office, and be succeeded by Johnson."

But Williams has also considered the U.S. chart in

making his forecast. Before the President's death, he had told me, "I felt that Kennedy would be elected, because I foresaw Nixon surviving, and the next President, whoever he was, was not fated to live out his term."

The U.S. chart, conceived nearly two hundred years before, posed no problem to Louis.

"That's strongly predictable, because of the Saturn-Jupiter conjunction governing the office of the Presidency. It's called the Great Mutation conjunction, and since 1840 or so, the conjunction has returned every twenty years, leading to the prediction that any President elected in the twenty-year cycle period since 1840 would die in office."

The first had been William Henry Harrison in 1840, and he had been followed by Lincoln, Garfield, McKinley, Harding, Roosevelt, and now Kennedy—elected respectively in 1860, 1880, 1900, 1920, 1940, and 1960.

It seemed a discouraging prospect for anyone contemplating the nation's highest post in 1980. "The conjunction will be changing just about then," Louis observed, "and the next President may be able to ride it out, though I don't think it likely. Since they're slow-moving planets it takes a while for them to move off to a point where their influence won't be felt."

How were planets many millions of miles away able to govern human destiny on this tiny planet of ours?

"There're only theories," Louis said, stroking his chin. "And some of these have been advanced by college professors who have noted the impact of the moon on the tides, human behavior, and even the menstrual cycle. One doctor in Tallahassee, Florida, discovered, for instance, that his patients bled more during the phase of the full moon, some even hemorrhaging, so he suspended surgery during these periods."

I was familiar with Dr. Edson Andrews' study. He had made surveys of some one thousand cases, and then had his research confirmed by another Florida physician, who similarly surveyed his own patients in surgery.

"But what of the planets—the Saturn and Jupiter conjunction, for instance, or that lineup of Mars, Uranus, Pluto, and Saturn—how can they have all this impact on us earthlings?"

"The same way the Moon does, theoretically," Louis pontificated. "At certain head-on positions, as in squares, oppositions, and conjunctions, the malefic planets affect the Sun with their magnetic field, and this, in turn, affects the responses of earth organisms, including man."

"In other words, man has a magnetic field responsive to the planets' magnetic fields?"

"Exactly," Louis said, "and the impact of these planets, at certain times, as has been proven over the centuries, is enough to shape and alter mass thinking to a point where wars, social upheavals, and financial depressions can ultimately develop." Louis laughed reflectively. "After all, if the Moon can move oceans, why is it so surprising that several planets combined shouldn't move people around whether they like it or not? Are we bigger, stronger, or more important than the vast tides that cover most of the earth's surface?"

"So why worry about earthquakes?" I said. "We can't do anything about them, if that's what the planets have in store for us."

"It's all part of the universal order," Louis conceded, "just like Halley's Comet showing up every seventy-five years. It's inevitable."

"What else is inevitable?"

Louis poked his nose into his charts. He was examining the charts for Soviet Russia, born November 17, 1917, with a series of convulsive contractions, in riot-ridden Moscow, and for Red China, hatched October 1, 1949, in plague-ridden Peking.

"Within fifteen or twenty years," he said, "there will be such a gradual worsening of relationship between China and Russia that armed conflict will be inevitable."

"That's the way it looks from reading the papers."

"That may be true," Louis said, "but astrologers were predicting this break five and ten years ago, when the two countries looked to be cozy with each other. Besides, there's another development, which the political wiseacres haven't caught up with."

"And what's that?"

"As the rupture between the two Red giants widens, the United States will line up more and more with the Soviet."

"Do you see a war?" I asked.

"That's quite possible."

"That's not very definite."

He nodded. "Actually, I see a whole series of skirmishes between Russia and China before the big blowoff."

And where would we be?

"With Russia, of course. The Chinese leaders don't care a bit for human life, they have seven hundred millions to throw around, and life is accordingly cheap."

"And where are you, the individual, in all of this?"

The question seemed to catch him off guard. "What do you mean?"

"How will all these earth-shaking events affect you?"

Louis still wasn't sure what I meant.

"Your family life, financial future, and little things like that."

He frowned for a moment. "Obviously," he said, "our stocks are going down with nearly everybody else's, and these financial pressures may put a certain stress on our marriage."

"How about your marriage house?" I asked.

"Actually, the stresses on the marriage house are mostly in Marcia's chart, because of her afflictions to Saturn, ruler of her seventh house."

"How can there be one unhappy partner in a marriage?"

"My chart shows a marital impact on me in spring of 1965, in reaction to Marcia's chart; but I will be only tangentially affected."

It was hard, obviously, to be objective about one's self.

While Louis put an optimistic interpretation on his own chart, he was inclined to be pessimistic in his delineations for others. Accused once of being a male Cassandra—a prophet of doom— he rebutted, logically, "This is the kind of a world it is; I only report what I see." He made a face. "Would you want me to tell you what is going to happen or what you would like to see happen? After all, everything isn't set. You still have choices, knowing what is coming."

"Like getting out of the market?"

"Exactly," he said. "Astrology is a guide. It lets you know when your good and bad periods arrive, when to plunge into something, when to withdraw or mark time. It reveals your weaknesses and strengths." His eyes focused on me vaguely. "You Taureans, for instance, have weak throats and necks, and have to guard against soreness and stiffness. You're also inclined to have stomach or digestive problems because of your Mars and Neptune in Cancer."

As nearly every astrology buff knew, Mars and Neptune were two of the ten guiding planets (counting Moon and Sun), Cancer was one of the twelve signs of the zodiac, and the twelve houses, each occupying a slice of the zodiac, were the seats of the different conditions affecting man. Marriage, for instance, belonged in the seventh house, death in the eighth. Louis thought of the horoscope as a play. "The planets are the actors or protagonists, the signs of the zodiac in which the planets fall determine the roles the planets play, and the houses, each occupying a sector of the zodiac, fix the scene of the action. The angular configurations of the planets are the plot."

Some of Louis' "plays" were on the dramatic side, and none more so than the one he staged for Linda, the blue-eyed Hindu from Boston.

One day Linda burst into the Concord ashram, crying, "Don't tell me I'm not going to be married for seven years."

Louis followed, apologetic. "I'm sorry, Linda, but that's what I see."

"You better take another look, that's all I can say," said the fuming Linda. "Because that's not the way it's going to be."

Louis scratched his thick mop of hair. "I've checked your horoscopes against each other, and it double-checks, Linda. What more can I tell you?"

"You can tell me nothing," she said warmly.

"It's really not at all bad, when you look at it philosophically," Louis said. "When you do marry, you are going to have a good marriage, and it will be on the spiritual side, too."

Linda and Louis seemed totally unaware of the rest of us.

"Maybe," I interposed, "you're going to marry another Hindu."

She gave me a scathing look. "I'm beginning to get my Irish up," she said. "Nobody is telling me what I'm going to do or not do."

"But they're your stars," Louis protested. "I didn't put them there. I only delineated them."

"You'd better undelineate them," Linda snapped.

Seven or eight people, all old enough to be Linda's parents, had been following the colloquy. "What's so bad about not getting married for seven years?" a sweet-faced matron asked. "You'll still be young, and you'll know more what you want."

"Because I'm engaged to a wonderful guy, that's why," Linda shot back.

"Oh," the woman said.

Louis held his ground, though on the defensive. He scanned the two charts in his hand, then shook his head. "With some people, it's not quite as clear; but Linda's Pluto is exactly on her seventh house cusp ruling marriage, and that makes it particularly decisive, especially when you compare the two charts." The second chart was her fiancé's. Louis wagged his head. "They really shouldn't get married."

"You're saying they shouldn't be married, which has

nothing to do with whether they will or not," I observed.

"Well, they won't be; they'll probably have a row before they get to the altar; that's in their stars."

"That's sure a lousy thing to tell anyone," Linda said.

"Not at all," Louis said, "when you consider that in 1971 all the signs are favorable for a good marriage, where it would have to be bad now, even if she did marry."

By now the whole room was absorbed in discussions of Linda's hypothetical nuptials.

"What is going to make her get married seven years from now?" a middle-aged yogi asked.

"She will marry in 1971," Louis replied, "when her progressed Venus reaches her seventh house cusp and the planet Pluto."

Linda snorted. "Don't keep telling me what I'm going to do."

Louis eyed Linda evenly. "You're not looking at it the right way, Linda. You should be happy to learn that when you do get married, you will choose an unusual partner of great spiritual power and wisdom."

At this point, Marcia walked into the room, blithely wondering if everybody was comfortable.

Louis appealed to her. "Look at these charts, Marcia, and tell us whether these two people should be married."

Marcia's eye quickly ran over the two sheets of paper, and she shuddered. "My God," was all she said.

Six months later, Linda was married to her young man. But Louis was not ruffled in the least. "Astrology," he said placidly, "can only show the way."

They all laughed when Jody Sheehan announced she was about to take up Yoga. Jody was what the teen-agers would call a senior citizen. She was in her early forties, weighed twenty pounds more than she should, and had just cracked up a leg in an accident. She was on crutches, her leg was stiffening from hip to knee, and she could see herself hobbling around for the rest of her life if she didn't do something.

But she couldn't see running around in a gym suit, tiring herself out at her age with a lot of calisthenics geared for people half her age. Yet she wanted to exercise and keep flexible. And so she came to Marcia's ashram on the Assabet.

In one week she was doing the Cobra, Locust, and Bow. In two weeks she was doing back bends and front bends. In a month she was doing the shoulder stand.

It took her three or four months to really get down to the headstand.

And after six months, she was still working on the Lotus posture, and she might never be able to do it. But she would always keep trying, for it was the effort, not the performance that paid the dramatic dividends.

For in six months, all stiffness had disappeared from Jody Sheehan's leg, she had lost twenty pounds, and everybody at her office had remarked on the new verve and vitality of their administrative assistant.

Besides all this there was an extra dividend. Without looking for it, Jody had gained the ability to relax and ease her tensions almost at will.

I had observed Jody working out next to me in Boulder Grove, as I came to think of the ashram which Louis had so generously staked out with rocks. She moved easily and freely, with evident zest and good humor. No exercise fazed her. If she couldn't do it once, she tried again, and she didn't give up until the hour was over and she collapsed into the prone Sponge posture with the rest of us.

She did not think of herself as a senior citizen. She hadn't felt or looked better in years.

She meditated quietly after the exercises, her thoughts prayerfully akin to those experienced in worshiping in her own church. Yoga, by disciplining her and making her capable of immobility at will, had elevated her mind for communion with God and nature.

Six months later, I was going through pretty much the same beginning routine that Jody Sheehan had.

However, I went through the same pitfalls, discouragement, and frustrations that almost anybody in his forties would. But, more important, the exercises taught me quite a bit about myself.

"Because of the pressure of the abdominal muscles," Marcia observed, "many students refrain from a big meal at least three hours before exercising. Hungry students can get a pickup with a tablespoon or two of honey in milk or hot water an hour before class."

Though the headstand was considered an ideal exercise, not everybody could do it, either for psychological or physical reasons. It was commonplace that some people could do some exercises better than others.

Two frail secretaries were doing the headstand in two weeks, though their arms and shoulders weren't strong enough to support the three preliminary push-ups that some teachers insisted upon as a prelude to a headstand. Yet, there were big brawny men in the same class at the Boston YMCA who had not been able to accomplish the headstand in months of frustrating effort. It was a matter of concentration and flexibility, not muscle. And it gave students a psychological lift. "When I finally got up there," a man of fifty told me, "I felt as though I was master of all I surveyed, which was all the sky above."

Some yogis claim that the headstand also strengthens the eyes, hearing, smell, even the hair growth. But there is no question that it develops lower back and pelvic vitality, relieving congestion by pulling up through reverse gravity organs that have dropped out of place over the years.

While some teachers feel the headstand should be avoided by heart and blood pressure cases, others feel it relieves the heart of its pumping burden. Some of Marcia's pupils once suffered rheumatic fever, leaving the remnant of a heart condition. Even more dramatic was the report of Goldie Lipson, a Yoga instructor in New York's Bronx. After her husband had recovered from a major heart attack, she taught him patiently to stand on his head. Two years later, at sixty, his health had improved strikingly.

But, healthwise, the headstand continues to be controversial. Somebody once asked a Hindu physician whether he thought the headstand was a healthful exercise. He smiled. "All I know is that only a very healthy man can do it."

Apparently, one is never too old to profit by the headstand. After reaching the age of seventy, Israel's doughty prime minister, David Ben-Gurion, took up a course of Yoga-like exercises, including the headstand, and found his physical prowess remarkably improved. His teacher was Moshe Feldenkrais, brilliant head of Israeli electronics, who wrote authoritatively of the tie-in between emotional instability and postural rigidity.

Reading Feldenkrais, Ben-Gurion sent for him. In his biography of Ben-Gurion, correspondent Robert St. John points out that the Jewish leader had never before been interested in physical exercise of any form. However, he was familiar with the Yoga concept that man can progress, intellectually and spiritually, through body control.

"How many lessons will it take?" he demanded of Feldenkrais.

"Ordinarily, one lesson a week for a year is enough," Feldenkrais rejoined. "But I have never had a pupil over seventy before."

Ben-Gurion limbered up with yogic discipline. Feldenkrais ordered him to lie on his back, and with eyes closed, raise one leg and turn it slowly in half-circles, concentrating on visualizing the movement.

Similar slow rhythmical exercises followed. The prime minister noted quick results. After the second lesson, St. John reports, he told his teacher, "Maybe you have something. For months I have had such pain in my hip joints that I wake up every fifteen minutes during the night, but last night I slept for several hours."

Ben-Gurion's wife, Paula, worried about this sudden excess of exercise. "I don't like people who are too much interested in themselves," she told Feldenkrais. "You are making my husband too conscious of how he stands, walks, and sits."

But in time, as her husband lost surplus weight and stopped wearing a corset support, she was won over. He was like a young man again. He could get up from a prone position with agility, and standing on one foot, as he tied a shoelace, he could laugh and say, "It's been thirty years since I've been able to do that."

Feldenkrais, yoki-like, encouraged bodily awareness. "Standing on the head," he observed, "is not an aim in itself. It is merely one of a hundred ways of getting to know oneself thoroughly, a road to greater awareness."

Ben-Gurion's grim determination had much to do with his mastering the headstand. "His feat was all the more remarkable," Marcia pointed out, "because older people who don't exercise have generally stiffened with time and have all kinds of kinks in their backs."

But even younger students, in their twenties and thirties, have already experienced some curvature of the spine, Marcia noted. "This curvature is so common that students often arch their legs to compensate for the curve in the backs."

She would keep after them to straighten their legs, and they would complain about feeling crooked. "Actually, they were not used to feeling straight. But little by little they are compelled to straighten their spines to maintain their balance, and in a year of practice, they are as straight as the day they were confirmed."

Not all students did the headstand, nor was it essential for yogic development.

At the ashram in Concord, I had noticed that one of the most proficient students didn't attempt the headstand with the rest. He was a man of sturdy build, who seemed to slide into such difficult postures as the Crow, the ear-knee pose (the Fetus), and the Bow with smoothness and precision. His name was Victor Best. He was a well-known Boston radio and television commentator, who headed up a school of broadcasting. There was a reason for the omission. Victor had suffered a severe whiplash injury, centered above the nape of the neck. "If anybody has had a lasting neck injury," Marcia said, "I don't give them the headstand; there's always a chance the neck might buckle. The shoulder stand, done long enough and well enough, can accomplish as much without stress."

"How about my whiplash?" I asked.

"Yours is centered in the ridge of the lower neck and shoulders, but even so that's why we emphasized neck-strengthening exercises."

Many authorities on Yoga make miraculous claims for the headstand—eliminating headaches, clearing the brain, and even curing piles; Marcia is loath to use the word *cure*. "Let us say it helps, with Nature doing the rest."

It is an exercise that she does exclusively for five to ten minutes a day, with leg-bending variations, when she has time for but one exercise. "It is an example of perfect rapport between body and mind," she points out, "and it stretches every muscle from head to toe—and with stretching comes a certain innate tranquillity."

The headstand should never be done against the wall or any other support. "If a person has a tendency to fall forward or backward," Marcia points out, "he just isn't holding himself properly."

Some have injured themselves, crashing against the wall; others, to avoid the wall as they fall, have twisted themselves into a sideways fall, pulling muscles and ligaments.

After a while, with the wide choice of exercises, the student gets to know the exercise, or exercises, that best suit his mood or mystique.

Observing one of Marcia's pupils, a Lexington, Massachusetts, psychiatrist, as he launched his workout, it was usually possible to know what kind of day it had been for him. "He would do an advanced Plough, with his knees drawn back across the ears—a fetus-like pose in which he figuratively crawled back into the womb and shut out the outside world," Marcia observed. "Then I would know he had had an unusually rough day with the juvenile delinquents and the Roxbury courts."

Many of the exercises, combined with the deep breathing, seemed to build up resistance generally, and relieve certain psychosomatic symptoms. The mother of a ten-year-old boy who had been asthmatic from early childhood, told me that her son's asthma disappeared after a few weeks of Yoga. "Asthmatics," Marcia pointed out, "generally do things in a spasmodic, jerky way, reflecting their emotional nature. They breathe shallowly, off the top of their lungs; the deep breathing of Yoga, which becomes automatic after a while, helps by relaxing the nervous system so that breathing becomes even and rhythmical."

The boy's mother drew a more graphic picture: "When my son started to go into a spasm, choking for breath, I would start him breathing in deeply and slowly, filling his lungs layer by layer from top to bottom. Soon he would quiet down. Then he would alternate-breathe, as practiced in Yoga class, breathing in one nostril, holding, and exhaling out the other, gaining confidence and quieting panic as he gained control. The attacks grew fewer and less troublesome until they vanished."

With Yoga, circulatory problems are minimized. Yoga students seldom catch cold. Some of Marcia's advanced pupils hadn't experienced colds in years, though they had once dreaded winter and long bouts of chest congestion, coughs, and sniffles. Louis hadn't had a cold in four or five years, and Marcia had experienced but one hint of a cold, when, ignoring her own advice, she overdid herself entertaining, while still managing her household and classes. Even so, she was able to abort the infection in a day, doing headstands, shoulder stands, and a few back bends, which brought freshets of blood to the head, nose, and throat.

I had an unexpected opportunity to test the effectiveness of these exercises, together with an additional one, the Lion, after being exposed to a draft one night during a temperature drop of some thirty degrees. The next morning I felt the familiar malaise of a budding cold: clamminess in body and limb; a sore, scratchy throat; and tender glands.

Normally, I would have taken aspirin, rested, and hoped for the best. But Marcia had other ideas. "We'll do a shoulder stand for a couple of minutes, making a special effort to keep the body straight up, the chin down in the jugular notch, and the breathing deep and relaxed."

I also did the Plough and the Fish, stimulating the spinal cord and stretching the back, while the blood surged to the head. And then Marcia introduced me to an utterly repulsive exercise known as the Lion. She didn't give it normally, as it was more therapeutic than preventive, more dramatic than developmental.

Sitting down, clasping the knees firmly, I stuck out my tongue as far as it would go, reaching for the bottom of my chin, as I tensed throat and even eyes. The idea was to look like a hungry lion.

"The purpose," Marcia said, trying not to laugh, "is to strengthen the ligaments of the throat, and draw the blood into that area, washing away the germs in a wave of antibodies."

I stuck out my tongue six or seven times in succession, repeating the maneuver every few hours during the day until it hurt. Toward evening, my throat no longer bothered me, the glands were no longer tender, and I had put in a full day at the Remington, sitting in the consciously upright posture that Marcia urged as an exercise in itself.

"You do the Lion wonderfully," Marcia complimented. "Tension comes naturally to you."

The Lion was a notable exception. Generally, even in the most intricate posture, the student is reminded to keep his face relaxed and even smiling. "When facial muscles tighten, there is a tendency for the whole body to go rigid," Marcia stressed. "While tensing the muscles involved in specific exercises, we try to keep others relaxed and immobile, practicing control and detachment as we minimize wear and tear, while increasing stamina and endurance."

Regardless of age—and particularly with age—the student of Yoga should never overdo. Between exercises he should lie prone in the Sponge position, resting until completely recovered from exertion, no longer able to hear the beat of the pulse of his head. As a rule of thumb, it is generally wise to spend as much time resting between exercises as doing the exercises, giving the body not only a chance to assimilate its lessons but to replenish its reserves.

As a moderating force, Yoga has countering exercises for nearly every excess. When I complained of gas pains once, Marcia had me get over on my back, lying out flat, and pull my knees back to my chest, raising my head, shoulders, and neck a trifle at the same time. After doing this two or three times, I tried it with each leg separately, and noticed oddly that the backward thrust of the left knee invariably expelled the greatest gas. This the Hindus called the Wind-Relieving Position.

At home or in a studio the neophyte should dress loosely, without shoes, belts, cinches, elastics, or anything else that would restrict movement. Women could wear a leotard or shorts; men, baggy fatigue trousers, or trunks, with sweat shirts or T-shirts if the room was cold. Preferably the skin should be exposed to air and sun, as it will allow the pores to breathe more freely.

Excesses of enthusiasm or depression in the first weeks should be guarded against. In my own case a burst of early optimism was almost my undoing. After a couple of weeks I thought I had found a miraculous cure for my sinus, and that all I had to do was go into a shoulder stand to cure a headache.

Marcia had warned, "You will have good days and bad for the first few weeks, but don't expect too much right away."

On the first cloudy low-pressure day, when my sinuses flared up again, my spirits sagged and I felt like chucking the whole thing. "Remember what I told you," she said, "about cultivating detachment."

For the Western mind, the relaxation that was part of Yoga was often the most difficult going. One middle-aged woman, for instance, had driven up to the Concord ashram in a big Cadillac, demanding to know when the classes got underway. She was interested in slimming her hips and firming her bust.

Told the class would not begin for a half hour, she restlessly leafed through some magazines, nervously paced the room consulting her watch every few minutes, and gasped out "At last!" when the rest of the class showed up.

She threw herself into the exercises with such vigor that Marcia cautioned her to take it easy. "She was obviously trying," Marcia said, "to take off all the weight in one place at one time."

As the workout ended, Marcia asked her students to lie flat, on their backs, and mentally talk to each part of the anatomy.

"Nothing will happen right away," she said, "but as you keep suggesting relaxation to toes, calves, knees, thighs, arms, and stomach, after a while they will react subconsciously to the repetition."

The woman with the Cadillac drew herself up on her elbows. "How long do we have to lie here like this?" she asked.

"I recommend ten minutes for my classes," Marcia said.

The woman's jaw dropped. "Lie here wasting all that time?" she snapped. "Not on your life."

She picked up her things, and without another word, stomped off to her car and drove away with the wheels screeching their protest.

"We never saw her again," Marcia said. "She was too busy to do the thing she needed most—to relax and detach herself long enough to discover her reason for being."

There were many weapons in the war on fat. The side bend variation of the Fountain was almost a specific for eliminating the top-of-the-girdle roll. Designer Suzy Wright, tutored by Marcia, found this simple exercise gave her hip line a boyish trimness, commensurate with the dress styles she was pushing. All Suzy did, standing, legs a few inches apart, was slowly raise arms above head, interlocking thumbs, palms out, with elbows straight and close to the side of the head. Then inhaling deeply, holding her breath, she bent slowly to the side from the hips, bringing head and shoulders down, and then as slowly returned to upright posture—finally exhaling. The exercise was repeated on the other side.

"Doing it but once a day," Suzy said, "will give the ladies the kind of figure that doesn't require a girdle—no matter their age."

Cosmetic-wise, Yoga has an appeal for beauties who want to stay beautiful. One popular rejuvenator was the arm lift practiced by Mrs. DeVries in her Nyack ashram. It nipped at crepey underarm flesh—dowager fat—and required little practice or skill. The hands were brought to the shoulders, and then raised, palms up, with a slow, resisting lift as high as possible, building up pressure on the cords of the inner arms. Then hands were slowly, with studied resistance, returned to shoulders, and the movement repeated five or six times.

In keeping with the popular Marilyn Monroe—Jayne Mansfield image, many women have an abiding interest in building up their bust lines, though they usually make their inquiries in the most offhand way.

There are many chest developers—the Crow, Bow, Bridge, Fish, Wheel, and Twist, to list a few. But Marcia expressly advocates a simple exercise in which the arms are held immobile, straight out from the shoulder, as the shoulder blades are pinched together five to ten times. The exercise is aptly known as the Blade. "What it does," Marcia explained, "is to firm muscles so that sagging busts regain their upward tilt, making the bust line appear larger and more dramatic."

"How about exercises for women who want to reduce their busts?" I asked.

Marcia was amused. "Nobody has ever asked about this."

My guru was careful not to tire or confuse the new student. If an exercise seemed particularly difficult, she would defer it until the student was more proficient, substituting one more easily grasped. For some reason, beginners seemed to favor some exercises and balk on others; for instance, my block on Suryanamaskar, the Sun exercise.

So rather than discourage me early, Marcia took me on to exercises I could clearly visualize. "It's like learning anything else," she said; "you can get too much too fast."

Instead, I did several simpler exercises with functions similar to Suryanamaskar. The Pelvic Stretch I could do within a few days. I doubled my knees under me, bending backward from the hips, pelvic area thrust forward, supporting myself with the palms flat on the ground near the feet. With the head hanging back, allowing gravity to do its work, resting on the elbows, it was an advanced Fish. It was good for thyroid and gonads, while strengthening the back.

I also took quickly to the Twist, which seemed more complex than it actually was. It was presumably beneficial for the adrenals, releasing fountains of energy, and for toning liver, kidney, and spleen. "Sit upright," Marcia directed, "and cross the right leg over the left knee, which is bent back. Plant the right foot firmly in front of the knee, then touch the left hand to the right ankle and bring the right arm around the waist, twisting to the right, looking over the right shoulder." The idea was to anchor the pelvis, getting the desired stretch.

Even as I write this, the Twist sounds impossible, but illustrations, in the Appendix, together with a fuller description, should simplify things. There was a reason, apparently, for all this complexity. "The more knotted you get physically," Marcia explained, "the less knotted you get emotionally. In Yoga, you tie yourself in knots to get nerves unknotted."

Nearly anyone can practice Yoga, according to my pretty guru, provided they have been cleared by a doctor who has no prejudices about exercise of a relaxing sort.

Recovered heart cases and people with high blood pressure can usually do the simpler stretching and balancing exercises without strain. "Many of these people," Marcia pointed out, "have faulty circulation in legs and feet, with ankle swelling." They can exercise safely as a rule in motionless positions. "Balancing first on one leg, then on the other, will tighten the muscles of the thigh, forcing blood down through the legs." This is the Stork. And then there is the Rooster, balancing on the toes of both feet simultaneously with the arms straight out for better balance, with the eyes closed in the advanced stage. "We call it the Rooster," Marcia stated, "because people flap their arms like wings trying to balance, though it's actually their feet, legs, and ankles that get toned up."

The debilitated, trying to regain flexibility and circulation, can begin with the Pump, tailoring it to their own needs. They can lie on their back and slowly bring up their leg, stiff-kneed, from the hip, and slowly down, alternating each leg. As they grow more flexible, they can ease stiff joints by gently but firmly clasping hands behind the knee and squeezing the leg back short of strain.

While all ages profit from Yoga—semi-invalids, dyspeptics, the distraught, the weak, and the strong—two groups gain the greatest good: my own age bracket, from perhaps thirty-five to fifty, and people of any age who want to stay young and vital.

"As people get older," Marcia pointed out, "they often stiffen up not only with wear and tear but with the dreary feeling that their lives have run their course. They secretly feel they have nothing to look forward to.

"People who can stretch, regardless of whether they are seventeen or seventy, still are reaching out mentally and spiritually with courage and resolution." But many, my guru found, particularly the older folk, could not even extend their arms freely when they first turned up at the ashram.

"They couldn't even stretch over their heads or out from the shoulders, but poked out in timid, tentative motions, which reflected the irresolution that had come with age or neurosis."

She found it necessary then to build up visual images to break down inhibitions and evoke movement.

"In many instances," Marcia said, "these older people had been very successful. One particularly was quite wealthy, and at seventy, semiretired. He seemed to have withdrawn into a cocoon of comforting materiality. He prided himself on his valuable art collection, made a sumptuous repast of each meal, had servants tending his least want. But he couldn't stretch to save his life."

And so Marcia appealed, visually, to the acquisitive nature which had brought material success. "You are dying for air," she said, with the fervor of a Bernhardt, "greedy for oxygen; you must get it or die. Reach out, reach out before it is too late."

As he had all his life, when motivated by gain, the rich man reached out. His arms formed two wide arcs, trying to sweep in all the air he could. Two or three times, this visualization was repeated. And then, his mind having set up a body pattern, he was able to stretch normally in class.

Often it took very little to relieve physical complaints, especially of a rheumatic nature. "Crossing the legs, squatting into the Perfect Posture, stretches the hip area gently, and has relieved many students troubled with sciatica," Marcia pointed out. In the Perfect Posture, one heel found a comfortable notch in the other, the two snuggled back into the crotch. In two or three weeks, I found my heels locking comfortably, bracing my lower spine and making me supremely aware of the junction of hip and thigh.

Two other exercises, shown me by Mrs. DeVries, appeared effective for a sacroliac condition. Before getting out of bed in the morning, I did the Pump five or six times, slowly pulling the leg straight up, then bending the knee and squeezing my lower leg toward the chest. Straightening the leg, I brought it down slowly, and repeated with the other leg.

Then, still flat on my back, with my knees bent back so that my feet were a foot or so apart, I slowly arched my lower back, feeling the hip tighten as I breathed out, simulating a sigh. I repeated six or seven times, and could see where it was also excellent for tightening the buttocks.

Marcia had found one gentle exercise helpful for bursitis—the Pendulum. The sufferer bends easily from the hips, and with head facing the floor, allows the affected arm to roll with the natural motion of a pendulum for about a half minute, and then brings the arm back with a wide swing ending in a stretch over his head. This is repeated with the other arm, to avoid imbalance and a sympathetic ache.

Even the finishing schools have borrowed a page or two from the 840,000 exercises collected in the name of Yoga in the last five thousand years. "It was amusing," Marcia pointed out, "to see these proper young Bostonians walking around on their toes, stretching their backs and arms upward, as though they were hanging on to an imaginary rope."

This didn't strike me as a particularly impressive exercise.

"It has not only a physical but a psychological effect," she said.

She mentioned by name two of her own students, secretaries. "Have you noticed their tendency to round their shoulders? That's a carry-over from adolescence, when they hunched over to minimize their bust line, from self-consciousness. Any old-line finishing school—or Yoga—would have changed that, making them proudly aware of themselves."

Yoga is the basis for many therapeutic movements now being "discovered" by science. Marcia had given a simple twisting and bending exercise, which her female students appeared to particularly enjoy. It was called the Triangle posture. One day she spotted an article from the *American Journal of Obstetrics and Gynecology* describing this exercise in detail. "It was being advocated by a Philadelphia physician to relieve painful menstruation in teen-agers," Marcia said. Dr. Leib J. Golub of Philadelphia's Jefferson Medical College reported the exercise had helped 90 per cent of some two hundred girls to whom it had been given.

It was an easy exercise. With arms out straight from shoulders, the body is twisted to one side at the waist. The doctor's directions, reading like basic Yoga, follow: "The knees are kept straight while the girl, twisting and bending the trunk, touches her foot with the opposite hand (right foot, left hand; left foot, right hand). An attempt is made to reach around the outer side of the foot till the heel is touched."

Marcia was quite impressed. "I have been giving this

exercise for years, just thinking it toned people up generally and relieved congestion in the abdominal area."

Dr. Golub specified the exercises three times daily, working up from four to ten repetitions on each side.

Women seemed to respond with particular verve to Yoga. They could manage the Lotus posture better, for instance, as they were more flexible in the pelvic area, nature's way of preparing them for childbirth. And after they gave birth, there was additional cartilage stretching, further increasing flexibility.

From what I had observed myself, working with Marcia's classes, young potential mothers became noticeably shapely and supple, radiating health, energy, and good will, all combining to form an ideal booby trap for the susceptible male. And after marriage, Yoga students seemed to take childbearing in stride.

One pupil, the wife of a young college professor, kept working out until the fifth month. And she was looking forward to a natural birth, without hypnosis or drugs, because of Yoga. "In these births," Marcia said, "the mother regulates her breathing rhythmically with the contractions of labor, simultaneously holding her breath, and relieving the pain."

Yoga has a tendency to jog up the whole system. "The shoulder stand isn't called the good-for-everything exercise for nothing," Marcia commented. "It strengthens the abdominal wall, stimulating peristalsis, while the Bow and Cobra, arching the lower back, tone both the digestive and reproductive systems." She laughed. "With these exercises, and the forward bending, I don't see how anybody could be constipated if they wanted to."

Without realizing it, some modern teen-agers help what should come naturally. They call it hunkering, sitting on their haunches, knees pressed back toward the chest, and feet flat on the ground in front of them. "It has an almost specific laxative action," Marcia observed.

Most Yoga exercises have more than one effect. The stomach lift, for instance, while advocated for constipation, also tones up the urogenital tract and gets rid of a paunch. As she demonstrated the stomach lift, Marcia put a belly dancer to shame. "Standing," she said, "bend slightly forward, pressing palms against mid-thighs, and then breathe out, emptying the lungs. Then, without breathing in, pull the abdominal muscles up from the pelvis, rolling them up as though trying to push the stomach against the backbone.

And then roll them slowly down again." Salome could not have done better.

Although an hour, with plenty of rest periods, forms the ideal workout, many Yoga students work but fifteen minutes a day with a few exercises they prefer. Some make their bedrooms their ashrams, others do snatches through the day, in the office, car, or kitchen.

The housewife sitting in her car, waiting for her children at school, can revolve her neck two or three times, getting out the kinks. It can be done at any time during the day. "Time the complete roll to the holding of single breath," Marcia advises. "In time it can become an automatic response to fatigue. The tense muscle sends a signal to the brain requesting the release that comes from a good stretch. After a while, people stretch without conscious thinking."

Eye and neck rolls are particularly useful for motorists. "They combine to increase peripheral vision; the driver's neck is so much more mobile that he can swing it around without stiffness or pain. And swinging the eyes from side to side soon gives a broader view of the road."

The only limitation is the individual's ingenuity. "Standing at the kitchen sink, doing the dishes," Marcia says, "the housewife can relieve lower back strain by stretching back one leg and then the other a few times in a variation of the Locust."

Marcia tells her girls at the telephone to "talk all you want as you exercise." She suggests standing up, a hand on one hip, the other holding the phone, circling the upper part of the body from the waist, slowly to the tune of the conversation, which is undoubtedly a dull one. "In this way you break up the tension caused by an unnecessary call."

For weary stenographers, there are the neck rolls, when the boss isn't looking, and squaring the shoulders, extending arms and touching hands behind the back, and pressing the shoulder blades together. "It gets at all those nerves at the base of the neck, and permits girls to leave at five without aching backs from bending over a hot typewriter all day." Also, as Marcia had previously noticed, this movement strengthened the pectoral muscles.

Because of student demands on her, Marcia sometimes wishes she were a psychiatrist, but she consoles herself with the thought that psychiatrists come to her, too.

In one day, recently, three women consulted her about constipation problems. One woman, about forty-five, was more distraught than her condition appeared to warrant.

"Can you help me?" she cried.

"There are any number of exercises you can pick up in class." It seemed no great problem to Marcia.

The woman had no time for class. "Just give me an exercise or two."

Marcia suggested meditation and self-analysis, and perhaps a little psychiatry, and an occasional class. "You didn't have to be a psychiatrist to know that she was containing everything—hence the constipation." She never saw her again.

Not long after, a pupil whom she had not seen for a while phoned with a similar problem. She had just been through surgery, and the anesthesia, affecting peristalsis, had made her sluggish. The doctor had prescribed laxatives and assured her she had no obstruction.

Over the phone, Marcia described the stomach lift and the squat—teen-age hunkering. "I also told her to contract her sphincter muscle from time to time during the day."

Within twenty-four hours the problem had vanished.

"Just doing the squat would have been enough," Marcia said, "since it wakes up just the right muscles and organs; it is no wonder that the East Indians have been going to the bathroom this way for thousands of years."

In a modern sense, it didn't seem quite practical.

Marcia laughed. "In India, I was amazed that many houses and hotels didn't have toilets. They just had holes in the floor, and slop buckets nearby. The Indian believes it's unsanitary to have contact with an area that somebody else might have contaminated."

"Didn't they know about modern plumbing?" I asked.

"Even where modern plumbing abounds, the Indian still has his mistrust of the commode. Recently I got a call from a graduate student at Radcliffe. She was living with an Indian girl, and was quite baffled by an incident that occurred in the rooms they shared together. In her dilemma she turned to me, since I had both lived in India and knew her well enough to be trusted."

The Radcliffe girl, being a gently reared young lady, had been embarrassed even to discuss the enigma over the phone. "What I can't understand, Marcia," she finally blurted out, "is how dirty footprints are forever turning up on the toilet seat. It's uncanny."

Immediately picturing what had happened, Marcia burst into a storm of laughter. She visualized the Indian girl, housebroken in the East, carefully perched on the toilet seat in her sandals, leaving the footprints that made a proper Bostonian feel she was up against a mystery of Sherlockian proportions.

"She is only doing what she has done all her life," Marcia said.

The Radcliffe girl recoiled in horror. "The least she could do," she said indignantly, "is take off her shoes."

Why, if Yoga was so great, and had been known through India for close on five thousand years, was India a land of filth, disease, illiteracy, and lack of hope?

Why had the caste system persisted all through those centuries to a point where the untouchables, the unmentionables of India, the hopeless ones, were not even exposed to Yoga instruction? It belonged to the three other castes, exclusively, and the upper class, the Brahmins, had monopolized its discipline for generations on end.

In this country it had made no great strides, but in India, where the religion was largely Hindu, it was a technique employed by members of that faith to attain union with God. Why, if it was a force for good, had its impact not been greater in the land of its origin?

Marcia recalled a parable from the story of Gautama, the Buddha, founder of a faith which incorporated some of the disciplines of Yoga.

"A friend came to the Buddha and asked why he did nothing to convert the people of his home community.

"The Buddha smiled.

" 'Visit the houses in any street,' he said, 'and ask the people in them what they want most.'

"So the friend went knocking on the doors of strangers, asking what they wanted of life.

"He returned to the Buddha with his report.

" 'And what did they tell you?' the Buddha said with a smile.

" 'One wanted a new hunting knife, the second wanted record crops, the third wanted enough rupees so he could stop working, the fourth wanted to marry his daughter off to a rich man.' "

And India has not changed through the ages. For it is axiomatic in Yoga that "when the pupil is ready, the teacher will arrive."

I wondered how many yogin, teachers of yogi, or swamis were operating in India these days.

Marcia smiled. "In three years in India, from Calcutta up to the Tibetan border, I only met one that taught the physical disciplines of Hatha Yoga." There might be a few hundred or so, but no more.

"Perhaps," I said, "the people of this country are more ready than the Indians for the tranquilizing message of

Yoga; for when man's stomach is full and his heart is empty, he looks for more than bread."

In a way, the homegrown purveyors of Yoga were their own worst adversaries. In their own land they were often vain, haughty, and materialistic. And in this country, with rare exceptions, they made no effort to adapt themselves to the Western temperament, or practice simple courtesy.

Many, dining in homes where they had a chance to influence Western thought, gloried in bad manners, making loud, belching noises as they ate. Ostensibly, this was to show their indifference to such material things as food, but all it conveyed was the remarkable arrogance of total indifference. Prevailing on a group of proper Bostonians to meet a swami who was on a lecture tour, Marcia had promised, "Now you will meet a spiritual person."

The guests watched in fascinated horror as the swami ingested his food with all the spirituality of a python swallowing a pig, wielding the cutlery as though it was a weapon and talking with his mouth open as he masticated his food.

"Unfortunately," Marcia said, "the West judges spirituality by externals as well as the intrinsic."

Years before, Marcia had gone to India full of plans for the subcontinent. Long before, she had dreamed of Indian cities and peoples, not knowing the locations, and now she was to arrive at Benares and see the stone steps rising up in a steep bank from the Ganges before she realized that her dream was actuality.

In Kashmir, Shantiniketan, and Kalimpong, she wandered through familiar streets and villages that she had never seen or read about before. Kashmir was the first stop, in the city of Srinagar, famed as the Venice of the East, and near the Gardens of Shalimar.

Wherever she went in India, Marcia was struck by the blind and the lame, the beggars, the moving caravans of refugees. There were swarms of homeless people. Women with infants stretched out beside the railroad tracks for a brief respite. In Shantiniketan, they would knock on doors and then strip off flimsy rags to the waist. "This was to show," Marcia said, "that they were too thin to nurse their children."

Marcia had arrived to reform the land, but she didn't know where to start. She was received by Nehru's sister, Gandhi's granddaughter, a fading royalty, and members of Parliament. All were quietly amused by the youthful eagerness of the Radcliffe girl who wanted to change India.

Somehow she felt that the poverty problem was connected with the lack of female status. In Kashmir she had been struck by the Indian women toiling in the fields with their matted hair looking like birds' nests. If only she could get them to take an interest in themselves!

In Srinagar she got her first awakening. She turned to an exquisitely groomed Indian princess and said, "Some of these poor women look like they haven't combed their hair in months."

The Princess lifted her delicately penciled eyebrows. "Combs?" she said. "What would they be doing with combs?"

The Indians had a curious social ambivalence. "They worshiped women as goddesses, but didn't give them as much freedom as the sacred cows. At parties in Shantiniketan and elsewhere, the women were herded into separate rooms after the refreshments. Ramakrishna, the great Indian saint, had warned that women and gold were twin delusions leading men from the path of righteousness, and the Indians took this as their cue."

Many Indians indignantly denied the servile role of the woman, stressing the influence of their mothers in their lives.

Marcia laughed. "They say they put woman on a pedestal; actually, it's a shelf. True, the mother-in-law or mother is often a domestic tyrant, but her influence ends there. In the street she frequently walks behind her husband, and rarely, if ever, goes any place alone."

Multitudes of their women had no greater value than beasts of burden. On a high narrow road, Marcia saw three bedraggled women in rags trying to wrestle a large piano uphill. "Why," she asked, "don't they use a mule?"

The answer was to the point. "Because at twenty-one cents a day they are cheaper than mules."

In Kalimpong she rented a commodious ten-room house with the grandest view in the world for forty dollars a month. Her chief housekeeper and cook got fifty cents a day, an assistant twenty-one cents a day. The ayah, taking care of the children from morning till night, got twenty-one cents. The part-time help—bathroom cleaners and washerwomen—were also paid twenty-one cents.

The new India was trying to raise its head, with resulting conflict within the women themselves. "They have been so brainwashed over the ages," Marcia observed, "that they feel uncomfortable when given any freedom."

Old marriage customs still persisted despite new laws.

There was still a dower among the poor, and marriages were arranged by parents. Change was slow, slower in the country than the city. All classes were resistant. In Shantiniketan, Marcia had become friendly with Mohandas Gandhi's granddaughter, Tara Gandhi. "Tara," Marcia recalled, "had reached a marriageable age, and was confused at the prospects of choosing her husband. She confided that she would almost rather have her family pick a husband for her, as her grandfather's bride had been picked when both were thirteen. But then a Prince Charming came along in the form of a young attractive Indian schooled at Stanford, and she found picking her own husband the most natural thing in the world."

There was a curious dichotomy about India that suggested an almost schizophrenic personality. "There was a division between men and women. There was a division between father and son, though the son played the dutiful role. There was a cleavage between religion and reality. And everything was extreme: the mountains were the highest, the plains the flattest, the weather the hottest and the wettest. There were fifteen different official languages and two hundred dialects."

In their love of role-playing, the Indians tried to fit their castes, religion, and women into roles framed thousands of years before. "The old order was so rigid, so remote from reality, that there was no organized thought about adjusting to changing conditions," Marcia observed. "When an Indian woman married, she was told to be like Sita, or like Savitri, both goddesses, both completely effacing themselves for their husbands. But they were never told to be themselves."

As part of the tragic make-believe of India, widows for centuries were not allowed to remarry, and proved their virtue by throwing themselves on their husband's funeral pyre. "There were innumerable child brides whose marriages were never even consummated," Marcia pointed out, "and when their young husbands died they might as well have died with them. As women, their lives had ended." Within living memory, this custom still prevailed. "In some districts, not until the 1890s did the first high-caste Indian widow remarry. And she and her husband left their family homes so that they would not subject them to social ostracism."

For all their vaunted worship of a goddess woman, the Indians believed that while woman was pure, she was hopelessly weak and had to be protected against herself.

She could do nothing independently
even in her own house.
In childhood subject to her father,
in youth to her husband,
And when her husband is dead to
her sons,
She should never enjoy independence.

With all the new talk of feminine equality, Marcia had
a rather revealing glimpse of woman's true status in modern India. One day she was being guided by Indian students
through the plain country near Calcutta and asked about
the Indian woman's new freedom. One of the guides, a
good-looking young man, smiled engagingly. "Just let me
say that if you were an Indian woman, and not an American, you wouldn't be seeing India as you are today."

The downgrading of women was a subtle carry-over from
ancient tradition. "In feudal India," Marcia observed,
"once an unmarried girl lost her virginity she became a
liability. Sex was a religious duty designed for the fertility
of Mother India. Nobody asked the young bride what she
wanted or how she felt. Intercourse was to begin within
eight days after the time she stopped menstruating, and
that was that."

Like the Japanese geisha, the old-time Indian wife rubbed
her husband's feet; she rose before him, retired when he
was comfortably snoring, and ate after he got through.

Marcia saw India through the eyes of a number of unusual women of various nationalities. Lila Ray, an American from Texas, had married a Bengali scholar, and lived
in Calcutta and Shantiniketan for twenty years. She was
fortyish and had four children. Through Lila Ray, Marcia
saw clearly the great paradoxes of the women's position.
Birth control was a burning necessity and yet Indian men
pointed out with disarming smiles that there was no population problem since the women wanted lots of children
and, of course, their wishes had to be gratified. "With not
enough food for hungry millions of people, they were still
adding new mouths at the rate of ten million a year,"
Marcia commented wrily. "It was a population explosion
without a corresponding agricultural explosion."

The provident mother was the Indian woman's great role,
and she found it convenient type-casting regardless of her
inner feelings. "Having children," Marcia observed, "was
about the only way women could gain a modicum of status,
and many had nothing else to do."

But abortions were not uncommon. "The woman who lived next door in Shantiniketan had a husband who worked for the post office and made fifty rupees a month—thirteen dollars. She had four children and could barely feed them. She had two abortions, aborting herself, and a friend had to come to us for a little rice so she could recover her strength."

Often girls appeared to be considered with as little sentiment as chattel. "During the battle with Pakistan over partition many Hindu girls had been abducted by the Moslems. They were never accepted back by their families, even though they may only have been kept overnight and had not been violated. They were labeled unclean through no fault of their own, and made homeless."

The Calcutta papers ran agonizing ads from girls seeking to be reunited with their families. When they didn't hear in return, many turned to prostitution. It was all that was left to them.

Marcia was amused by the Hindu's quixotic attitude toward chastity. "The Indians idealized their women to a point where they would turn on them furiously if they acted human."

Because of the formalized attitude between the sexes, the men often seemed more at ease with their own sex. "Public demonstrations of affection between men and women were rare, but it was quite usual to see men holding hands in the street."

Aside from her pupil relationship with her Yoga teacher, Marcia was not able to bridge the traditional gulf between the sexes. She made only a few male friends.

Still, she was not as badly off as the American girl studying in India who lived in with a high-caste Indian family. At dinner one night, the head of the clan delivered himself of an opinion; his wife and daughters nodded perfunctorily and ate on in silence.

But the American ventured to disagree mildly.

A look of disbelief, then anger came over his face. His family stirred uneasily, and he turned on his brash guest. "Don't you know that the women in this household call me God?" His voice was like ice.

The poor, bewildered American girl did not know whether to laugh or cry, but averted a storm by saying she meant no disrespect. The crisis passed, but thereafter the American in India stopped reading and talking about the new India; she knew better.

Even the vocabulary reflects the suzerainty of the male.

Significantly, swami means lord, master, even god in some areas of India. "And the word for husband," Marcia said, "also means master."

Even in gaining the vote, woman's low estate was strikingly revealed. "When they registered many didn't even have names to put down, since they were known only as the wife of so-and-so."

Old India shook with indignation as women began to poke into books. For centuries it was taken for granted that Indian women had no reason to read. "Educated, informed women might not be content to remain in their homes," Marcia observed drily.

But even on their pedestal, a terrible apartness traditionally saddened them:

> In silence my hopes rise and sink,
> In silence I find my heart's delight,
> In silence I walk through eternal night,
> In silence I bear my defeat and triumph,
> In silence I die.
> And in silence am born.

As a nation of paradoxes, India was humming with talk of social reform—and little more. There were drawers of statistics on power plants, new highways, factories, dams, schools, and they stayed in the drawers. "When you complained that there wasn't enough family planning, they would show off their clinics. You questioned their sewage facilities, and they dug out surveys on new drainage systems and rural reconstruction."

Indianophiles were burning with zeal to help their adopted land. But they were overwhelmed by a national inertia which Marcia found hard to appraise at first. And then, as she got around the country, the explanation of the negative attitudes on women, class systems, social reform, all dawned on her. It was rather a shock, but it seemed inescapable, in view of all she had witnessed. "Essentially," she said, "there was a deep-running lack of love, of caring, of concern for others."

In a land once committed to Yoga, this was a massive contradiction, since Yoga was calculated to make man piously efface self and bring about union with God. Instead, disunity and disharmony prevailed as leaders spoke mechanically of God and love and peace. "They were still playing a role, supremely conscious of the image they were creating," Marcia observed.

The caste system was much blamed for India's backwardness. But actually, it was more result than cause. "Traditionally, the four major castes had stemmed from a desire for separateness. They had been based on color, originally; the Sanskrit word for class, *varna*, also means color. The Aryans invading the subcontinent from the north were white and they introduced the caste system. Generally, the darker the people, the lower the caste, and it was often considered a mark of social success to marry into a lighter family."

The country was so huge and disorganized that almost any effort at improvement was swallowed up in the bland indifference of the millions scraping along on empty bellies. Ineffectuality was the rule.

Another who helped Marcia see India clearly was the Indian parliamentarian, Rukmini Devi, widow of George Arundale, English-born president of the Theosophical Society in Madras. Rukmini, an ardent antivivisectionist and vegetarian, had vigorously campaigned against the slaughter of sheep, goats, and cattle. With all the children starving in India, Marcia couldn't help but wonder why this clear-sighted woman was devoting herself to the salvation of animals.

But Rukmini's primary concern was the brutalizing of people. "The animals died slowly and painfully in the slaughterhouses, and the little children would play in the blood and the muck, even playfully picking up the gory heads and tossing them around. So hardened, how could they grow up with any kindness for their fellow man?"

Viewing India with a tender if critical eye, Marcia sometimes thought that the land's very indifference was its considered defense against change. The missionaries who had come with their God appeared sublimely oblivious that Hinduism embraced portions of Christianity, Judaism, and Buddhism. They behaved as though India was their backyard.

"In Kalimpong," she said, "the missionaries would march to the center of town, set up a phonograph with a loudspeaker attachment, and play records blaring the gospel in English. It didn't matter whether anybody understood English, or what their inclinations were; here was the gospel being jammed down their throats." She laughed. "They were not only trying to make them Christians, but Englishmen."

Kalimpong was fair game for competing Europeans, all convinced of their superior image. "In the square there was a tired old statue of Queen Victoria and nearby were posters with the hammer and sickle, proclaiming the Communist virtues. But most provocative were the leaflets showing an Englishman sitting comfortably in a chair, the light shining from a lamp over his left shoulder as he read from his Bible. It didn't occur to the missionaries that many in Kalimpong not only didn't have chairs but had never seen one."

The squalor of India, vested with tradition, triumphantly resisted all intrusion. In Kalimpong, as in other areas, American influence, despite hundreds of millions of dollars of aid to India, was meaningless. The aid itself appeared to have been swallowed up in chaos. "Practically everybody in Kalimpong suffered from anemia, and there was a tragic dearth of supplies and medicines. The undernourished, hearing vaguely of vitamins, applied at the clinics, and they couldn't understand that the vitamins would be ineffectual without the diet to go with it."

One child she knew had an ailment for which the clinic did have helpful drugs, and if she didn't get these drugs she would die.

The clinic turned down a mother's plea. "We do not have enough for our own people," they said, "and they too will die."

Marcia inquired about the cost of the medicine. It came to two cents a day.

"Did you see any sign of American supplies?" I asked.

"Oh, yes," she replied, "they sent in large quantities of surplus cheese to Shantiniketan, not knowing or caring, apparently, that the Indians can't stand cheese. However, it did serve some purpose. A Hungarian woman, running a hostel for Europeans, put in for the cheese and fed her pupils."

Although she thought of India as her spiritual home, Marcia found it difficult for America—and Americans—to navigate amidst a network of homebred Communist sympathizers. As Americans, she and her first husband, author Simons Roof, had trouble obtaining visas to get into the country. They were held up in New York, again in England, and then in Pakistan, before the Ramakrishna Mission, a high-level, Yoga-inspired religious organization, vouched for them and made nonadmission awkward. Meanwhile, as Americans were being rebuffed, Uncle Sam was pouring goods into India to make friends and influence people. Even so, the Commies made our largesse look like a Fascist plot.

In Shantiniketan, Marcia saw great containers destined for India's hungry. "I see you're at least getting our powdered milk," she remarked to a sulking guide.

"It's poisoned," he said. "Some children died from it up north."

Up and down the vast subcontinent, the Commies told similar lies, the Red propaganda filtering in from China and Tibet. Shoestores in Kalimpong were a favorite cover-up for Red espionage nests, so much so that Marcia found it difficult to buy shoes. She walked into one store, picking out a pair in the window. They were sorry but the shoes couldn't be removed. She tried another store; they had a similar rule; and in still another, the same. Neighbors laughed when she told of her experience, "They never sell their shoes," she was told.

Happily, she was introduced to Hatha Yoga at this point, just as her nerves were beginning to fray. She met her Indian instructor, Roman Datta, at a social at the Scottish-Presbyterian mission school in Kalimpong, chiefly serving Anglo-Indian children. One boy was named Michael Corporal. His Indian mother had gone with an American corporal; nobody could remember his last name.

Datta was then fifty, a successful Calcutta businessman summering in Kalimpong. He was the best-looking man Marcia had ever seen. He spoke immaculate English, was tall and charming, and looked no more than thirty or thirty-five. In the fifteen years he had been practicing Yoga he had not aged a day outwardly. He was a theosophist by belief, holding that man progressed and evolved through a succession of reincarnations. He was perhaps the most impressive man she had met in India, and the only yogin. "It was ironical," she recalled, "that the most holy man I met in India was a businessman with a wife and child."

Like so many Indians, Datta had not bothered with Yoga—until something bothered him. After thirty-five he had noticed a painful constriction in the lower back. He couldn't sit or stand comfortably, and walking was agony. He needed help to lift himself out of a chair. All the doctors agreed; he had an acute, crippling sciatica. He tried a number of remedies, from a nonacid diet to soaking in a hot tub. Surgery at the base of the spine was recommended as a last resort, and then Datta balked. He knew a little about Yoga, enough to know it had helped other people with muscular and nervous problems. He found a good Yoga teacher in Calcutta and began painfully working out.

One exercise, he discovered, helped his particular problem, stretching and relieving the taut muscles. As he sat on the mat, crossing his legs, the stretch given the hips appeared to ease his pain almost immediately. "And by the time he could perfect the Perfect Posture, crossing his legs and folding his ankles together, the sciatica had disappeared," Marcia related.

Marcia was eternally grateful that Datta came along when he did, for she was beginning to realize that while she could do very little about the world swarming around her, she could do something about herself.

She gave up her rounds of the hospitals and clinics, no longer attended the meaningless meetings on rural reconstruction and sewage disposal, traveled no more with the literacy crews in their discouraging tours of the towns and villages.

She stayed at home, practiced Yoga, and looked at the stars. They were sparkling and clean, and they made her feel there was something far beyond the dirt and squalor engulfing the miserable masses. But believing in reincarnation as she did, she now felt that she understood India completely, and out of comprehension—not futility—had come the decision to leave the subcontinent to itself.

After years of so-called freedom, India was nowhere near ready to cope with its mundane problems. The people were still starving and still multiplying. In July of 1964, after almost a generation of Indian liberation, *The New York Times* reported food hoarding, black marketeering, long food lines, and riots over spiraling food prices. In Uttar Pradesh a farmer committed suicide because he could not bear watching his children starve. Around Lucknow hungry peasants ate the seed they had set aside for planting. In Agra a thousand rioters broke into food shops and looted them of grain. Half the flour mills in the Punjab, a rich wheat-growing area, had closed because they had no grain to grind.

It was the same old India because, basically, nothing had really changed. "Distribution," *The New York Times* reported, "is frustrated by poor planning, an overworked transportation system, hoarding, profiteering, interstate jealousies, inefficiencies, some apparent indifference and occasional dishonesty."

If, as the reincarnationists believed, people had a karmic debt in one life for the delinquencies in another, then India, Marcia felt, had an especially heavy burden. "India is pay-

ing for its centuries of inhumanity to its poor, its downgrading of women, and, above all, its repudiation every day of
its own sacred teachings of love and selflessness."

But the day of reckoning was not distant. "There is a
tradition in India, as old as the mountains, that when all
four castes have had their cycle of rule, then India will be
torn by confusion and chaos. And then, but not until then,
will the Golden Age dawn."

The last of the cycles was at hand. "First came the
Brahmins, the reign of the priests, back in the time of the
Vedas; then the warriors, the Emperors Asoka and Akbar;
then the merchant class, with Gandhi as their spokesman."
The ghost of a smile stole fleetingly over Marcia's face.
"And now the cries of the rabble are heard above the voice
of the turtle."

She turned to me with a rather sardonic laugh. "What
took Mother India some three thousand years, we are doing
in three hundred."

I regarded her inquiringly.

"First, the theocracy of the Puritans, the Boston Brahmins; then the soldiers of the Revolution, the wars of expansion, and the Civil War. After the Civil War, the
Industrial Revolution and the new merchant class, the
Rockefellers, Harrimans, and Hills." She smiled. "And now
the pendulum has swung to the workers and the mob, and
there is rioting all over the land."

She shrugged. "Armageddon may be a lot nearer than
we think."

India, apparently, wasn't the only country building up
karma.

"How do you explain Mozart's composing music at the age of five?" Louis thought he had me.

"I can do better than that," I said. "How about the Polish prodigy Josef Hofmann, who was playing the piano at a year and a half—tripping off classical numbers when he could hardly sit up at the piano?"

And then there was the Negro youngster, even younger than Hofmann, who could run off any jazz tune on the piano after having heard it only once.

"Because we don't understand these things," I pointed out, "doesn't mean they are evidence of reincarnation."

Only that morning I had watched the children's cat move forward on his belly, and pounce on a bird which noticed him only too late. "There is a case of genetic memory. Nobody taught that cat how to track that bird; it's a matter of evolutionary development over countless generations."

I laughed. "Would you say that Rover [the cat] was a reincarnation of a previous cat because he knew what to do about birds the moment he saw one?"

Louis was amazed that I didn't believe in reincarnation.

"Why should you be surprised," I said, "when in a nation of nearly two hundred million, only a comparative handful believe that we were born before and shall be born again?"

"Most of the world believes in reincarnation," he said.

"Sure, and in India the untouchables believe that the Brahmins can make them return as worms in their next incarnation if they give offense to the Brahmin."

"But wouldn't it be a pretty idiotic world," he said, "if this was all there was to it, and we didn't have a chance to profit by the mistakes of this life?"

I laughed. "Many people believe it is an idiotic world."

"I don't see what's so astonishing about rebirth," Marcia put in. "Matter is neither created nor destroyed, so why should the spirit be?" She paused. "When you visit the Bellevue Hospital morgue in New York and see a body laid out, it makes you realize how much more tangible the spirit is than the body. Without the spirit, the body is a slab of meat."

She frowned. "If you think about it, it is just as surprising that we are here at all. As Voltaire said, it is just as remarkable to be born once as twice."

"That is Voltaire's opinion, not evidence," I said.

"I've seen people regressed to the point under hypnosis where they discussed their past lives, mentioning names and places that they could never have known about if they hadn't been there themselves at one time," Louis observed.

"I can give you better than that," I said. "I've heard psychic Peter Hurkos under hypnosis speak Russian with an accent, though he never studied or even read the language, and came from Holland where he had never heard anybody speak Russian."

I mentioned an even more fantastic case, where a well-known psychiatrist had regressed a woman with the drug LSD until she began to talk falteringly in Icelandic of the past life. "The doctor," I pointed out, "was completely baffled because she spoke in a dialect prevalent some hundreds of years ago, and now almost extinct. Like Hurkos she had no previous familiarity with the language, had never consciously heard it spoken, and had no known antecedents in Iceland."

Louis' face brightened. "How else can you explain that?"

"There are many explanations, once you rule out fraud. Hurkos, or the woman—obviously operating out of their subconscious—could be tuned into what psychics call the Universal Mind, a sort of subconscious register of everything that ever happened or will happen. They might be drawing, too, on genetic memory, atavistic recollections from forgotten forebears, just as they—or the cat—inherit certain instincts. Or," I added, "they could be imagining it all."

Louis grimaced. "You don't imagine something that happened hundreds of years ago that you had no way of knowing about."

The brilliant Swiss analyst Carl Jung had advanced the concept of a collective unconscious, suggesting a broad sweep of memory going back to the beginnings of the race and cropping out unpredictably in different people at various times. But, of course, this was as hypothetical as reincarnation itself.

Marcia smiled placidly. "How do you account for an uncanny feeling I had that I had been in India before, as I walked through the streets of Kalimpong, and could describe the market place before I ever saw it?"

I shrugged. "Instances of déjà vu are commonplace; people are always having uneasy feelings that they have been somewhere before."

"But how do you explain it?"

"They might have seen an illustration or a motion picture that had slipped their conscious memory, or they might have read a description of a place with such vivid detail that it burnt itself on their brain. Or failing that, granted you accept the psychic, it could have been a precognitive dream, foretelling a future incident.

"Chauncey Depew, the president of the New York Central, saw himself in a dream nominating Teddy Roosevelt at Saratoga—and six weeks later made the exact nominating speech he had heard in his dream, recognizing strange faces on the nominating platform that he had seen only in his dream."

I thought for a moment. "To be really scientific, of course, we must consider that the explanation of remembered experiences could be none of these things, including reincarnation, but X, the unknown."

Louis' brow furled. "What do you mean by that?"

"Just that we shouldn't limit any explanation to our limited understanding of the universe."

Like many who had explored the work of Edgar Cayce, the late sage of Virginia Beach, Louis had been fascinated by Cayce's delving into past lives in legendary Atlantis. Pointing out that the mystic had also accurately forecast volcanic eruptions, new land formations, and drastic climatic changes, Louis argued, "If he was correct, psychically, about the future, he was probably right about the past."

It was true that some reputable geologists had granted that Cayce could very well have been correct about Atlantis having sunk under the Atlantic, and his revelation in trance of women living in the monasteries of the Essenes had been recently confirmed by the Dead Sea scrolls.

"It shocked everybody at the time," Marcia commented, "but Cayce correctly observed that they were only servant women."

Marcia was eying me speculatively, obviously debating with herself.

"What is it?" I asked.

Even then she hesitated. "You have mentioned the lack of scientific evidence for reincarnation."

"That's right."

"Well, as a reporter, what do you consider evidence?"

"Eyewitness accounts by independent witnesses having nothing to gain or lose by the evidence."

"How about Thoreau and Emerson and Alcott—they all felt that they had lived before, and could remember the past when 'a lively chord in the soul is struck, when the windows for a moment are unbarred.' "

"They were mystics, rapt followers of the Bhagavad-Gita and spiritual descendants of the Indian Brahmins," I noted.

She smiled. "Would you call Benjamin Franklin a good witness? After all, he was a newspaperman."

"Don't tell me that Ben was a reincarnationist."

"Listen," she said, "to the apostle of thrift and honesty:

" 'When I see nothing annihilated [in the works of God] and not a drop of water wasted, I cannot suspect the annihilation of souls, or believe that He will suffer the daily waste of millions of minds ready made that now exist, and put himself to the continual trouble of making new ones. I believe, in some shape or other, I shall always exist and with all the inconveniences human life is liable to, I shall not object to a new edition of mine, hoping, however, that the errata of the last may be corrected.' "

"Still, that's only one man's opinion," I said, "undoubtedly motivated by wishful thinking toward the end of his life."

She thumbed through the pages of Whittier:

> A presence strange at once and known
> Walked with me as my guide;
> The skirts of some forgotten life
> Trailed noiselessly at my side.

She looked up. "There's a remembered experience."

I shook my head. "Poets are notoriously unfactual."

She smiled. "Haven't you ever met anybody you felt you had known all your life?"

"People who fall in love often have that feeling, but that doesn't mean they knew each other in a previous life."

"Perhaps not," she said, "but I like what Tennyson has to say about it:

> Although I knew not in what time or place
> Methought that I had often met with you,
> And each had lived in other's mind and speech.

It was a pleasant thought, prettily said, but still no remembered experience.

Marcia said, "Louisa May Alcott had many such experiences."

"She may have been influenced by her father, Bronson."

"Bronson had little influence on her writing, and was amazed that *Little Women* should be a best-seller. She was an independent thinker."

Louisa May Alcott had apparently dwelt to some purpose on reincarnation:

> I seem to remember former states and feel that in them I have learned some of the lessons that have never since been mine here, and in my next step I hope to leave behind many of the trials I have struggled to bear here and begin to find lightened as I go on.

Even in pagan times they were "remembering." The Greek mathematician Pythagoras, a leading scientist of the pre-Christian era, spoke often of previous lives. His biographer Diogenes Laërtius said he was first born as one Aethalides, then came back as Euphorbus, son of Panthus, and was wounded at Troy by Menelaus, husband of the fair Helen. Next, as Hermotimus, he entered a temple of Apollo and picked up a shield which he remembered from his Euphorbus days. It had been the gift of Menelaus generations before.

That was a pagan version, but, still, what evidence was there? Wasn't it significant that the Judaic-Christian tradition, accepting a certain immortality, should still spurn reincarnation?

Marcia picked up a copy of the New Testament. "Let's turn to Matthew . . . ah, here it is:

> Why then do our teachers say that Elijah must come first? He replied, Yes, Elijah will come and set everything right. But I tell you that Elijah has already come, and they failed to recognize him, and worked their will upon him . . . Then the disciples understood that He meant John the Baptist.

"And again, Matthew:

> When he came to the territory of Caesarea Philippi, Jesus asked his disciples, Who do men say that the Son of Man is? They answered, Some say John the Baptist, others Elijah, others Jeremiah, or one of the prophets.

All this seemed in the dim long ago, with little bearing on our modern frame of reference.

Marcia asked, "Have you ever heard of Heinrich Schliemann?"

Memory stirred. "You mean the German archaeologist?"

"As a small boy in Germany, Schliemann dreamed of ancient Greece and the day that he would find the lost city of Troy. It became his lifelong mission, even though there was little evidence outside of Homer's *Odyssey* and *Iliad* that Troy had ever existed."

Schliemann dedicated his early life to making money so he could finance a search for the legendary city. He quickly learned Greek by reading the same books in French and Greek and comparing the languages; and then, preparing for his expedition, he took a Greek wife almost thirty years younger than himself. They named their two children Agamemnon and Andromache Schliemann.

All this seemed like the harmless idiosyncrasy of a man who had fallen in love with antiquity.

Marcia plodded on. "The other archaeologists scorned him as a rank amateur, but he never wavered. He seemed to know exactly what he was doing. At great personal expense, he hired scores of diggers, after taking a year to clear things with government officials, and headed for a desolate northwest corner of Asia Minor. There, he was convinced, he would find the Troy of Priam and Hector, of Ulysses, Achilles, and Agamemnon. He felt compelled. The professionals laughed and turned their backs. Schliemann was flying in the face of all scholarly opinion. But the German who trained for archaeology as a merchant prince shrugged and went ahead.

"With his wife, he went through great hardships for a year; anybody with less conviction would have given up, but he kept his men digging, even as they regarded him, privately, as being out of his senses."

And then, one day, a shovel grated against gold, and Schliemann had found his first buried treasure of ancient Troy. Before he got through there were nine Troys, one under the other.

And what was the point of this little lesson in archaeology?

Marcia shrugged. "Schliemann wasn't guessing; he obviously knew where to go and what to look for, when all the savants were floundering in the dark. He remembered, vaguely at times, but he remembered."

Evidence? Of an unerring instinct, perhaps. But of what lay behind it, who could say?

Of all the remembered experiences, Mark Twain's were

the most vivid. His remembrances came in dreams, and I had had some acquaintance with the humorist's dreams. They were uncanny.

In St. Louis once, as I related in *The Door to the Future,* as a young riverman, he had dreamed that he saw his brother Henry lying in a metal casket, a red rose on his chest. The dream was so vivid that he told his sister about it in a state of great depression and bid Henry be careful as he took the boat down the Mississippi the next day. There was an explosion near Memphis, as Twain had feared, and his brother was killed. Touched by Henry's youth and good looks, the women of Memphis had contributed to a steel casket, while all the others were of wood. And as the author was standing by this casket, pondering with melancholy the vagaries of his dream, an elderly woman came along and put a red rose on his brother's chest. The dream was complete.

Now it developed that all his life, Sam Clemens had dreamed of a girl whom he had loved in different lands at different times. She had many names, and her eye color and hair changed, but she was always the same girl, and he was always the same young man. Sometimes he was George, and she Alice; sometimes she was Agnes, and he Robert. And they were always the same age—he, seventeen, she fifteen.

Twain called his dream experience "My Platonic Sweetheart," and it appeared after his death in a volume titled *The Mysterious Stranger*. He had put the manuscript away, hoping to treat the dreams philosophically, but he died at seventy-five before he could do anything about it. He was born with Halley's Comet and went out with it, a circumstance he was prepared for—perhaps from another dream.

The dreams began to materialize when he was a young man, continuing for over forty years and recurring once every two years. They were alive with detail, fraught with emotion, more real than life.

"I did not meet her; I overtook her," he begins. "It was in a Missourian village which I had never been in before, and was not in at that time, except dreamwise; in the flesh I was on the Atlantic seaboard ten or twelve hundred miles away. The thing was sudden, and without preparation—after the custom of dreams. There I was, crossing a wooden bridge that had a wooden rail and was untidy with scattered wisps of hay, and there she was, five steps in front of me; half a second previously neither of us was there. This was the exit of the village, which lay immediately behind us. Its

last house was the blacksmith-shop; and the peaceful clink-
ing of the hammers—a sound which nearly always seems
remote, and is always touched with a spirit of loneliness
and a feeling of soft regret for something, you don't know
what—was wafted to my ears over my shoulder; in front
of us was the winding country road, with woods on one
side, and on the other a rail fence, with blackberry vines
and hazel bushes crowding its angles; on an upper rail a
bluebird, and scurrying toward him along the same rail a
fox-squirrel with his tail bent high like a shepherd's crook;
beyond the fence a rich field of grain, and far away a
farmer in shirtsleeves and straw hat wading knee-deep
through it; no other representatives of life, and no noise at
all, everywhere a Sabbath stillness."

Never had the author viewed a passing scene with greater
richness, never with stronger empathy. When he awakened
the vision remained startlingly clear, his teeming subconscious apparently brimming over into his conscious. Had he
met anybody like her in the street, a meadow, or a parlor,
he would have felt an immediate tug of recognition.

"I remember it all—and the girl, too, and just how she
walked, and how she was dressed. In the first moment I
was five steps behind her; in the next one I was at her side
. . . I put my arm around her waist and drew her close
to me, for I loved her. She showed no surprise, no distress,
no displeasure, but put an arm around my waist, and
turned up her face to mine with a happy welcome in it, and
when I bent down to kiss her she received the kiss as if she
was expecting it, and as if it was quite natural for me to
offer it and her to take it and have pleasure in it . . ."

There was a sweet contentment about their love, the
endearing affection of a long-time relationship. "We strolled
along, across the bridge and down the road chatting like
the oldest friends. She called me George, and that seemed
natural and right, though it was not my name; and I called
her Alice, and she did not correct me, though without
doubt it was not her name. Everything that happened
seemed just natural and to be expected. Once I said, 'What
a dear little hand it is!' and without any words she laid it
gracefully in mine for me to examine it. I did it, remarking
upon its littleness, its delicate beauty, and its satin skin,
then kissed it; she put it up to her lips without saying anything and kissed it in the same place."

They came to a log house, and it seemed as though everything was waiting. "The food was steaming on the table,

and a cat curled up in a splint-bottomed chair by the fire-place. But there were no people, just emptiness and silence. Alice went to look around. So I sat down, and she passed through a door which closed behind her with a click of the latch. I waited and waited. Then I got up and followed, for I could not bear any longer to have her out of my sight."

With a sudden chill, I relived the somber scene with dreamer Twain:

"I passed through the door, and found myself in a strange sort of cemetery, a city of innumerable tombs and monuments stretching far and wide on every hand, and flushed with pink and gold lights flung from the sinking sun. I turned around and the log house was gone. I ran here and there and yonder down the lanes between the rows of tombs, calling Alice; and presently the night closed down, and I could not find my way. Then I awoke in deep distress over my loss."

Alice had died and Sam Clemens was inconsolable. But she was to return ten years later. He was again seventeen, and she fifteen. "I was in a grassy place in the twilight deeps of a magnolia forest some miles above Natchez, Mississippi; the trees were snowed over with great blossoms, and the air was loaded with their rich and strenuous fragrance; the ground was high, and through a rift in the wood a burnished patch of the river was visible in the distance. I was sitting on the grass, absorbed in thinking, when an arm was laid around my neck, and there was Alice sitting by my side and looking into my face. A deep and satisfied happiness and an unwordable gratitude rose in me, but with it there was no feeling of surprise; and there was no sense of time lapse."

Bombay, London, Athens, Hawaii, occupied his dream world as clearly as Natchez or his own Missouri. "I was in Athens—a city which I had not then seen, but I recognized the Parthenon from the pictures, although it had a fresh look and was in perfect repair. I passed by it and climbed a grassy hill toward a palatial sort of mansion which was built of red terra cotta and had a spacious portico, whose roof was supported by a rank of fluted columns with Corinthian capitals.

"I passed into the house and entered the first room. It was very large and light, its walls were of polished and richly tinted and veined onyx, and its floor was a pictured pattern in soft colors laid in tiles. I noted the details of the furniture and the ornaments—a thing which I should not have been likely to do when awake—and they took sharp hold and remained in my memory; they are not really dim yet, and this was more than thirty years ago."

She was in Athens, waiting. "There was a person present —Agnes. I was not surprised to see her, but only glad. She was in the simple Greek costume, and her hair and eyes were different as to color from those she had had when she died in the Hawaiian Islands half an hour before. But to me she was exactly her own beautiful little self as I had always known her, and she was still fifteen, and I was seventeen once more. She was sitting on an ivory settee, crocheting something or other, and had her crewels in a shallow willow work basket in her lap. I sat down by her and we began to chat in the usual way. I remembered her death. But the pain and the grief and the bitterness which had been so sharp and so desolating to me at the moment that it happened had wholly passed from me now, and had left not a scar."

Many distinguished Greeks passed through his dream, among them Socrates, whom he recognized by his nose. How he gloried in the clearness of his images! "When I think of that house and its belongings, I recognize what a master in taste and drawing and color and arrangement is the dream-artist who resides in us. In my waking hours, when the inferior artist in me is in command, I cannot draw even the simplest picture. But my dream artist can draw anything, and do it perfectly; he can paint with all the colors and the shades, and do it with delicacy and truth; he can place before me vivid images of palaces, cities, hamlets, hovels, mountains, valleys, lakes, skies, glowing in sunlight or moonlight, or veiled in driving gusts of snow or rain, and he can set before me people who are intensely alive, and who feel and express their feelings in their places, and who also talk and laugh, sing and swear. And when I wake I can shut my eyes and bring back those people, and the scenery and the buildings, and not only in general view but in nice detail."

Was Alice or Agnes his eternal soulmate? Was he reliving clairvoyantly in his dreams all that which had happened before?

"In our dreams—I know it—we do make the journeys we seem to make; we do see the things we seem to see; the people, the horses, the cats, the dogs, the birds, the whales are real, not chimeras. They are living spirits, not shadows."

He had suffered more with Agnes than with anybody in this life. She was terribly real. "This glimpse of her carries me back to Maui [Hawaii] and that time when I saw her gasp out her young life. That was a terrible thing to me at the time. It was preternaturally vivid and the pain, the grief and the misery of it transcended any suffering I have known in waking life."

Yet, hopefully, death might be only another stage in the road to truth and ultimate understanding. "When we die we shall slough off this cheap intellect, perhaps, and go abroad into Dreamland clothed in our real selves, and aggrandized and enriched by the command over the mysterious mental magician who is here not our slave, but only our guest."

The Platonic Sweetheart was not fiction, not to Mark Twain; obviously, he had toyed with the idea of reincarnation. Sometime later, intriguingly, he was to take a character out of New England's nineteenth century and arbitrarily dump him back a thousand years and more into the England of Camelot, when knighthood was in flower. The result: *A Connecticut Yankee in King Arthur's Court,* a rather arbitrary one-man regression.

The humorist had come along before hypnosis, LSD, and the tape recorder had made a vogue of reincarnation, and had not been influenced much by the philosophies of the East. It was his own subconscious, stewing around for creative ideas, that had been the prod.

On the other hand, Louis' and Marcia's absorption with reincarnation had verged naturally out of their Yoga, since Yoga in its philosophic aspects assumed an endless wheel of life.

Louis was no Mark Twain. He had not had any dramatic inner experiences. But as part of the Bridey Murphy vogue, people claiming to be psychics had delved into his so-called past lives. And Louis had been impressed that their reports had pretty much dovetailed.

"Three different times," Louis said, "by three different people I have been told that I was a Spanish don."

He was certainly not the Latin type, with his rugged redness that extended from the top of his head down his stalwart frame to the very bottom of him.

"It might have been wishful thinking," I said, "and they dredged it out of your subconscious."

"I couldn't even begin to imagine myself as a Spanish don," Louis said.

"Not even a Don Juan," I said. "That might subconsciously be the way you would like to see yourself, and being clairvoyant perhaps they picked it out."

"I didn't even know who these people were, and they didn't know me, yet separately they all said the same thing about my past lives."

He turned to Marcia. "Tell him about the fellow they regressed over at Canterbury, New Hampshire, last week. That seemed rather definite to me."

Marcia shrugged. "I really don't know how impressive it is as evidence."

The subject, a professor at a small Vermont college, had been regressed under hypnosis by Dr. Kenneth Lyons, a Boston psychologist. "At first," Marcia recalled, "the hypnotist took his subject back to childhood. And the subject saw himself as a first-grader, at his second day of school, anxious and apprehensive, racing for his home on the top of a hill with a sense of freedom the moment he was let out."

When he came to, and was told what he had said, he realized he had perfectly described in trance the house he had lived in as a boy—the school, the teacher, his own remembered impressions.

Passing on from childhood, the hypnotist turned suggestively to the professor's past lives. In a halting voice the professor saw himself living in the time of Henry the Eighth in London. He was an orphan boy, and he grew up a thief, trying to live by his wits. As the sequence of events in the life of the thief unfolded, a look of alarm came over the subject's face. "The audience reacted uneasily as he started to squirm in his chair," Marcia recalled, "his hands going to his throat as he moaned darkly. In a voice choked with fear, he was describing an attack on himself; he was being clubbed by two assailants, and he was reliving the furious fight he had made for his life."

His anguish was so real that some in the audience thought he should be awakened. But suddenly his mood changed. A blissful smile spread over his face.

"What happened then?" Dr. Lyons had asked.

"I don't know," he said, "I didn't stay around to find out." His face was sublimely serene. He had crossed over.

He heaved a sigh of relief. "I don't want to look back," he said. "I am floating in space, between the stars; I can almost reach out and touch them. I am searching for someone, always seeking someone, I don't know who, but I need this someone badly." He was seeking God.

The regression continued. At the hypnotist's suggestion the subject went back another fifteen hundred years. He was in Rome now, a Christian youth of sixteen, carrying the message that Paul was coming to Rome to lecture the faithful on their holy obligations. He had a feeling of being aggrieved, wondering why the Christians couldn't enjoy the same pleasures as other Romans. He was not at all happy about Paul's coming.

That was about all there was to this regression. It was not terribly impressive, though Louis was ready to be convinced. There was no fact, or shred of fact—no place name, building site, or human relationship that could be traced back.

Dr. Lyons had induced other regressions at this session, sponsored by the New Hampshire Society for the Study of Psychic Research. One subject was a housewife, Mrs. Pearl Rosborough of Belmont, Massachusetts.

As Marcia recalled this regression, Mrs. Rosborough, in trance, had been taken back to a so-called life in India, a land where she had never been or read of to any extent. She mentioned the names of people she knew then, and the village in which she had known them. It was a hardly pronounceable name. In even tones, still in hypnotic trance, she went through the various stages of her life, the joys and sorrows, the good and the bad, and then she came to the climax—a fire. In this fire her hands were mutilated, and she perished, suffering dreadfully for two days, and moaning about her disfigured fingers.

Later Marcia, seated behind her, had leaned forward and asked casually, "Have you any feeling about fires?"

"I've always been afraid of them," she said, a not unnatural reaction.

"Have you ever had any psychological feeling about your hands?"

Mrs. Rosborough held up both hands. "Look," she said, with an enigmatic smile, "I have no joint in either thumb."

An effort was made to check back on the names that Mrs. Rosborough had recalled. It was impossible to dig back hundreds of years into little-known personalities. "However," Marcia said, "they did find that such a village as the one she mentioned had existed long before, though it had since disappeared from the map."

Marcia's report was rather sketchy, I thought.

"Why don't you check for yourself?" she suggested. "There were dozens of people there."

Actually, as I looked into it, I found that sixty people had been present during the regression at Canterbury, New Hampshire, and Pearl had been chosen as a subject quite by chance. Initially, Dr. Lyons had experimented with the entire group to find the best hypnotic subjects. "As we held out an arm," reported eyewitness Dick Snow of the New Hampshire group, "we were told that it would get rigid. Perhaps a dozen women found that they couldn't bend their arms, and from these three volunteers were chosen." One of these was Pearl.

Lyons regressed his subject, in deep hypnosis, gradually, taking her back first to her fifth birthday. It was a big day. She described her family taking her on the trolley to Rowe's Wharf in Boston, and then for a boat ride to Provincetown.

As her sleep became deeper, Lyons suggested she was back in infancy. As she mentioned that she was four months old, sitting in her crib, her hand went to her throat, and she began gasping, "I can't breathe, I hit my head."

"That choking feeling will disappear," Lyons suggested, and Pearl became calm.

Now the keenly awaited moment had arrived.

"You are going into an ever deeper sleep," Dr. Lyons said, "and you are going to feel very good; you will let your mind be free to roam back and forth in time; now take your thoughts back to a time before you were born in this body."

There was a dramatic pause. "Where are you?"

Pearl replied softly, "India."

The year was 1212 A.D., and she was twelve years old. Her father was a silk merchant, and her maiden name was Chango, which seemed more Chinese than Indian. At twenty, she married a university professor, and went to live in a community called Targon or Taigon or some similar name—it was hard to tell which from her slurred pronunciation under hypnosis.

Lyons tried to take her to her fiftieth year. She shook her head, "I'm dead."

She had "died" seven years before, in a fire that swept her home, dying amid the horror Marcia had already mentioned.

As Pearl described her two days of dying, her face and body writhed in agony, and she glanced down at her hands in terror. "I long for my release," she gasped.

Then the look of anguish was replaced by one of serenity. She had found her peace. She was dead.

And where had she gone, between lives, waiting to return again in spirit?

Dr. Lyons had received the question from the audience, and he passed it on.

Pearl hesitated only slightly. "I feel suspended in light,

air and sky. The heavens are above me. I see no people anywhere, but I feel vibrations, rhythms and pulsations on all sides."

It was certainly not evidential.

She had no previous life apparently, because she could not go back further under hypnosis, but she could go forward, some four hundred years, in fact. She was living in the town of "Crowford" near the southern coast of England. Her name was Abigail Trehune and she was living with her father on a farm. She was twenty-one, and very unhappy due to the religious oppression of her people by the Crown.

The year was 1636, and Charles I, who was later to lose his head, was presiding over the land.

Mrs. Rosborough was asked, "Were your people Catholics?"

"No, Puritans," she said, "they were feeling the brunt of Catholicism."

Since Charles was the titular head of the Protestant Church of England, it seemed a complete washout.

On this indecisive note, Pearl was returned to the twentieth century. As a posthypnotic suggestion, Dr. Lyons advised that she recall everything that had transpired while she was under and feel good about it. The session had lasted for five hours and everybody was tired except Pearl. She could have lived another life or two; she was exhilarated by the remembered experience.

She was now so interested in her past lives that she became an amateur investigator, along with her husband Ray, a practical businessman. She looked through all the almanacs, but could find nothing close to Taigung or Targon in India or Burma—Burma having been an Indian province at one time. And there was no Crowford or anything phonetically akin in the English atlases.

And then, suddenly, exciting things started to develop, exciting for the Rosboroughs in any case. They had written away to the British Museum in London. And soon a letter came back from Helen Wallis, the Museum's assistant keeper. "We find in John Adam Index Villaris, 1680, the town of Croford in Somerset." And Somerset, as it developed, was a coastal county in south England.

This was by no means conclusive of anything, and I was highly skeptical of Catholic discrimination against Protestants in a Protestant country. It didn't jibe.

But meanwhile from an unexpected source came news that threw a little light on Pearl's "first life" in India.

Evelyn Boynton, a librarian at Colby College, had attended the session in New Hampshire, and had left highly skeptical. But two weeks later, she was not so sure. She had made a discovery that indicated that the city of Targon or Taigon, or Taigung, depending on the pronunciation, had really existed at the time of Pearl's regression, though it had since disappeared from the face of the map.

Reviewing her own impressions, she made a report of her research, however scanty, to Charles (Bud) Thompson, head of the New Hampshire psychic research group.

"I attended the meeting in a lukewarm frame of mind," she wrote, "and came home fascinated but certainly uncommitted. Knowing the wiles of the subconscious mind makes one prone to doubt any demonstration of this sort—however skillfully managed."

Nevertheless, out of curiosity, librarian Boynton had browsed around in her college library. At the session, almost doodling, she had listed the names of the places where Pearl had supposedly lived in India. Because she had not spoken as distinctly under hypnosis as ordinarily, Pearl's words had often seemed slurred. And, besides, the place names were strange to the American ear. Variant spellings included Targon, Taigon, Taugong, even Tygong. And none of these appeared in any of the current geographies. But, as luck would have it, Evelyn Boynton one day plucked a book off a Colby library shelf. It was a *Handbook for Travellers in India, Burma and Ceylon* by John Murray, published by Scribner's in 1938. And in it appeared the following:

"About fifty miles above Thabeikkvin, Tagaung is reached on the bank of the Irrawaddy, one of the oldest and most important capitals of Burma, sometimes spoken of as old Pagan. As Tagaung ceased to have any importance some hundreds of years ago, there are no ruins to be found, though the mounds in the marshes near it may in the future yield important results."

The city of Tagaung went back to the ninth century B.C., and apparently retained its Indian and Burmese influence until 1287 A.D., when the encroaching Chinese finally moved in and took over.

The Rosboroughs took Pearl's past lives in stride. They lived in a modest two-family house which they owned, and it was modestly furnished. "The only costly thing around here," Ray Rosborough said with a wave of the arm, "was the bill I got for the flameproofing. We fireproofed everything, from drapes to slipcovers." He smiled quizzically.

"Ever since I've known her, and that goes back a lifetime, Pearl has been mortally afraid of fire."

I had not been impressed by Pearl's English experience. "Why should you have felt persecuted in England in 1636?" I asked.

She shrugged indifferently. "I only know what I said at the time—you can't prove anything by me now."

Mrs. Rosborough had been invalided once, wearing a supporting brace to compensate for a neck and spinal weakness. Doctors thought it might have come from a blow on the head when she was young, but she couldn't remember the injury. I recalled her memory of bumping her head in the crib, as she was regressed.

She shrugged lightly. "I would have been too young to remember anything like that, consciously."

Later, leaving the Rosboroughs, I still pondered the unhappy persecution of one Abigail Trehune of old Croford. I found myself turning to the *Encyclopaedia Britannica*, to Charles I. Charles was a Stuart, and the family tradition was Catholic, though he dutifully embraced Anglicanism. But his Catholic sympathies were nearly always brimming to the surface, and had much to do with his unpopularity. The encyclopedia noted: "Charles further increased the popular fears on the subject of religion by his welcome given to Panzani, the pope's agent, in 1634, who endeavored unsuccessfully to reconcile the two churches, and afterwards to George Conn, papal agent at the court of Henrietta Maria [of Spain], while the favor shown by the king to these was contrasted with the severe sentences passed upon the Puritans."

Pearl Rosborough, in her regression, had discussed America with a Puritan friend who had just returned from there. But, still, it proved little.

Yet, the year 1636 was an odd choice, for in this year Charles produced a prayer book which stirred many Protestants to open rebellion. "In 1636," the *Britannica* reported, "the new Book of Canons was issued by the king's authority, ordering the communion table to be placed at the east end, enjoining confession, and declaring excommunicate any who should presume to attack the new prayer book."

In Scotland it was attacked as "English and popish"; in England, as merely "popish."

But neither England nor India seemed to awaken any conscious memory in Pearl Rosborough. She was no Marcia Moore, who felt more at ease in India than in even Concord. Just as Heinrich Schliemann had dreamed of ancient Greece, so did Marcia dream of India. "When I first saw Benares, on the Ganges, the city the Hindus called the 'Navel of the World,' I realized that I had dreamed of it many times." Everywhere she traveled through India, she had the feeling that she was meeting her own people. It was easy for her to learn Hindi and even Sanskrit, the sacred written language which was a key to the holy writings of India—the Vedas, Upanishads, and the Bhagavad-Gita.

An astrologer who was mediumistic told her of two previous lives in India, one fifteen hundred years ago as a temple dancer—devadasi, a Servant of God—and again as a Buddhist. She had also lived in Tibet, but even before she was told this she had felt strangely drawn to this area high in the Himalayas, and had settled longest in Kalimpong, where she studied Tibetan philosophy and visited with Tibetan monks.

It was an interesting story, nothing more, but there was no doubt about Marcia believing it implicitly. However, without wanting to belabor the point, I didn't see the significance of it all, except that it made people believing in reincarnation feel better about dying.

"Not at all," Marcia said with a smile, "it's living that it makes more understandable, really.

"I know of this young woman, unhappily married," Marcia continued, "who went to a trance clairvoyant—a past-life reader—and was told that in an earlier life in ancient Greece she had been poisoned by her husband. It was a horrifying thought, but as she got to thinking about it she began to understand her own home life better. Her husband, in this life, was oddly enough the same she had back in olden times when she was a courtesan, and he was now constantly accusing her of poisoning him. Before tasting the soup, he would insist that she try it first, and he would eat nothing that she hadn't sampled first. It was all very nerve-wracking, particularly since there was no germ of truth in it. But once she understood the subconscious basis for his fear of poisoning—for his own guilt complex carried over from a previous life—she relaxed about the whole thing, and became so sympathetic in attitude that he gradually began to relax."

However, the marriage deteriorated in other areas. Ironically, the husband stumbled across the written past-life readings. Reading that his wife had been a courtesan, he took the report to his attorney, and threatened to use it in a divorce action. It needed all the sage counseling the lawyer could invoke to talk him out of producing this as evidence of infidelity.

Reincarnation, as Marcia saw it, was an integral part of the cycle of life. "Without it," she said, "there wouldn't be much order in the universe, and even Einstein, an avowed atheist, acknowledged Universal Order."

Still, where was the evidence? I wondered how their own research had impressed the men with the tape recorders—the hypnotists and regressors—the so-called scientists. What did they consider evidence?

Dr. Kenneth Lyons was a good-looking man of middle age with a shock of wavy iron-gray hair. He looked like a solid businessman, and he was. Besides practicing regressive hypnosis, he was the personnel director for a large insurance company. His wife was an attractive woman of youthful appearance who had mothered three children, and conveyed the impression, sardonically, that this was world enough for her. Dr. Lyons seemed the last person to be sold on reincarnation.

"Actually," he explained during a visit to Concord, "my interest developed in rebuttal to Bridey Murphy. I was out to prove reincarnation so much nonsense. Instead, I found that as I regressed people a pattern began to appear: they talked of leaving their bodies the same way, and of being reborn the same way."

There was the young American girl, regressed but two generations, who reported a remarkable affinity to a young married couple. She hovered in spirit about them, not knowing exactly why. One day she saw the young mother wheeling a carriage with a male infant inside, and she suddenly realized, "That's going to be my baby brother."

Regressively, hypnotically, her spirit entered the womb a few days before her own birth.

It sounded like an overvivid imagination to me, hypnosis or not.

In another regression, a Wilmington, Massachusetts, man went back to the Spanish-American War period. He couldn't understand why he was so anxiously following the romance of his son and a pretty girl friend. Only when they finally decided to get married did he relax with a sigh.

"As it developed," Lyons said, "he was slated to return as his own son's grandson, so he was in a sense waiting for his own father to materialize."

I laughed. "That sounds like the old Tennessee hillbilly song that goes, 'He was his own grandpaw.' "

Working with a team of brother scientists, Dr. Lyons

had painstakingly produced one regression which he thought clearly indicative of reincarnation. In this case, the regressee was a Wilmington electrician, some forty years old, with no interest in reincarnation. He had volunteered for hypnosis without knowing that he was to be taken back in trance and asked about previous lives. There was no chance of a setup, Dr. Lyons felt.

"And the unusual thing about it," the psychologist said, "was that in regression we finally found somebody whose previous life was not laid in some distant setting, where it was virtually impossible to check."

Then and now—a hundred years ago—the electrician had lived in the same area. He had been a farmer in Andover, Massachusetts, in about 1850, and then had moved to Wilmington. And it was the Wilmington of that period he discussed, in trance, for Lyons and his tape-recording team.

They had hypnotized him and taken him out to the Wilmington graveyard, which went back to old Colonial times. On the way over, he kept pointing out houses, naming the tenants who had lived there a century earlier.

In the cemetery, still in trance, he picked out the location of the graves of his period, naming the dead. Then he turned and pointed, saying, "There is a red stone there."

Investigation developed, Lyons said, that the stone had been there once, but had been moved to another part of the cemetery.

Again he pointed to a mound, and there was no mound. "They are waiting to be buried there," he said, naming a couple who were alive in the year 1850.

Again, said Lyons, investigation verified the information brought out in the regression. "There had been such a mound, heaped over a vault intended as the last resting-place of the people he had mentioned. But before their death, the pair had replaced the mound with a couple of urns."

To check old grave sites, the investigators led by Lyons had scoured the local Wilmington library and come up with a book which listed burial records confirming much that the electrician had said under hypnosis.

"That book," Lyons stressed, "had not been taken out of the library for forty years, not since our subject was born."

"It could have been read there, with copious notes taken," I observed.

"That is true," he said, "but our subject had no interest in reincarnation, and was not the library type."

There was one point that puzzled me. En route to the cemetery, the subject had paused before an old, dismantled railroad crossing, and cautioned Lyons and his group to be careful.

"What kind of tracks," I asked, "did they have in 1850, when railroads were just spreading out?"

"It was apparently a pioneer line," Lyons said.

As in Bridey Murphy, the regressions posed many alternatives to reincarnation. "Anything consciously or unconsciously picked up by the subject could come through under hypnosis," I pointed out. "He might be clairvoyant, tuning into the past through the so-called Universal Mind, or he could be the beneficiary of Jung's collective unconscious. Or, scientifically speaking, it could be the unknown, X."

Lyons was familiar with classic recalls in India, where reincarnation was accepted as casually as Westerners accept normal birth. One, Jagdish Chandra, living in Bareilly, India, was three years old in 1926 when he began talking about automobiles his family had owned during a recent past life in Benares. He described the family house with amazing detail, gave the complete names of his mother and father. He made only one mistake, and it was the mistake that confounded the critics. He had given his grandfather's name as his father's, and actually, as Lyons pointed out, he had lived with his grandfather until the age of twelve, when he died. He had never known his own father.

Lyons dug up another case. The little Indian girl Shanti Devi, living in Delhi in 1936, claimed a past life in Muttra, a nearby community which she had never seen. She recalled details of previous homes and relatives, all of which checked out. But the clincher apparently came when she mentioned a place where she had hidden some money. The hiding place turned up, but not the money, and then the surviving husband—of the previous life—confessed that he had carried it off after her death.

Reincarnation was largely responsible for the fatalism of the East. For the kindred doctrine of karma made the wickedness of past lives accountable for the misfortunes and evils of this one. Conversely, the better one's life, the higher his development the next time around. It was a comforting philosophy, and provided many people with a ready explanation for their own shortcomings. "If you foul up the nest," I said to Dr. Lyons, "I suppose you can al-

ways blame it on your karma, or"—looking to Louis—
"on the stars."

Lyons smiled. "It's not quite that simple. The performance of good can still offset the results of a bad karma."

There were broader implications, too. The rationalists tried to explain away virtually all contemporary social injustice in terms of a perpetual debit and credit ledger. And since the spirit survived, and the body was no more important than any other container, the deaths of helpless children, the persecutions of millions of innocents—including the chosen of God—famine, flood, and pestilence, all these were merely surface ripples in the ceaseless tides of never-ending life.

"Understanding that there is a continuous life cycle, accepting the evidence for it, makes it easier to bear tragic circumstances that might otherwise be unbearable," Lyons said. "The subconscious, with its vast untapped powers, may very easily be the key to the riddle of the universe."

We had been sitting around at the Concord ashram for better than an hour now, talking reincarnation. And Louis was beginning to show signs of impatience.

"Would you mind regressing me?" he asked Lyons.

The psychologist smiled. "I can always try."

But Louis was not a good subject. Lightly hypnotized, he was taken back to the age of six, his first year at school, and then he balked. It had been a bad period for him, almost traumatic, and he had defensively snapped out of a shallow trance state.

Marcia also submitted to hypnosis, but taken back to age two, she jumped up from the couch.

Marcia's daughter, Loulie, had been watching the proceedings with interest. As Dr. Lyons pointed out that the atmosphere apparently wasn't conducive for deep hypnosis, Loulie announced that she would like to be regressed.

Lyons looked doubtful, but when Loulie's face fell, he capitulated. "It can do no harm," he said, and shrugged.

Loulie seemed a more plastic subject than her grownups.

It required only a few moments to induce a trance. "You will go to sleep but still be aware of what is going on around you. Nothing will harm you." Lyons spoke with professional crispness and detachment. He took Loulie back a little at a time.

"It is your fourth birthday, Louisa," he prompted. "Describe that day for us, please. Your fourth birthday."

Loulie's face was composed; she responded evenly. "I

had a party with a cake and candles, and George and Debbie and Ann were there."

Her mother nodded confirmingly; the regression continued.

"Let us take you beyond that, earlier in this life, the first thing you can remember."

Loulie frowned slightly, but she did not falter. "I see lights and confusion," she said, "and there are a lot of people moving around me. I don't know any of them."

"Was your mother there?"

Loulie shook her head slowly.

Lyons shot a glance at Marcia. She appeared to be thinking. "It might be the hospital where Loulie was born. I objected at the time to the fact that they put the newborn babies in a nursery with such dazzling lights."

If this was true, Loulie had been regressed to a few hours after birth.

Beyond that, of course, was the great unknown. But not for long.

"Let us take you back now to before that," Lyons said. "You are going back, back, tell us what you can remember, Louisa."

Loulie frowned, and her voice came haltingly. "I see the ocean," she said, "lots of beach. I'm spending the holiday with relatives."

"How old are you?"

She hesitated. "Sixteen." That was a year more than she actually was.

"Where was this holiday?"

"On the Riviera."

"In France?"

"No, Italy, I had come from France for the holiday."

"When was this, Louisa?"

There was a long pause. Finally, "In 1764, the year 1764."

Lyons looked pleased, and I became mildly interested.

"Were you Italian?"

"No, French, my parents were French."

"What was your name?"

"Matilda."

"Matilda what?"

"Argente, A-r-g-e-n-t-e."

"Can you speak French?"

"Yes."

"Say something in French."

Loulie softly sang off a few words in French.

Lyons looked significantly at Marcia.

She whispered back through her teeth, nodding, "She knows French."

"Can you speak Italian?" Dr. Lyons asked.

Loulie hesitated. "I'm learning."

"Can you say something in Italian for us?"

My interest perked up, for Loulie knew no Italian.

She stirred around uneasily on the big davenport but did not answer.

"Louisa," Lyons repeated, "can you say something in Italian?"

Again she did not answer.

"All right," Lyons said, "let us go back to the Italian beach in 1769."

I did not know whether Lyons' slip was deliberate. But Loulie corrected slowly, "1764."

Lyons shot us a glance, and then stepping over to Loulie, tapped her shoulder, taking her completely out of trance.

"You're all right now, Louisa," he said, "you're right back where you were before."

Loulie seemed none the worse for the experience. "I would like to try it again sometime," she said. "It was kind of pleasant, floating back like that."

For all I knew, of course, the regressions did represent past lives. But even so, what difference did it make, if these lives couldn't be consciously remembered?

And there were other questions that had not been resolved. Where did the spirit dwell, waiting to re-emerge, and why did it come back? Wasn't one life experience enough in this vale of tears and disillusionment?

A visiting English witch, Sybil Leek, a confirmed reincarnationist, offered a provocative theory. "Think of it in scientific terms if you like," she said. "Nothing in nature is lost. We know now that matter and energy are interchangeable. So if we accept the physical part of this equation, we have to accept the intangible—the energy force."

"Matter is physical and visible, but how do you harness a spirit?"

She smiled. "How do you harness a thought? Actually, the spirit is a thought form—and thought is energy. When we say an idea can move mountains, we are thinking in terms of the thought's energy form. Could anybody draw a picture of that thought, or put it in a box? Yet it exists, and makes itself felt."

She pointed to a tree growing outside the window. "The Orientals wisely talk of the tree of life. It is a perfect life symbol. The leaves bud, flower, and fall, fertilizing the soil, and return in a violet, a rose, a tomato, or perhaps even in insect life."

I laughed. "We may return as a leaf, insect life, or a carbon atom, without reincarnation."

"But that is the physical; I am talking about the energy force, the surge of life that makes the blade of grass struggle to reach the sun and the rain, and which in man is inherent in the drive to finish his life experience."

And how did this surging thought form, this nebulous, immortal spirit, finally come to earth after its astral sojourn?

"Like any thought form, it is not very far away. The spirit moves in as part of the surge of life, the parents having their children as accessories in the continuous cycle of nature."

"Then why do so many children resemble their parents so closely?"

"The physical nature may be shaped by parents, but not the experience the child must undergo. In some families, the children may resemble a father physically, but seem almost alien in nature."

She laughed. "How many fathers find themselves saying in bewilderment, 'How could a son of mine have done anything like that?' "

She looked up. "You have two grown children; how much alike are they?"

"They're as different," I said, "as day and night."

If anybody had told Gordon Myers that he had lived before as somebody else, he would have smiled politely and gingerly moved away. Myers was a concert singer, born and bred in Iowa, now singing and composing out of New York. In Iowa, they didn't talk about things like reincarnation, and in Manhattan, musical circles were more concerned about next month's bookings than theoretical existences in ancient India, Egypt, or Greece.

Myers had a feeling of dissatisfaction within himself; he had shown considerable promise, but it had not been fulfilled. At thirty-nine, he felt he was a failure. Classmates and friends with less ability had gone on to lucrative positions, and here he was, verging on middle age and still struggling.

He knew nothing about reincarnation, but a friend, Alice Wightman, had mentioned that clairvoyant Betty McCain, visiting from California, had been helpful in getting people to understand themselves and their problems. Having an interest in the psychic, he was receptive.

On meeting Betty McCain, Myers had no realization that his whole life was about to change. There was nothing about the clairvoyant to indicate that she was in any way extraordinary. She was middle-aged, of nondescript appearance, except for the eyes. They had a penetrating quality, and for a disconcerting moment, Myers felt that she could read his most private thoughts.

Betty McCain was not a medium; she thought of herself as a channel, subconsciously tuned into a Universal Mind or register of events. In trance, as I was to later see myself, she breathed hard, as in the Kapalabhati or Recharge, and was completely renewed when she came to. She had no recollection of what she said, but a tape recorder quietly preserved her message.

Like the late Edgar Cayce of Virginia Beach, Miss McCain would put herself in trance, and then, with her subconscious, explore an individual's past, present and future. The idea was apparently that what one had done in a previous life, in another body, had shaped or prepared one for this life, building up a karmic debit or credit. Myers wasn't interested in reincarnation, but having a reason, he was willing to proceed, framing the questions to Miss McCain in keeping with her past-life beliefs.

"What is my past-life karmic relationship with my wife, Harriet, and how can I help her?" he asked. "Are there special talents or abilities which indicate practices of profession? What is my major purpose for this lifetime and how can I best fulfill it?"

And then Myers sat back and waited.

Betty's voice came back deeper than normal—her High Self voice—between rhythmical gasps:

"You have come to learn the meaning of freedom within self to choose that which you can accept without dominance or force, that you may spread freely among others this feeling of equality. This is your purpose.

"You could have been a physician or a minister. You could have been a singer in this life. You have all these talents. We will bring unto you awareness from where they have come that you may understand."

Myers was startled. Betty knew nothing about him, and yet she had mentioned his singing. And he had once thought seriously of becoming a Methodist minister, as his grandfather and great-grandfather were before him.

He didn't have much time to think about this, however. Soon she was advising him to discuss his secret misgivings with his wife. "It would bring a oneness. Respect her feelings, and also by respecting her feelings have your own respected. If it be a religion in which she believes or anything else, respect it. This will draw you closer, and make you more of a team." She mentioned his concern for a child by a previous marriage, and this again gave him pause, for she had not only not known about the child, but correctly described his innermost feelings.

But Myers' new-found interest began to wane when the clairvoyant got into past lives. They seemed remote and meaningless. He had once lived in Atlantis and died in an eruption there. It seemed thin and implausible. He had also lived in other bodies in India, Egypt, and the England of Richard the Lionhearted. A variety of formal religions ran through his lives, this supposedly to make him more tolerant of others' faiths and give him a desirable universality.

But how could you check on spiritual ancestors centuries back, when you didn't even know such people existed? Wasn't there anything more recent—even theoretically?

"We see where you have been a Methodist minister," Betty was saying. "We would say this was a very late life in the late 1700s or early 1800s. We seem to see you follow the Wesley clan. We see this, whatever it means. Yes, it was in England. Also it was in Ireland." Betty's voice droned on. "We get your name as Philip Embury. It seemed that you experienced that. You went to Canada and America to teach this. This is another of your experiences where you stood strong for that in which you believed, to experience these sufferings, and, shall we say, tensions, of teaching religions."

There was one explicit thing, one tangible, a name, Philip Embury—a name which Betty McCain herself had no conscious recollection of. It did not strike a responsive chord with Myers, but surely it could be checked. Myers knew something of the Methodist Church because of two known forebears who had been in it, and he himself had been an active Methodist once.

He couldn't check on lives in India, Egypt, and Atlantis, but he could on Embury. Betty had been so right about his relations with his wife, his feelings about his ex-wife and son, who knows but what there might be an Embury.

He thought about it a while and called on Methodist Church headquarters in New York City, contacting a Dr. Wade Crawford Barclay, who was compiling a history of the Methodist missions. He couldn't quite get up the courage to give his real reason for calling. "Dr. Barclay peered at me closely when I expressed interest in Philip Embury because of a possible 'family relationship,' and his inquisitive gaze didn't lessen when he learned I was not acquainted with the name 'Embury' as being important in 'our Church.'"

However, in one of the many coincidences that was to mark Myers' search, Dr. Barclay reached across his desk and handed Myers a card that he had prepared just that morning for a biographical encyclopedia. They were requesting information on Philip Embury.

Embury, a local preacher from Ireland (there was Ireland for you), conducted the first Methodist service on the mainland of America. He had been converted from German Lutheranism in 1752 by John Wesley, the founder of Methodism, and had sailed for the colonies in 1760, settling in New York. He worked as a carpenter, as he had back in Ballingarane, Ireland, and began his preaching in homes. As the congregation increased, a church was built on John Street, now the heart of New York's financial district, and Embury helped construct the building and made the pulpit with his own hands.

In 1770, he left New York and settled in Camden, Washington County, above Albany, and organized a small Methodist society. In 1775 he died from injuries suffered in an accident while mowing in his meadow.

Myers' interest was piqued. He scouted through second-hand book stores and came up with Simpson's *Cyclopedia of Methodism.* The *Cyclopedia,* put out in 1883, carried a picture of Embury, showing an even, serene countenance with regular features. The mortal remains of Embury had been installed in the Methodist burying ground at Ash Grove, near Cambridge, New York, where a marble tablet announced, "Philip Embury: The earliest American minister of the Methodist Episcopal Church here found his last earthly resting-place. Precious in the sight of the Lord is the death of his saints."

At any rate, there was an Embury. Myers was intrigued by their common Methodism, and considered with a start that Embury was a carpenter. Carpentry had long been one of Myers' avocations. He had made his dining-room table, his infant child's crib, the bedframes, and was constantly absorbed in woodwork, but of course there was nothing conclusive about this.

Yet, he was interested enough to want to know more about Embury. He came upon a history of Methodism by the Reverend James Youngs, published in 1831, who had talked to people who had listened to Embury preach. Prodded by his cousin Barbara Heck, who was scandalized by the card-playing and dancing in the young New York, Embury held the first Methodist meeting in his apartment on Augustus Street. He encountered "the scoffs of the ignorant, the sarcasm of the worldly-minded, the contempt of the more wealthy class of people, and the stern opposition manifested by partisans of old established persuasions," the Reverend Youngs reported.

"At their first meeting only six were collected. They sang and prayed, whilst Mr. Embury instructed them in the doctrines of salvation. Influenced by the spirit of holiness, they enrolled their names into a class, and resolved to attend regularly at his house for further instruction."

The first Methodist church was dedicated on October 30, 1768. Embury delivered a discourse from the pulpit, declaring that the best dedication a minister could make was to preach a faithful sermon. "In the preaching of Mr. Embury," Reverend Youngs noted, "there was something extremely affecting; he generally shed tears in the midst of his subject, and on all occasions showed himself a perfectly sincere Christian. His occupation was that of a house carpenter; but no business could detract his thoughts from heavenly things; and he was often heard singing hymns in earnest devotion, and at the same time busily plying the implements of his trade." The new church was called Wesley Chapel, honoring the founder of Methodism.

By now Myers was hooked on Embury, if not reincarnation. Slated to appear with the New York Pro Musica at Tanglewood in the Berkshires, Myers drove up a day early to northern New York to look at the resting place of old Embury. "When I arrived at Cambridge, I spotted a large cemetery. Toward the south end of the grounds, a winding road led up a hill, and as I rounded one of the curves, my eye fell upon a monument some fifteen feet in height. And although I could not read from the distance the two names inscribed upon it, I knew this was the spot I had come to see.

"The grave was on the side of the hill, overlooking the valley, where the town of Cambridge lay nestled among the trees. The late morning sun was warm, and mingled with the soft breeze was the sound of a lawn mower, buzzing in another part of the grounds."

It was a stirring moment for the pilgrim. "As I walked up the hill toward the plot, I found myself singing softly 'Blest be the tie that binds.' " Myers felt a friendly eternity all around him, an unseen presence that he couldn't explain, any more than he could explain why he had suddenly burst into song, singing that particular hymn. Thinking of it, though, he recalled having sung it twice as a boy and having been oddly moved.

As he stood at the grave, meditating, the thought came to him, "If reincarnation be true, then these are the bones I once used. I am being privileged then to stand over my own grave." And then, perhaps influenced by Betty McCain, the idea struck him, "Might this experience not be for reasons of teaching me that the soul does live after bodily death?"

Philip Embury probably had little inkling of the great movement that was to fan out from his humble effort. "This, too, might be a lesson," Myers considered. "Shun not the humble deed—for we never know how much good may result from little things we do for someone."

Myers was still not sold on reincarnation, but he was increasingly entranced with his own research. Somewhere he had read that Embury's copy of Cruden's Concordance was in the Wesley Theological College Library in Montreal.

In the spring of 1959, a year after his first session with Betty McCain in a New York hotel, a concert tour took Myers to Montreal. There he discovered that Wesley Theological had become part of McGill University. And in the library's rare book room, he found Embury's Concordance. As always, near anything of Embury's, he became strangely pensive. "I sit in the Divinity Hall Library, and before me on the table in good condition, though obviously much used, rests the copy of Cruden's Concordance which was published in 1769, and which was presented to Philip Embury by his congregation when he left New York City."

Inside the book was a typewritten note left by a nameless researcher. It said: "The widow and children of Philip Embury who died in 1775 came to Canada with a handful of other loyal Methodists on the outbreak of the Revolutionary War, and brought this Concordance with them. This little band became the founders and pioneers of Methodism in upper Canada as they had been in the U.S." (and here was Canada as Betty McCain had said).

With mixed emotions Myers fondled the heavy book. Could he actually have been Embury? It seemed fantastic. But if a man could be said to have an empathy with an object, he was experiencing that empathy now. Again he felt strangely moved, as the feeling came over him that he had been through all this before. "Now I can say I have held this dear book in my hands, and I can fit the fingers of my left hand in the worn places on the front cover—the way he must have held it, half opened as he leafed back and forth, looking up and copying out reference after reference with his right hand." The volume had been given in love, and tenderly used in love. "It was a good friend, and he used it well. It was a useful tool in helping others toward building a spiritual life—the same as the hammer and saw and the measure he used with his hands to build a house."

In spite of himself, Myers was beginning to become emotionally involved with the dead Embury—and to dwell on reincarnation. It almost seemed at times as though Embury was trying to convey a message. Perhaps Myers' imagination was playing him tricks, but the vague feeling of being in tune with a filmy presence hung on. "Oh, that we could pierce the veil that hides from us the memory of soul," he reflected, "then might such pages out of the past be recognized as truly old friends. Then, too, might we prove more surely that the spirit of man does continue after death, only to return to earth to live again in another body, in another time, and with another opportunity to serve mankind for higher evolution."

On the hillside, contemplating Embury's grave, he had felt a new strength for living and for coping, a surging faith in a continuing soul. "Perhaps," he speculated, "the soul-memory is pointing out to my conscious memory what Embury the man chose to do in his lifetime to build toward higher evolution of soul. And that in this way I am now being made aware of these values, so that past spiritual gains are not wasted or forgotten, but are preserved, expanded and developed even more."

Although he was not conversant with Yoga, he was beginning to entertain the Eastern idea of a never-ending cycle of life that Betty McCain had presented as part of Nature's orderly process.

While considering reincarnation as a possibility, the workaday Myers was sufficiently practical to keep his interest to himself as he pursued his inquiries. Emotionally stirred as he had been in encountering Embury's personal articles, he had deliberately avoided the church Embury had founded. Finally, though, sixteen months after he had first heard Embury's name, he telephoned the Reverend Dr. David Chamberlain and made an appointment to visit the church in John Street, the third on the original location.

Dr. Chamberlain, a pleasant young man, who had been pastor for only a few months, guided his visitor through the church, showing him the pulpit which Embury built and Embury's old rocking chair. On the wall behind the pulpit was a big grandfather clock brought from Ireland, bearing the inscription: "Be ye also ready, for in such an hour as ye think not, the Son of Man cometh."

As Myers prowled through the basement, two portraits among numerous other paintings and etchings caught his eye. One was of Philip Embury, the other of his wife, Margaret—both done shortly before Embury's death. A chill ran up Myers' spine. "There is no reason why," he told himself, "or evidence that physical characteristics carry over from one lifetime to another, granted there are other lifetimes." However, gazing on the portrait of Philip Embury, he noticed that his face and Embury's had a startling similarity in the eyes. "The shape of the lower face chin line, mouth, and the lines around it, were also strikingly similar."

Intrigued that he might be effecting a completed circle, and feeling that Embury may have left his church prematurely, Myers decided to close out the circle. In November, 1959, on tour through the Middle West, he stopped off in Cedar Rapids, Iowa, to arrange for transfer of his all-but-forgotten Iowa church membership to John Street Methodist Church. Shortly thereafter, he was formally inducted into the New York church. At a luncheon which followed the regular services, Dr. Chamberlain, being acutely aware of Myers' interest in the church's history—without quite knowing why—handed his new parishioner an old book. "This," he said, "is Philip Embury's Bible."

Just as the Concordance had stirred an unexpected surge of emotion, so now the touch of this Bible shook Myers' very core. "Little could Dr. Chamberlain know that he caused a tingle in both my heart and hands, and I had to fight back an overpowering emotional response, which I managed by looking long into its pages, turning them slowly one by one and pretending to read passages which my tear-filled eyes prevented me from doing."

Coincidences continued to pile up. The copy of the Methodist magazine *Together* arrived. In it was a picture of Philip Embury preaching at home. Later, Myers received a card in the mail announcing: "Be it known that Gordon Myers is a friend of John Street Church, New York, Oldest Methodist Society in America—and joins me in supporting the unique ministry of this national shrine." Below was a rubber-stamped signature—the facsimile of one inside Embury's Concordance. The undersigned name was "Phil. Embury."

Meanwhile, Myers, as his quest went on, had additional sessions with Betty McCain, visiting from her psychic headquarters in Los Altos, California. She mentioned that he was growing in confidence and spirituality, and that musical compositions would soon be pouring out of him.

He wondered aloud, as she lay in shallow trance, whether any music had survived that Embury had liked enough to sing. She replied immediately, citing the hymn, "Oh glory of God who still liveth." "And one day," she went on, "you are going to have an inspiration to write something of this nature." She saw still another hymn favorite of Embury. "We will just bring you what we find here. 'Blest be the tie that binds.' That is what we get. That was very much unto him in his feelings."

And now, with a little shiver, Myers thought back to that peaceful summer day in northern New York when he had marched toward Embury's grave unaccountably singing, "Blest be the tie that binds."

He had mentioned his experience to no one, confiding it only to a secret diary, and now Betty McCain had introduced a new tie that binds. Could the clairvoyant have been reading his mind, could it have been coincidence? He went poring back into hymnal history. "The Tie That Binds" had been formally introduced to words and music by the Englishman Fawcett in 1772—three years before Embury's death.

Was it possible that Embury could have learned to love the hymn in so short a time? And yet, in 1770, he had been presented with a Concordance published only the year before. Could he have not as quickly familiarized himself with a new hymn book, or could not the hymn have been one traditionally passed on long before its formal composition?

Anyway, there it was, and whether Embury or not, he had lately been turning out a steady flow of compositions —cantatas, choral pieces, and the like. He no longer thought himself a failure, no longer considered material success, but his own outlook, his own sense of creativity as the measure of his own personality development—and his niche in this life. His own growth was the important thing.

In the fall of 1964, when I met him, Myers was a tranquil, well-adjusted man, happy with his wife Harriet and their infant son. He had a healthy sense of humor and a hearty laugh, and this humor extended to himself as well as Philip Embury. "He couldn't have done more for me," he smiled, "if he had been my own father. Just thinking about him straightened out my thinking and reinforced my faith in the plans of the Almighty."

Betty McCain was pleased that Myers had been helped. She was a quiet, manifestly sincere woman who made no claims. She had read for several people I knew, giving them the same kind of life reading she had given Myers. There was no way of verifying these things, of course. But one thing was sure. Betty McCain had flashes of clairvoyance. Reading for Mrs. Hiram Blauvelt, a society belle who had been a professional singer, she told her what few knew, that she was planning a new singing career, and then turning to the state of Mrs. Blauvelt's health, she said, "There is a vegetable juicer on a shelf in your kitchen— use it." The juicer had been sitting there neglected.

She discussed another person's two marriages, related why they had failed, and then as he sat stubbornly unconvinced, added, "As a young man I see you walking in the rain, your coat buttoned only at the top, and a hat snapped down over your eyes."

He had worn such a hat in college, and had never worn a hat thereafter. "And," he recalled grudgingly, "my top button was the only one I managed to keep on my rain-coat."

He finally, too, agreed she was right about his marriages and the peculiar circumstances that had brought them to an end. It gave him pause. "How can I say she was wrong about anything," he observed, "when she was right about the things I knew about?"

It seemed like a good question.

Spooks of all types passed in and out of the Concord ashram. Even the cleaning woman had revelations, and though the Hindus frowned on psychism in Yoga, it was obvious that the two went together—Western-style.

We were besieged by witches, fortunetellers, astrologers, hypnotists, psychic researchers; and Marcia's daughter, Loulie, with the aid of her Hebrew lessons, read a mean tarot card.

Having done one book on psychics, like the scientists—Einstein, Carrel, Jung, and Freud—I was constantly intrigued by manifestations of telepathy, clairvoyance, and especially precognition, the ability to foresee the future. Einstein, before his death, had received psychics at Princeton, and appeared to toy with the idea that psychic ability was linked with the Universal Order of things. Alexis Carrel, a Nobel prize winner, had said that when we understood how people did *know* the future, we would be on the brink of solving the mystery of man's existence.

But many, less scientific, reacted angrily to the thought that psychics could peer into the future.

"If people can predict the future," a wealthy, material-minded friend protested, "that would mean the future is fixed."

He could not accept Einstein's order of the universe, though he accepted Einstein, and he did not believe in God. Reincarnation, of course, was so much hogwash; there was continuous life, no hereafter, and before he was through expostulating, there really didn't seem to be much present.

My own approach was that of an observer, and I was intrigued to find myself in a home where the psychic was regarded with as much equanimity as Sanskrit, the headstand, and New England fish chowder.

Jody Sheehan, a classmate in Yoga, was one of my favorite sensitives. As they said back in the Ould Sod, from where her ancestors peregrinated in 1840, Jody had "the gift." She was a serious office administrator by day, played the fiddle in bands by night, and in off moments read the cards for friend and foe.

She brought out the cards for me regularly, and she was seldom wrong in picking out a vexing situation. And her predictions were not always reassuring. The cards, of course, like crystal balls and tea leaves, were only a focal point, detaching the subconscious, but Jody always managed to find the card her ESP was reaching for, whether it was the grim ace of spades, the death card, or the ten of diamonds, the traditional money card.

Like the proverbial bus driver, Jody liked to be "read" herself in her spare time. She had a file on the leading psychics in the Boston area, grading them with stars. She was particularly fond of the nonagenarian Mrs. Florence Maines, who held forth in Waltham, and Mrs. Kay O'Connor of Revere, but deplored the fact that time seemed to have dulled Mrs. Maines' fine edge.

The three of us—Marcia, Jody, and myself—drove one night to nearby Waltham for our rendezvous with Mrs. Maines. En route, Jody warned that the dean was given to garrulity, and might not read for all of us in the allotted time. "We'll defer to you," she said genially.

Mrs. Maines lived over a corner drugstore in an undistinguished neighborhood. We walked up a flight of stairs, and were met by an elderly woman with a friendly smile. "That's Verna, Mrs. Maines' daughter," Jody whispered.

The house was simply furnished, scrubbed clean, the rooms small. From the kitchen we were ushered into a front room. There, quietly, sat a silver-haired, wrinkled figure of a woman who seemed to be praying to herself. Her lips moved inaudibly and her face was composed. She didn't seem aware that anybody had come into the room. I noticed that her lids drooped over her eyes, and thought fleetingly that she might be blind.

Jody seemed to interpret my glance. She leaned over and whispered, "Her eyelids refuse to stay up, the muscles just won't hold. She's been to many eye doctors. But the last one, a famous ophthalmologist, decided there was no medical reason for this lack of muscle control. "All I can think of," he said, "is that because of the nature of her work she is not meant to keep her eyes open to material things but to concentrate spiritually on the sight that comes from within."

We sat quietly for several minutes before the old woman stirred. She made an effort to open her eyes, but one remained completely closed, and the other was a narrow slit. She peered straight ahead, not attempting to focus. She seemed as old as the hills, but when she spoke finally, her words were clear and coherent. Her voice was high-pitched, and wavered at times, but she quickly took hold of herself. She showed no inclination to get to the readings. She talked about herself for a while, the foibles and vanities of

people, and the wonders of God. "I have been in this work
for sixty years," she said, "and have helped many people,
but I take no credit. Without God's help I could have done
nothing."

She was quite plainly of a religious turn. Several pictures of Jesus hung from her walls, and a photograph of
a middle-aged nun stood on a mantel. This, it developed,
was Mrs. Maines' granddaughter. "She's at Guadalcanal
now," the old woman said with a sigh of pride, "helping the
poor souls there." She had apparently intercepted my
glance.

She was in no hurry, and considering that her fee was
only a dollar, I did not see how she managed to eke a
living out of her work.

She rambled on for fifteen minutes, and I began to grow
restive. Then she said suddenly, "Who is it going to be?"

Marcia and Jody graciously left the arena to me, Jody
muttering as she walked out, "She's read me so often I
feel like an old newspaper."

In years of research, I had come to know hundreds of
psychics, from Peter Hurkos to Jeane Dixon, Florence
Psychic, Arthur Ford, Maya Perez, and Cayce. They all
worked differently. Some went into trance or peered into
crystals, others held a subject's personal possession or read
cards and palms. But most functioned like Mrs. Maines.
She just sat across from me, trying to tune in to what
psychics called the individual's vibratory force.

She came up with nothing breath-taking, perhaps because nothing of this nature was in the wind. Many of the
things she told me, as she got started, did not seem to
apply at the time, nor did she seem to get into the crux
of my life and work. She talked about phone calls and
letters I was about to receive, trips I was to make, and
mentioned names which meant nothing to me.

"You will get a telephone call from New York City
about your work next week," she said.

As it was, I averaged two or three calls a day from New
York. But it was mildly intriguing that she should pick
New York as having some connection with my work, with-
out knowing my name and address.

She cupped her hands over her eyes. "I see a letter.
Something special, a special delivery stamp." She strained
as though to see better. "And air mail—special delivery,
air mail." This letter was also to arrive next week.

She seemed to catch a glimpse of my Yoga program, but
it was no more than a flash, which she could not fit into

a finished picture. "I don't know what you do for a living," she said, "but I see you studying and reading about the physical body, and it is something you don't ordinarily do."

She asked no questions, looked for no hints, and made no apologies. She was an honest woman, offering whatever came, hoping it might be of use.

At one point, I thought she had dozed off. But she bestirred herself with a clack of the tongue, and dabbed at her eyes. She poked a bony finger at me. "You wake up a lot at night," she said, "with ideas of all kinds bursting in, not letting you get back to sleep. Write them down, they will help in your work."

I laughed in spite of myself. Actually, only a few nights before, I had begun waking in the middle of the night for no good reason, my mind brimming with thoughts about Yoga.

"I see you lecturing," she said, "though I don't get what you do. But you will give talks about things you have concerned yourself with in the past."

I had two lectures on my schedule, both on psychic research. But I still had heard nothing of significance. A silence fell between us, and then, as though reading my thoughts, she said suddenly, "You have been working on something with which there have been difficulties, but it will materialize sucessfully in October. Mark that date down—great success."

She said almost querulously, "I like my people to write down what I tell them; otherwise, they forget."

"I have a photographic memory," I assured her, "and seldom take notes."

She nodded, reassured.

It had been a long reading, because of the long pauses and intermittent ramblings, and I was afraid she was getting overtired. I started up, but she waved me back into my chair. "I get something else," she said. "Don't try to do so much. Do one thing at a time, and you'll do your best, and get credit for it."

She chuckled in evident satisfaction, and then her mood shifted suddenly, her face twisting into a frown. "I see the name Bradbury. Funny, I never got that name before. If you haven't met somebody by that name, you're going to hear about them."

There was a long pause, and I started up from my seat. She held up a restraining hand. "You're in New Hampshire," she said, shading her eyes with a gnarled hand, "and you're riding through the White Mountains. You've had a pleasant time and are saying the trip was well worth it."

I had never been to New Hampshire, and had no plans, so far as I knew, to travel there.

The reading was over.

Obviously, Mrs. Maines was psychic, and may once have had great powers. Equally obviously, the passage of years had made it difficult for her to join the images that flashed across her vision into integrated prophecy. And I was sure, as with other psychics—and people, generally—that she had some days that were better than others.

I had looked for general predictions about war, politics, business conditions, and earth changes, such as volcanic eruptions, earthquakes, and tidal storms, so that I might compare them with other forecasts and the astrological alarms of Marcia's Louis.

I had a well-stocked file of predictions.

Recently, in New York, psychic Bob Rhodes had predicted that within two years the streets of Manhattan would run with blood from racial riots; he, like Cayce, had seen great eruptions and catastrophes, visualizing a wall of water sweeping in on the city of Seattle, and great areas in California, coinciding with predictions of California quakes by the Dutchman Hurkos. Predicting world events was the prerogative of the provocative seer. Bronx sensitive Zara Lakes, a spiritualist, astrologer, and soothsayer, had correctly foreseen the death of Nehru. But Mrs. Maines had concerned herself with none of these things.

When I emerged, finally, Jody had her cards on the kitchen table and was reading for Verna Maines. "Have cards, will travel," she said lightly.

Marcia inquired about my session.

I laughed. "She saw me in New Hampshire, to give you an idea."

Marcia smiled. "But you are scheduled to lecture at Concord, New Hampshire."

Marcia had arranged the talk; all I had known was that it was within easy driving distance. "It's in the foothills of the White Mountains," Marcia said. "We might just ride through them."

That next week, Friday, June 5, a special delivery, airmail letter turned up. It was from the psychic Bob Rhodes. It was the only "special" letter I received in more than two months at Concord.

Also I did get a telephone call specifically connected with my work, from my literary agent Sterling Lord. It concerned the sale of two past books into paperbacks, and came the first day of the week.

But who was Bradbury?

Mrs. Maines was a spiritualist. She had guides, who were always "they," and they were her source of information. Why they should be interested in trivial phone calls and letters, I could not understand, when there were so many urgent things we would like to know. I suspected that the spiritualists, like other psychics, might only be dramatizing their subconscious, but I had additional opportunity to judge.

At least, they were in fundamental agreement. Three others besides Mrs. Maines saw "great success" in three or four months; two identified me as a writer who would be lecturing. There was no questioning their sincerity. Their fees were small, and they gave liberally of their time and energy. They had no smooth patter, and often groped, or paused, better to hear their voices and see their pictures.

"Do you ever feel somebody in spirit looking comfortingly over your shoulder?" asked the spiritualist Kay O'Connor of Revere, a Boston suburb. It was a rhetorical question. She had just told me that a woman on my mother's side was close—momentarily close.

"I think of my grandmother often," I said. "She brought me up."

Mrs. O'Connor's blue eyes responded with a smile. "Would the name Sarah mean anything to you?"

"That is my grandmother's name."

She paused. "She wants you to know that in November things will clear up for you. You will always be protected, she wants you to know that." It was now early June.

I could think of no possible comment. But with a Presidential election looming in the fall, I wondered what Mrs. O'Connor's spirits thought about it.

The answer was rather surprising. "The Republicans will be split; Johnson will win." This, weeks before the Republicans nominated Senator Goldwater.

Another evening I found myself sitting across from spiritualist Gertrude Beach in suburban Somerville. Mrs. Beach, a kindly lady in her eighties, was born a Baptist. She had been weaned to spiritualism by her visions. They appeared as symbols. For instance, as her eyes fell on mine, she said, "I see a door opening into stairs, and you running up the stairs."

What did it signify?

"That means great success, personally and professionally,

and soon, since you are running." I would see this success materialize in three months.

Optimism seemed Mrs. Beach's forte, but only time could vindicate her prediction.

"I am not a fortuneteller," she was saying. "I try to help people with their problems." Suddenly, her gaze shifted from me to the wall beyond. "I see somebody over your shoulder," she said. "Could it be your grandmother would have a message for you?"

I shrugged, not knowing what to say.

"Does Sarah mean anything to you?"

"That was my grandmother's name."

"She has a message for you."

I sat waiting.

Mrs. Beach spoke quietly, in an ordinary tone. "You don't see how right now, but great happiness will be yours. Put yourself in God's hands. When we try to force things, they generally don't work out."

I assumed Mrs. Beach had reference to a personal situation.

Mrs. Kathryn Dellicicchi of nearby Newton also "pulled in" my grandmother, with the aid of cards. She was a card reader who apparently had spirit contact. As she laid out her cards, she frowned. "Every time you go through a personal crisis, you think of your grandmother."

She frowned. "Who is Sarah? I see a woman with white hair parted down the center."

My grandmother had worn her silvery hair that way.

Three spiritualists had picked out my grandmother by name. Could they have dredged up my subconscious? The alternative I could not contemplate realistically.

Later I summarized the three readings for Marcia, and she asked, "Did your grandmother ever say anything consistent with these messages?"

The memory of my grandmother's deathbed was a vivid one. "As she lay dying, she said that she would always be with me, and that great happiness would one day be mine."

The Moore-Roof-Acker household did not confine itself to ordinary psychics. They had witches for weekends, and not just ordinary witches, but the chief witch of all of England's six thousand witches. Her name was Sybil Leek, and she came from the New Forest in England, not far from Salisbury. She had ventured from the forest long enough to make a tour of the United States, inspecting the few witch covens in this country.

I had never met a real-life witch, though as a schoolboy I had been fascinated by tales of witchcraft in Salem and by the good and bad witches of *The Wizard of Oz.*

Sybil, it should be known, was a good witch, though she had been known to cast a dark spell when she had a grievance. She was fat, forty-two years old, a mother of two teen-agers back in England, and hearty-looking until she got down to business. She had visited with Marcia and Louis for a few days before I got there, tipping tables in a midnight seance, and now she was returning for a return match.

"They have invited me to Salem," she told Marcia on the phone from New York, "and I really can't go back to England without paying a social call to the famed old Witch City of Massachusetts."

I expected that she might fly up on her broomstick, but Marcia drove down and got her instead, stopping alongside the parkway to do her headstands and sundry other postures as flying motorists tooted their horns in wonderment.

She drove the nearly five hundred miles in one lunge, arriving with Sybil by three in the afternoon. She was not at all tired from being up and grinding through traffic since five that morning. "My exercises set me up perfectly," she said. "I could drive back to New York this minute."

Sybil too appeared inexhaustible. She was a picture in purple—purple shoes, hose, skirt, blouse, and jacket. "That's my trademark," she said with a bewitching smile. "Deep purple."

I had heard of her prowess, but had no way of checking the stories. She had been on television in England, under the auspices of the Independent Television Authority; and a producer, the story went, had reneged on the promised fee. All appeals to ethics were unavailing. Finally, Sybil's patience wore thin.

"If you don't pay me," she said at last, "you shall fall asleep at your desk every afternoon at three o'clock."

On the seventh day, the check was in the mail, and the spell removed. The producer had capitulated.

I was curious. "How did you ever do all that?" I asked.

"I just thought about it every day at three o'clock."

"How long did he sleep?"

"Just five or ten minutes—enough to let him know."

I saw no reason why he should get disturbed about a refreshing little nap in the middle of the afternoon. "I would have been more impressed," I said, "if you had woken him at three in the morning, and not let him get back to sleep."

She laughed. "That would have meant my getting up at three, too."

She wasn't much of a one for spells, though. Her primary concern was occult healing. She was credited with healing people of cancer and other degenerative diseases by just meditating with them on the wholeness of the body from afar. One case in point was in Rotterdam, another in Southampton.

I had the unhappy habit of not being able to accept any account of a psychic wonder without seeing it myself or checking with reliable witnesses. It spoiled many a miracle.

But I liked the Witch. As witches go she was a pretty good scout. She frowned on vegetarianism, nondrinking, and nonsmoking, and soon let the household know that abstinence was not necessarily a virtue.

"You mean you don't even eat eggs?" she said to Louis. "Now, tell me, what are you trying to prove?" She looked over at me. "A good belt of gin never hurt anybody," she said, "and nobody ever died of a medium-rare steak."

Louis started to say something, but she quickly silenced him. "Not doing anything is no virtue in itself. That's strictly negative. Moderation, not abstinence, is the word." She tossed Louis a tolerant smile. "Just don't go thinking you're superior because you eat vegetables and don't take a drink."

She showed some familiarity with Yoga. "In Yoga they teach you to examine the nature of your actions. If you're not-doing because of fear then you should admit it to yourself, and not consider it a virtue. It's a weakness and recognize it as such."

Louis finally got his chance. "I really don't care what anybody else does," he said, "nor do I feel superior."

"Good," she said, "then you won't mind my having a drink?"

She gave me a wink. "I guess we'll have Louis on our side yet."

"Not really," Louis said. "I just don't worry what anybody else does."

Obviously Sybil was a jolly old witch, but I still couldn't conceive of her as a faith healer, particularly when her faith was witchcraft, which was a faith unto itself and did not even recognize the existence of God. It was only natural that we should come to grips; we squared off in the living room not long after we had met. "How can you tell somebody is ill or afflicted?" I asked.

"I just concentrate," she said. "As you see a body's visible form, I see the pain, congestion, and damage within the body; I see an organ shriveling or expanding, squeezed, contorted, debilitated."

"How do you see it?"

"With just a flash of vision," she said.

I thought I would put her to a test. A half hour before, in doing the Fish, I had revived my old whiplash injury. My neck was beginning to throb at a point just to the right of the top vertebra. Marcia had not yet come in from the exercise glade, so nobody knew of the injury.

I regarded Sybil with an air of bland detachment. "You say you can tell where an injury is by just looking at the person?"

"Nearly always," she said.

"And right away?"

"Quite right."

"Then you shouldn't have any trouble with me."

Her eyebrows raised questioningly.

"I hurt myself exercising a short time ago." I smiled casually. "Now where did I hurt myself?"

She looked at me quickly, with no change in expression, and her left hand came over and touched a spot on her shoulder blades, just to the right of her top vertebra. "That's where," she said matter-of-factly. A diagram could not have found the spot more precisely.

I was ready to test the Witch's healing skills but she demurred after a sympathetic bystander had rubbed my neck.

"I can't help now," Sybil said. "Just leave it alone, and it will heal in a few days."

Sybil felt quite relaxed at the Concord ashram. Perhaps it was because she was a Druid, a high priestess in that esoteric cult which still observed its rituals at Stonehenge, near Salisbury. "I feel right at home," she said, "when I look out Marcia's window and see that grove surrounded by all those lovely boulders."

At the mention of Stonehenge, Louis' eyes kindled. "How big are the stones?" he asked.

She looked around the spacious living room. "The smallest," she said, "is about forty times the size of this room."

Louis' eyes boggled. "How did they ever move them?"

"Nobody knows, but they have established that this type of rock is quarried only in Ireland. And so that makes it

more of a problem as to how three hundred and sixty-five
rocks this size were moved that far four thousand years
ago."

Sybil was anxious to get off the next morning for a bus
driver's holiday to Salem. She waved a letter. I have an
invitation to come up and see what their old-time witches
were like."

"I'll drive you," I said, "if your broomstick isn't working."

"That," she said, "is like carrying coals to Newcastle."

We arrived in the Witch City for lunch, then called on
David Proper, the librarian of the Essex Institute, who
had issued the invitation.

He was a short, slight, surprisingly young man with a
sallow face. He was obviously overjoyed to see a live
witch. "I don't of course have to tell you anything about
witches, but then"—his voice dropped deprecatingly—"we
are not even sure our witches were the real thing."

"Oh, there was some witchcraft around in those days,"
Sybil countered, "but I don't think the Salem variety was
the real article."

The whole madness had lasted but six months, from
March to September of 1692. Hundreds of innocent women
—and men—were accused of casting satanic spells, and
eighteen were hanged on Gallow's Hill in old Salem. One
unfortunate man was pressed to death.

"That was Giles Corey," Proper said. "In a way, he
deserved it. He had testified against his wife, Martha; then,
when he discovered that her property wouldn't come to
him but reverted to the state because of her high crime, he
recanted and denounced the entire proceedings. He was
taken into an open field, stripped of his clothing, thrown
on his back, and buried under boulders."

Proper had a personal interest in the proceedings. For
one of his ancestors, Mrs. Mary Estey, was doomed as a
witch with her sister, Mrs. Rebecca Nourse.

The chief witnesses were children. They liked being the
center of attraction, and as their accusations were accepted,
they grew bolder. Some finally overstepped, accusing the
wife of the Reverend John Hale, one of the most zealous
witch-hunters. Knowing his wife was no caster of evil spells,
this misguided man of God had a glimpse of the truth and
of innocents imprisoned and hanged.

The nightmare ended in a spirit of revulsion. "One of
the leading witch-hunters was Cotton Mather, whose father,
Increase Mather, had been head of Harvard," Proper ob-

served. "In the repudiation that followed, Cotton Mather, rejected by the overseers, lost his lifelong ambition of becoming president of Harvard."

The Witch had been listening intently. "He didn't lose quite as much as those innocent girls did," she observed drily.

And so the jails were emptied. Boston, Salem, and Cambridge resumed an air of normalcy, but ill feeling and rancor persisted. In neighboring Salem Village, now Danvers, where the first charges were made, a historic marker on the lawn of the First Church testifies how deeply the current cut.

Sybil read from the marker with misplaced amusement: "To this church, rent by the witchcraft frenzy, came in 1697, the Reverend Joseph Green, aged twenty-two. He induced the mischief-makers to confess, reconciled the factions, established the first public school, and became noted for his skill at hunting game and his generous hospitality."

Back in old Salem, Proper guided us over a grassy sward to a high bluff overlooking one end of the city. This was Gallow's Hill. "Majority opinion holds that on this spot the executions took place, though some people, who may be interested in jacking up the value of the land, insist it was at a lower altitude."

Sybil took an appreciative look around, walked over to the precipice and examined the neighboring terrain. "This is the spot," she announced. "Witch-hunters always took the highest ground for their executions, to confound the low spirits."

She turned to librarian Proper. "These poor people weren't witches, or there wouldn't have been so many witnesses against them."

"What do you mean by that?" I asked.

She smiled slyly. "A real witch doesn't leave evidence lying around to confound her later."

Actually, the only evidence was blind superstition, hate, and malice, as revealed by an eyewitness account of the trial of Rebecca Nourse:

"Goodwife Nourse was brought before the Magistrates Mr. Hathorne and Mr. Corwin, about Ten of Clock in the Forenoon, to be examined in the meeting-house; the Reverend Mr. Hale began with prayer, and the warrant being read, she was required to give answer, Why she afflicted those persons? She pleaded her own innocency with earnestness. Thomas Putnam's wife Abigail Williams and

Thomas Putnam's daughter accused her that she appeared to them, and afflicted them in their fits. But some of the others said that they had seen her, but knew not that ever she had hurt them; amongst which was Mary Walcut, who was presently after, she had so declared, bitten and cried out in the meeting-house, producing the marks of teeth on her wrist." Thinking it over, Mary Walcut apparently decided it the better part of valor to join the pack.

Salem was forever stigmatized, and the city which once rivaled Boston as a port never regained its lost prestige. Some blame a harbor not as deep as Boston, but others point darkly to the spirit of Gallow's Hill.

"As for me," observed Sybil, "I think they were a bloody pack of fools." She turned to librarian Proper. "To give you an idea of how times have changed, you can't get people to take witches seriously today."

And how did a modern witch function?

England's chief witch regarded me somberly. "A witch subscribes to black arts that have been handed down from time immemorial, generally within her own family. She is in complete tune with the supernatural, believes in neither Satan nor God, only good or evil, which she can invoke at demand." Sybil was a good witch.

She was not sorry to leave Salem. "Rank amateurs," she said scornfully, and besides she had a table-tipping date back in Concord.

It would be her second venture. During the first, according to a wide-eyed Loulie and school chum Lynn Rawson, two legs of a heavy table had reared off the floor, and tapped out that they didn't like little girls.

I didn't see the point of table-tipping.

"It's not a very high form of the occult," Sybil agreed, "but it amuses some people."

She turned to astrology, mentioning that one day it would be generally recognized that the planets shaped the course of man's affairs. "This doctor I know in England has done considerable research on the Moon."

"What is his name?" I asked.

"Bradbury—Dr. Robert Bradbury. Ever heard of him?"

I smiled. "Not really." Mrs. Maines had only given a last name.

In Concord, everything was ready for the table-tipping. The guests had already arrived. In fact, they had over-arrived, and there were more spectators than participants. The Witch seemed upset by the turnout. "Too many people," she whispered. "I'll go through the motions, but don't expect much."

She called the turn. It was quite unspectacular. At one point, as several pairs of hands rested on the table top, one side seemed to lurch up as though it had life. It could have been magnetic force, innate energy, any one of a number of things. But one skeptic seemed impressed. That was Boston radio personality Bob Kennedy. "There couldn't possibly have been a trick," he said later. "It just came up by itself."

But Sybil was disappointed. "The vibrations weren't right. They don't like spectators sitting around, peering under tables."

The next morning England's top witch bid us a fond farewell. She took one last lingering look at Boulder Grove. "What a wonderful place," she sighed, "to commune with the spirits under a full moon."

She promised to be back. "You'll hear from me," she said, waving good-bye.

And so we did, sooner than expected. Two weeks later, Louis rushed in, brandishing the Boston newspapers. "We're on the front page," he cried.

A look of apprehension swept over Marcia's face.

"What is it?"

Louis kept waving the paper. "It's Sybil; they're throwing her out of the New Forest, and she's coming here."

Marcia took the paper slowly. There was a dispatch from Reuters, and a front-page picture of Sybil as big as life, carrying a broomstick.

The three children crowded around excitedly, as Marcia read aloud: "Britain's top witch, Mrs. Sybil Leek, who complained she had been persecuted in Britain like a Negro in Alabama, announced today she would seek a new life in the United States."

She planned to settle around Concord, where she had been so warmly received by her friends, Mr. and Mrs. Louis Acker, and perhaps start a witches' group in Boston. So went the story.

Marcia sighed.

Chris was beside himself with importance. "All the kids at school asked me about it," he said. "I didn't tell them a thing."

Louis picked up the paper and read through the story again. He seemed delighted.

Only Marcia seemed less than radiant. "I'm just wondering what our friends and relatives will think."

Chris's jaw dropped. "You mean they might not like her being here?"

"You know how people are," Marcia said.

Thirteen-year-old Chris knit his brow in perplexity. "But, Mom," he said, "didn't they all sign that declaration of welcome?"

"I refuse to grow old gracefully," Marcia said. "I insist on staying young."

She had been reading from an interview with perennially glamorous Gloria Swanson, by beauty columnist Arlene Dahl, no small beauty herself. Miss Dahl pointed out that the ageless Swanson, acting before I was born, had been a health food convert and a student of Yoga for years. Health was the basis of all beauty—and there was no reason why women should ever stop being beautiful. That was the burden of the interview. La Swanson sounded like an overage Marcia: "Women should pay careful attention to exercise and diet in order to prevent the heaviness so often characteristic of mature women who let their figures settle down as their birthdays pile up."

Miss Swanson was a food faddist. I recalled, as a newspaper reporter, inviting her to lunch one day, and her reply, "Fine, if you don't mind my bringing my lunch."

On the surface, her diet didn't seem drastic. She was strong on health foods, and like Marcia scorned refined white sugar and white bread. "All the flour in my food must contain whole wheat germ."

An integral part of beauty, this glamorous grandmother pointed out, was good posture and the graceful use of arms, hands, and feet. "Although she is petite," Miss Dahl observed, "she moves with the grace and assurance of a tall woman."

Marcia snorted as she read. "Of course she moves gracefully—anybody doing Yoga all those years couldn't help herself, and it's the greatest thing in the world for posture."

We were sitting on the terrace after a Yoga class, three months to a day after my first session. "Look at your own posture," she said. "You stand like a West Point cadet, your back is supple and young, your neck erect and head high. It is a miracle considering you were round-shouldered, fatigued, and all sixes and sevens, when you came to Concord."

She put the newspaper down. "I don't know where people get the idea that being short is a handicap as far as grace is concerned." She was only a little over five foot three herself, and I supposed sensitive. "Not at all," she said, proudly mentioning her own recent gains in height. In a way, she had reversed life's process.

"Haven't you noticed," she said, "how some people shrink as they get older? The cartilage loses its elasticity, and the next thing their minds aren't elastic either." She looked me over critically. "Well, you've reversed the process, and if you keep up your Yoga, you'll stay young and productive for the rest of your life. Right now you not only look ten years younger, but are ten years younger." She had warmed up to her subject. "With the control and dexterity gained from Yoga, it is virtually impossible for an advanced Yoga student to make an awkward gesture. They can even get in and out of a cab gracefully."

Grace and Yoga were synonymous in Marcia's ledger. "Every time I see a perenially youthful Hollywood or Broadway star," she said, "I would be willing to wager they were Yoga students." She looked up. "Look at Marlene Dietrich; at sixty or so, she is as sexy-looking and provocative as she ever was—and that's plenty."

Youthwise, I had apparently prospered. My neck was so flexible and strong that I could almost look directly behind me. All vestiges of the old whiplash injury had miraculously vanished. I could do any back-bending exercise without fear of strain. For the first time in years, my ankles, weakened in youth by torn ligaments, showed no sign of turning under pressure; I could sit for hours on end without my lower spine stiffening as had become its custom. I had become firm and hard all over, gaining a solid inch around the chest, losing two inches around the waist, with my stomach flat and hard. And while I had lost but five pounds, the symmetry was better and I was not fat anywhere.

I worked and concentrated better at my desk, had far more energy, seldom if ever tiring, and needed five or six hours' sleep at most.

My periodic indigestion, gas, and nausea had left me. I felt in such deliberate control of body and mind that I could invoke bodily resistance at will in case of a mass assault on my inner defenses by hordes of germs. And whether this confidence was justified or not, the fact remained that even eight or nine months later, continuing my exercises, I had not the hint of a cold or minor indisposition, an unbelievable rarity in my life.

My spine was straight, my shoulders square, and I held my upper body together without effort. I seemed to be aware of every muscle in my body. I also became more aware of the world around me, beauty in every form,

Nature and the conglomerate of peoples and their problems.

Even acquaintances noticed these changes in temperament. And though I was no Hollywood star, and realized that looks were superficial, I would have been less than human not to like the frequent references to my youthful appearance.

I was to think often of little Charlie Weiser, though I hardly knew him. Some of the things that had happened to him were apparently happening to me, the change in my attitude toward food, for instance. I enjoyed a good meal as much as ever, but I found myself thinking less of food. I had entirely given up the idea of three squares a day. I ate only when I felt like it, and this was less often than I would have thought. Evidently, I was making better use of what food I did take in. I might have only coffee or orange juice in the morning, a sandwich and a glass of milk later in the day, and not touch anything until a late dinner at night. I didn't consciously diet. I just didn't get hungry like I used to, yet my energy remained at an even level.

I had become more relaxed, and with it, more tolerant and optimistic. I still had periods of tension and irascibility —a writer's syndrome—but was more aware of the importance of controlling these lapses. There was not much point to controlling body and mind without controlling emotions —and the one seemed to follow the other naturally.

My shifting attitude toward Marcia's children was reflective of the changes within me. Their behavior had certainly not changed. They were normally active children, who naturally turned the household into a teen-age asylum. And I found it distracting, to say the least, in those first few weeks, of trying to adjust. Marcia was constantly apologizing. "I'm afraid," she said, "we're not a very yogic household."

As I meditated, I found myself dwelling on their need to express themselves. If I couldn't concentrate through it all, I was no better than the yogi whose meditations were disrupted by a woman's brushing past him in the town square. So I joined them instead of fighting it, and wound up playing cards with the boys or tossing a ball around with all three children, Loulie included.

Stressful circumstances did not bother me as they once had. I was able to withdraw, detach my mind, and put the problem from me until I was ready to meditate on it. It was not escape, but withdrawal for planned attack.

I was reaching out for peace of mind, but it was too elusive to be so easily snared. It could only come, I felt, through complete attunement with the universe around us, and this, it appeared to me, could only stem from a strong sense of individual purpose. The student needed a reason for being, and with it an understanding of the ways of the universe.

In meditating on the universe and its wonders, I had begun to fancy my place in it and my relation to every living thing that was part of it. If the trees and the flowers and the birds and the bees had their place in the natural rhythm of life, then, obviously, so had I. I was no less nor greater than the least or the greatest creature in an ordered universe.

In a way, I now understood Louis Acker's concern for the insects that had annoyed us as we exercised. If I were a hunting man, I don't think I could ever again raise a rifle to my shoulder. Indeed, I found myself picking ants off legs and arms and depositing them safely at a distance. I was not silly about it. If I had no choice between a fat mosquito and my hide, the mosquito had to go. But I could not be a willful agency of destruction—of animal, insect, or man.

Rover the cat did not seem to share my sensibilities. He seemed to delight in bringing young squirrels and birds to my study window, and appealing through the glass for my approbation.

I mentioned Rover's lack of yogic scruples to Marcia.

"I know," she sighed, "I've chased and scolded him, but I'm finally convinced it's his dharma."

Dharma was a new term for me.

"That's the individual's function or role in the universe. It's as natural for Rover to take after things smaller than he is, alas, as it is for a man to love a woman and beget children."

Meditating after a good Hatha Yoga workout made one wonder about man's dharma in a world that seemed to be fast getting out of control. What was man's dharma? Was it to kill and be killed? Were all the pestilences, quakes, holocausts, and wars staged for the express purpose of controlling man, of showing how small he was?

I got no sudden flash of illumination. All I did know was that I was so perfectly relaxed after an exercise session that I felt thoroughly unburdened. Body and mind seemed deliciously reprieved from the cares of the day, and I felt most in tune with Nature.

The meditations provided a pleasant break and left me refreshed and sometimes exhilarated. When I sat down, or stretched out, as the mood suited, I never knew what would flow through my mind. I was like a breathless out-of-towner making the round of Broadway first-nights. I had so much to see, I didn't know what to look at first.

From my own experience, I did not think it necessary for the student to have a tutor for the meditations, nor to deliberately set about meditating. It would happen or not, as he became ready through Hatha Yoga.

Many of Marcia's students, like myself, were wary of the meditations in the beginning, even when she pointed out that they could do no worse than provide an extra rest period. But after a while, as their confidence in the physical Yoga mounted, some became interested in the philosophic. "They became so relaxed," Marcia said, "that the idea of sitting after class and meditating was almost sensuously appealing."

As I found myself dwelling on the impersonal universe, my interest in the subconscious, and with it the psychic, grew. I was fascinated by new developments in what I had begun to think of as the John Conte Story. Seeress Lucille Joy's predictions were apparently unfolding, just as she had foretold, and Conte, once a confirmed unbeliever, was now convinced that he was a child of destiny.

As I recalled, the California clairvoyant had advised the actor that he would go to New York and work in an off-Broadway production that would soon close, but not before he had gained attention that would launch him on a new and greater career in mid-June. The show, I presently learned, was shuttered in four days, but Conte's performance so impressed the talent people that he was signed for a Broadway production on June 15. Other offers started flowing in—movie, Broadway, and television. Only time would tell whether his career would have the glorious thirteen-year span that the seeress had foreseen, but Conte was so radiantly confident now that it seemed likely that the power of suggestion might make the rest of it come true. Yet, in the twenty years I had known him, the actor had been similarly confident before, without his plans maturing. But now he felt certain of the outcome. "I am a child of destiny," he said with a grin. But I had a feeling that he really believed it.

The development of the psychic potential appeared a promising phase of Yoga. In the East, the frame of reference for the psychic was a belief in a continuous, orderly cycle of life, and, believing the future part of this patterned cycle, the yogis saw nothing remarkable about clairvoyants foretelling the future. In the pragmatic West, of course, there was a tendency to believe only the five senses. And even when these senses confirmed the psychic wonders of an Edgar Cayce or Betty McCain, there was a disposition by materialists and intellectuals—similarly dedicated to the nonspiritual—to mock and sneer.

I had noted some slight psychic experiences of my own in my yogic development. At times I got impressions without quite knowing how they filtered in. One day I was lunching with New York Police Commissioner Michael J. Murphy and his deputy, Walter Arm, when the Commissioner mentioned a departmental aide. "We came from the same place and grew up together," he said.

"Was that County Cork?" I asked, without thinking.

He looked puzzled. "No, Elmhurst," naming a section of New York.

"Didn't your family come from County Cork?" I persisted.

"As a matter of fact they did come from Cork?" He eyed me quizzically.

"Just a little ESP—extrasensory perception," I said lightly.

The Commissioner was still smiling in tolerant amusement when we made a date to meet again the following week.

A few days later the phone rang. It was Arm. "I know," I said, "you want to put the appointment over a week."

Arm laughed. "As a matter of fact, the Commissioner suggested I let your ESP figure out why I was calling." He grunted. "But you're right, we have to cancel out this week."

As Arm saw it, of course, it was all coincidence. And he could very well have been right.

It was obvious that a predictable future implied that the future was set, and a set future certainly indicated a definite order in the universe, applying not only to the movements of the planets but of man.

I grew to meditate on these and other matters with guidance from the great Indian teachers of the past. "How can the mind remain still without an object as its support?" said Dadu, the great saint of India. "It will naturally wander hither and thither restlessly. Let the wandering mind constantly remember God, and it will calm down."

Originally, meditating, I had visualized God in personal terms, once in the image of Leonardo da Vinci, but eventually I began to see Him in everything about me—a tree, a table, the tiniest blade of grass, in children and the aged, even in people I had no reason to be fond of. Somebody had asked, "Is God with you, or are you with Him?" I didn't see where there was any difference, as long as man sought to tune into God's universe.

It was ever the means that were important, Yoga stressed, and it became apparent in many ways how vital this stress was in the development of the individual. A young lady I knew, a backslid Catholic, had been taking instructional courses in her old faith in a vague effort to resolve her confusion and give herself a sense of purpose. After a few classes she wondered about going on. "Having been a Catholic all my life, and then leaving it, what assurance do I have that completing this course will give me what I need?"

In yogic terms the answer was clearly obvious. "Concentrate only on the means," a yogi advised, "make every lesson an end unto itself, and in time you will find that the means and the end are the same. The effort you make to find yourself in your faith will be its own reward, as long as misgivings about the result don't intrude."

Impressed, the young woman plunged into her classes. Yoga, ironically, helped a Catholic to find her Catholicism.

As indicated, the meditations refreshed and renewed me, and sharpened my thinking. But even feeling myself part of the universe, I had no idea where the universe was going. Nobel prize winner Alexis Carrel, acknowledging that some people could foresee the future, had postulated that when we understood how this was done we would know the kind of world we lived in. It seemed to me that we needed more to find peace, in and out of ourselves, by knowing how we fit into such a universe—and other Yoga students apparently felt the same.

"You just can't be at peace," a Concord student said, "and feel that you are a puppet dangled at the end of a string by a merciless fate. You must feel you are here for a reason, that you are part of things."

"And what is your reason?" I asked.

He smiled. "To live in such a way, improving myself in the sight of God, that I will advance in my next birth."

The speaker was no crank. He was an ordinary, intelligent businessman, yet he was obviously keying his life to a belief in reincarnation.

"Suppose you are wrong," I said, "and this is it?"

He grinned good-naturedly. "It is the only thing that

makes sense." And then he quoted from a little book he held in his hand. It was the Bhagavad-Gita. "Even as a man casts off worn-out clothes, and puts on others which are new, so the embodied casts off worn-out bodies, and enters into others which are new."

Though I did not reject reincarnation, even with all the research I had done I was not fully convinced by the evidence. The subconscious was known to play tricks, and what might seem verified remembered experience might be only examples of clairvoyance instead.

"At any rate," I rejoined, "reincarnation is useful if it causes you to lead a better life on this plane, even if there is no other plane."

Nothing I said could shake his confidence. He had watched me develop physically, if not spiritually, in the course of three months.

"Yoga has obviously helped you," he said.

I agreed.

"You not only look like a new person, but you are a new person—you are less critical, more compassionate, more understanding, and"—he smiled—"more open."

"That's only because I am more relaxed," I said.

His eyes gleamed. "Exactly," he said. "You came here tired and weary, you had an aching back, sinus, headaches, and now you feel strong and vigorous, with no aches and pains of any kind."

I wondered what he was driving at.

"Just this. Yoga did everything and more than you expected it to—and you are the living evidence of that."

I nodded. "I am grateful for everything it has done."

"Well, if it has been so supremely right, as far as we could measure the evidence, in your physical and emotional growth, why should it suddenly be wrong about the spiritual?"

I shrugged, still not getting his drift.

"Yoga says that the physical, mental, and spiritual are joined, and through this perfect joining we get a glimmer of truth in which we see the divine truths of an eternal universe."

That evening, I picked up a volume by the most cynical of contemporary chroniclers, Somerset Maugham. *The Summing Up*, an autobiographical account, delivered a masterful résumé for reincarnation:

"Some say that God has placed evils here for our training; some say that he has sent them upon men to punish them for their sins. But I have seen a child die of meningitis. I have found only one explanation that appealed equally to my sensibility and to my imagination. This is the doctrine of the transmigration of souls [reincarnation]. As everyone knows, it assumes that life does not begin at birth or end at death, but is a link in an indefinite series of lives each one of which is determined by the acts done in previous existences. Good deeds may exalt a man to the heights of heaven and evil deeds degrade him to the depths of hell. All lives come to an end, even the life of the gods, and happiness is to be sought in release from the round of births and repose in the changeless state called Nirvana. It would be less difficult to bear the evils of one's own life if one could think that they were but the necessary outcome of one's errors in a previous existence, and the effort to do better would be less difficult too when there was the hope that in another existence a greater happiness would reward one."

And then this admitted agnostic, yielding to the five senses, stated, "I can only regret that I find the doctrine as impossible to believe . . ."

If there was any purpose or design to life, certainly the part—man—should have as much purpose as the whole of the order, the whole being the sum of its parts. If the movements and positions of the planets were predictable, would man's fate be any less predictable? How could he be in the order and not of it? The secret of his existence, as the holy men of India divined, lay in man himself. All he had to do was see himself in Nature, as Nature—or God—saw him. It was a big order, but the yogis said it lay at the end of meditation's rainbow.

In India, some holy men claimed they knew the answer to life's mysteries, and knowing the answer they withdrew from the world, and kept their secret from the common man. Though my references to India may seem overly critical, I have the friendliest feeling for these troubled people. In appearing critical of India, I was merely showing, as the facts warranted, that India, incongruously, was not prepared for a discipline it had given the world thousands of years ago.

"India is a confused country," Yogi Vithaldas had told me with remarkable oversimplification. "They talk the old ways, but they ignore the disciplines of Yoga. They hardly know what Yoga is."

He had been rebuked by fellow Indians for so forcefully

expressing his opinions. "India," he rejoined, "will never get anywhere until it lives by the truth—and is not afraid to hear it."

Although the meditations become intriguing in time, many will prefer to discover Yoga—and themselves— through the physical exercises exclusively. They will find that the simplest exercises will not only be the easiest to remember, but will have the most saultary effect. In six months, I had not attempted such complex postures as the Tortoise, Peacock, or Scorpion. There were so many others that I could do with little practice that it seemed absurd to waste time on contortions, especially when the simpler exercises would confer similar benefits.

I worked out a pattern of my own—a series of exercises which seemed to yield the most for the least energy. After three and a half months of exercises I had developed a simple routine, which I recapitulate for the beginner wishing a ready reference. I began with two or three repetitions of the twelve-phase Sun exercise, good old Suryanamaskar, visualizing the rhythm as I worked. Then I went to the Pump, slowly raising each leg five or six times, pulling each leg back, hands behind the knee for additional stress. I did several warm-ups, generally preferring torso twists, or the side bend, and it was these tune-ups, together with the shoulder stand, which slimmed my thirty-four waist to a college-trim thirty-two.

Lying down, hunching up the knees, I would swing them to one side, twisting from the waist toward the other side. Another favorite, oddly, was that recommended for teen-agers with menstrual problems. Standing, I would bend from the hips, bringing one hand down to the opposite foot, the other arm meanwhile reaching for the sky.

After the neck rolls, which had erased all lines and circles from my neck, I would do the shoulder stand. I could raise myself easily on my shoulders for five minutes now, holding my feet perfectly still, and making my back straight. From this position I would bring back each leg separately, my hands supporting my back, and then bring both legs together, touching the mat behind me with my toes. This was the Plough, an exercise Yogi Vithaldas had recommended for those who wanted to stay sexually young.

To reverse the muscle pull, stretching contracted muscles, I doubled back on my heels, drawing back on my palms, arching the spine as I thrust the pelvis out. After holding the Pelvic Stretch for fifteen or twenty seconds, I shifted my weight from my hands to my elbows, bringing my head almost back to the mat in a variation of the Fish. I realized how much progress I had made when I recalled that at the outset I could not even slip back on my elbows.

I then went into a series of back stretches—the Cobra, Locust, Bow, and Swan, which was the Cobra with the knees up—finishing up the Swan with the Chinese ancestor worship posture, back on my haunches, a position of obeisance. I did the Cobra five or six times, feeling the successive stretch in each ridge of the vertebrae, to a rising count of nine, three for the head and neck, three for the chest, three for the lower spine, descending in the same rhythm, lower spine down first.

I put new emphasis on the exercises, visualizing them as they should be properly done, and, surprisingly, soon achieving the visualized state in reality. In the Locust, I had hardly been able to get both feet off the ground together in the beginning; I could now raise my legs almost perpendicularly, with my hands underneath my hips, and feel the flow of blood to the head. It was a great tonic for the entire pelvic girdle.

I found the forward bends relaxing from a semi-Lotus posture. With one foot comfortably bent back into the crotch, I would sit erect and then, bending from the hips, reach out for the opposite foot, angled away from my body. In time, I had become so limber that I could not only touch my toes and hang on for a few moments, rocking back and forth to accentuate the back stretch, but could lower my face to my knees. This was Paschimothanasana, the sitting forward bend.

I was then ready for the preliminaries to the headstand, cradling my head in my hands and walking bent over toward my hands as far as I could. The Cobra, forward bend, and the shoulder-stand back—all strengthening the back— were preparing me for the supreme endeavor.

My Crow was my one posture in the difficult classification. As I saddled my knees on my elbows, in a bent-over position, I could feel the strength building up in shoulders, arms, and chest. But even more important, as Marcia reminded me, was the mind-and-body union fostered by my rapt concentration. "Nobody," as Marcia pointed out, "can think of their unpaid bills and do the Crow."

Then came the alternate breathing, and relaxation, in which I almost automatically lost myself in meditation. I had temporarily discontinued the Kapalabhati, the pranayama breathing exercise marked by staccato expulsions of air from the diaphragm. Perhaps because I was not doing it properly, it seemed irritating to my bronchial areas. I suggest this exercise not be attempted without supervision. (But I later went back to it, with good effect.)

When I had time, I did the stomach lift, rolling my abdominal muscles up five or six times as my lungs remained empty. And I also did the Blade, knifing my shoulder blades back nine or ten times, imagining them pinching a dime, as I held my arms out straight and immovable. I felt immediately relaxed with these simple exercises; and the stomach lift, I found, was great for slimming the abdominal area below the waist—getting rid of the paunch.

This session took from thirty to forty minutes, varying with the rest periods. The beginning student, depending on age, will have to bear with aches, pains, and cramps for the first two or three weeks, and taking cognizance of these aches, should perhaps reduce his schedule. It is possible to overdo with even Yoga, if one adheres too closely to a fixed regimen at the start.

"Each individual is his own best judge," Marcia stressed, "of how fast he can proceed."

Uniquely, Yoga stretched every joint area from the top of the spine to the toes, giving the vital connective tissue the pliancy of youth. As I stretched, striving to bring hand to toe, or face to knee, I could feel my mind force straining with my ligaments and muscles. I found a new understanding of how my body reacted under pressure, and with this understanding came acceptance by body of mind and mind of body. There was a sympathetic response between the two, with the relaxed muscles inevitably conditioning the mind to relax with it. I had always thought of the mind relaxing or tensing the body, and now I discovered, through Yoga, that the reverse was equally true. A two-way interchange had been established.

This, I feel, is the principal distinction between Hatha Yoga and calisthenics—a different method and a different purpose. There are other differences and some similarities. Only Yoga preaches discipline through immobility. In holding a posture for five or six minutes, or even three or four, the student can almost feel the union between mind and body crystallizing.

Some calisthenics, of course, feature physical and mental concentration. Taking students through a body-building, weight-lifting course at his Rockefeller Center health club, physical culturist Harold J. Reilly invariably stressed, "Work slowly and think the exercise through."

Actually, this was an adaptation of the Yoga concept. But there was still a subtle difference in purpose that made the weight-lifting mechanistic, and the Yoga almost intuitive, tapping hidden channels of the mind.

Yoga is more efficient working with gravity; there is less wasted movement and more balance; muscles are strengthened and stamina is developed for the broad purpose of standing up to life, not standing up to weights or horizontal bars. Even if an exercise is not successfully completed, the concentrated effort toward fulfillment rewards the student with a resulting rapport between mind and body. And with a streamlined system, designed expressly for specific body areas, the Yoga student expends far less energy than he would with calisthenics; additional rewards are reaped by those who don't have that much energy to spread around. "I get more out of a few simple Yoga exercises," Manhattan restaurateur Richard Sheresky told me, "than I do with forty-five minutes of calisthenics."

Many teachers, adjusting to a different culture, give a modified Yoga. Manhattan's Madam Delakova, schooled by Israel's Feldenkrais, saw little point, for instance, to holding the headstand and shoulder stand for the ten minutes advocated by many Indian yogis. "The original purpose of some exercises has been lost in method," Madam Delakova observed.

"Some yogis stressed complete withdrawal for withdrawal's sake. For the more volatile Western temperament, we counsel withdrawal for renewal and participation—and we replace the stress on immobility with a controlled mobility, disciplining muscles to work independently of each other."

I finally got around to the headstand, and wondered how I ever considered it a problem. Six months after my first Yoga lessons, Madam DeVries put me through a testing workout at Nyack. I needed a little help getting my legs up at first, but once up, was able to balance for a minute with ease. "Once the student has achieved control," she observed, "the exercises become effortless; it doesn't matter what you do, only how you do it."

Marcia's teacher, the Swami Vishnudevananda, stood his students on their heads for ten minutes when they were sufficiently advanced, but Marcia—and Madam DeVries—had found that three minutes would convey all the benefits their students could reasonably absorb. At Concord I did five or six minutes of the shoulder stand once, just for the psychological lift it gave me, the Western zest for achievement being what it was.

But fundamentally, I was trained in the new style Yoga for the twentieth century—for the volatile Westerner caught up in the nuclear age, seeking some respite from worry, boredom, and frustration in martinis and promiscuity, wondering when the bomb will come and telling himself that he doesn't really care. It was a world that found it hard to pay more than lip service to God, and which when it thought of God at all, thought of Him as some impersonal stranger completely detached from a universe He had set into motion.

It was pleasant, I found, to meditate on God and the universe, and to think of Him as being inherent in everything we saw, heard, or felt. It was pleasant to think of Him as being at the heart of everything I did—of being the wellspring of body, mind, and spirit. It was also pleasant to exercise, feeling that the exercise was a sort of ritual, almost an acknowledgment of the hoped-for union with God and the universe.

Marcia was quite pleased with my new introspection and with my exercises. Indeed, she was rather surprised, since I had made such a poor beginning, physically, had hurt myself in an unfortunate neck twist, and then pulled a hip in an unrelated accident. It could not be said that I had had the easiest time. In my three and a half months with Marcia, I had exactly one hundred lessons—the equivalent of a two-year course with a regulation once-a-week lesson. I was not the best student in the world, but I am sure that no student felt better.

It had been an experience fraught with misgivings, marked with pain and the intrusion of personal problems, and it had been capped with a feeling of glorious rapport between my guru and myself. I took my leave of the Concord ashram with some sorrow. I would go on to a new teacher, nearer my New York home, but I would never have another guru. There could be only one real guru in a student's life—the teacher that had reshaped and remolded his outlook, personality, and physique. I did not fully accept reincarnation, yet I felt somehow as though I had been reborn.

"In the old days," Marcia said with a warm smile, "the guru demanded complete obedience and devotion, and in return would take on complete responsibility for the student. But if man is innately divine, he has the ability within

himself to be his own master. All the teacher has done is
guide him to himself."

And so we shook hands and parted, not good-bye, but
farewell. And whenever I thought of Emerson, Thoreau,
and Alcott, of bandhas, Karma Yoga, and good old Suryanamaskar, then, too, would I think of my guru back in
Concord. May the good Lord Krishna bless her and carry
her back one day to the land of her dreams, where she
stood before and will stand again—on the ridge of the
Himalayas looking down on her beloved India.

As for me, as my guru had said, I was on my own, detached and disciplined, confident and unafraid. For the first
time in my life I felt myself in harmony with the universe
around me. It was a good feeling.

APPENDIX

Rarely does a student fit into the "convenient" training tables, six-week courses, or "easy to follow" routines laid out in books. Yet guidance and a schedule are helpful and even necessary in the beginning. Therefore, we suggest specific basic exercises laid out in orderly sequence—for the beginner, the intermediate student, the advanced and specialized. After a while, he will learn through experience the exercises he individually needs and is capable of performing to greatest advantage.

In our training pages he can pick out whatever exercises he is up to, gradually working in more exercises to ever increasing counts. In knowing how strenuously to bend, twist, or stretch, for example, it is not a question of how many minutes or seconds are considered "safe" but rather of a cultivation of sensitivity so that one can judge for himself how far to go and when to stop. No teacher can feel another's pain threshold nor gauge subtle conditioning factors based on body chemistry, glandular balance, nervous coordination, and emotional environment.

By getting to know his own capacity, the student achieves one great aim of Yoga, self-knowledge.

Students should begin each exercise session with preliminary "warming-up" exercises, choosing those that suit them best as they get to know more about their individual capacity and need. These can be alternated for the sake of variety and over-all body coverage, and can be added to, or interspersed through the asanas, as the student progresses. Flexing is done from time to time, during the main exercises, to loosen muscles that have contracted during holding postures. Just as the Pump, limbering the hips, prepares for the headstand and shoulder stand, so, too, do the neck rolls frequently follow these postures to ease tautness.

Many conditioning exercises are adaptations of classical asanas (postures) requiring yogi-like deliberation and control. Because of the specific effect on the system, the teacher and the student can often spot weak, or potentially weak, points in his physique and psyche.

Simple though they may seem, many of these exercises are therapeutic. Together with the asanas, they tend to alleviate, or even cure, conditions as varied as constipation, gas pains, sunken chest, round shoulders, nasal drip, fallen arches, sciatica, bursitis, menstrual disorders, aching back, and aching psyche. Ancient authorities, sounding like modern-day admen, were fond of extolling the virtue of each separate position as a specific for dysfunctions ranging from death to dyspepsia. They even put emphasis on enhancement of sexual health, and just as subtly. Nowadays, with emotional instability and tension so much of a problem, there is a new emphasis in the West on the integration of body and mind as a whole. Essentially, though, Yoga is more of a preventive system, designed to make the subnormal normal, and the normal supernormal. Nevertheless, its principles are sufficiently sound to help almost anybody capable of being helped.

The "warm-ups" are not only useful before strenuous exercising but as a test of readiness. People getting on in years or who have been ill may very well experiment at first with the conditioning exercises. It will give them—and the instructor—an idea of how much they can do in the beginning.

Movements like the hand-clenching require more visualization and concentration than muscle, making them ideal for people limited physically. In more advanced Yoga, the secret of all true meditation is the power to visualize. Visual thinking becomes autosuggestive and facilitates contact with the unconscious.

Although Yoga students have been accused of "loving their bodies too much," the ultimate purpose is to make the body a humble but effective servant of the mind and soul. Therefore the true yogi never shows off. When headstands or shoulder stands or other dramatic postures seem inappropriate, the less unobtrusive conditioners may be suitable. Some can be done conveniently during coffee breaks or while waiting in a car or hanging on a telephone. Who knows but that one day an "oxygen cocktail," served up by rhythmical deep breathing, will be more revivifying than its alcoholic counterpart?

Stretching exercises are particularly helpful in relieving nervous tension, since all stretching is inherently tranquilizing. (All animals, unless alarmed, will stretch the first thing on rising.) Many people have become so emotionally and physically repressed, constricted, and inhibited that they cannot profit by ordinary exercise, calisthenics, dancing, or housework until they learn *how* to move with inner awareness and harmony. Attitudes of body often affect attitudes of mind.

Tensing exercises, contracting and strengthening the

muscles, are additionally effective because of their emphasis on breath control. Paradoxically, they help tense people
relax, since *controlled* tension often seems to lead to a similarly controlled letting-go. Stressing resistance, isometric
exercises, now enjoying a vogue, are yogic in principle and
excellent for people unable to tense in more imaginative
ways. However, they do not, as a rule, expand muscles
before contracting them, as Yoga does in attaining highest
efficiency.

Rhythmic bends and twists increase mobility of limbs,
stretching ligaments, lubricating joints, and creating a
supple, flexible spine. The yogis say that pressure on nerves
caused by subtle misalignments, and vertebral maladjustments, are often relieved. Gentle flowing motions synchronized with breathing obviously improve circulation and
coordination.

As a prelude to difficult postures, the balancing exercises
require the student's complete attention. In time, the habit
of concentration generally makes it easier to focus attention inside or outside oneself. The greater the concentration, the greater the mind's control over the body.

Whatever conditioners are selected, like the postures
they should never be overdone, with ease and comfort the
constant criterion. Spontaneity within limits and easeful
exertion are to be cultivated as a measure of inner grace
and poise. If, after some five or six weeks, the effort is not
to some extent enjoyable, the exercises are perhaps being
wrongly performed. In Yoga, one attaches even more importance to the means than the end. That is why they are
so often the same. It is not at all necessary to be graceful.
Feeling graceful is quite enough for the start. But even the
most awkward, unassured student can become graceful as
control, technique, and rhythm improve—as they will with
practice.

YOGA WARM-UPS

		Page
1.	Chest Expander	265
2.	Cat Stretch	265
3.	The Pendulum	266
4.	The Hugging Exercise	267
5.	Invisible Wings	267
6.	The Pulley	268
7.	Knee Presses	269
8.	Knee Squeeze	270
9.	Shoulder Squeeze	270
10.	Arm Lift	271
11.	The Flower	271
12.	The Roots	272
13.	Rock 'n' Rolls	273
14.	The Pump	274
15.	Neck Rolls	276
16.	Finger Flexing	277
17.	Ankle Bends	277
18.	Rippling the Back	278
19.	Rippling the Arms	278
20.	The Fountain	279
21.	One-Leg Stands	280
22.	Angle Balance	280
23.	The Rooster	281
24.	The Stork	281

STRETCHING

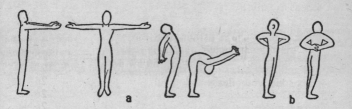

1. *Chest Expander* (An Instant Invigorator)

   a. Standing, first touch palms, arms extended forward, then bring arms slowly back to shoulder level, opening the chest box. Then clasp hands behind back, arms straight down.

   Inhale deeply, pulling shoulders back. Retain breath, bend forward, raise arms high over head.

   Exhale. Return to original position.

   Repeat up to three times.

   b. Clasp hands behind back.

   Swing arms slowly from one side to the other, twisting from hips.

This is a quick energizer, filling lungs with air, stimulating circulation to head and heart, loosening tense muscles of back and shoulders. In men's classes it is commonly called "chest expander," in women's the "bust builder." All movements must be done slowly.

2. *Cat Stretch*

   a. Kneel on hands and knees so that back is parallel to floor, arms and legs perpendicular like legs of a table, palms forward.

Inhale and slowly lower chest, trying to rest neck on floor. Variation: Pointing fingers inward, tips touching, repeat as before.

Hold five to ten seconds.

Exhale and return to kneeling position, humping back like an angry cat, sucking stomach up toward spine, then relax spine and release abdomen.

Repeat twice.

b. In "table position"—on hands and knees, back straight —inhale and raise right leg, stretching it back and up so that pull is felt all along spine. Keep head high. Bring leg forward and try to press doubled-up knee against chest while exhaling.

Repeat on other side.

c. Practice as in (b) except that on bringing leg forward knee is pressed against forehead.

The cat stretch was given Marcia by her obstetrician after the birth of her first child. While designed specifically to relieve pressure on inner organs and return uterus to normal position, it is also a wonderful back strengthener and apparently effective in alleviating "female complaints." If there is difficulty lowering chest to the ground it is usually a sign that the student's posture needs to be improved. Catlike neck stretch also firms sagging jaw lines.

3. *The Pendulum*

a. Stand erect. Inhale and bend forward, allowing arm to swing back and forth like a pendulum in front of you, fingers just missing floor.

Inhale deeply and straighten body, swinging arm up and stretching it behind you at shoulder level. Other hand rests on waist. Hold briefly, exhale, and relax.

Repeat on other side.

b. Repeat as in (a) except that two arms together swing down in pendulum and then up over head for backward stretch.

This exercise is given specifically for bursitis but it strengthens the whole back and shoulder region and improves posture.

CREATIVE VISUALIZATION

4. The Hugging Exercise

Visualize the air as an almost palpable, light-filled substance more necessary for survival than food, money, or shelter. In kneeling position stretch out arms and try to draw in as much of this precious essence as you can grasp. Inhale, reaching out for oxygen in every direction, clasping it to bosom and stretching out for more. Endeavor to feel desirous to absorb and assimilate all the air you can encompass with two arms. The more you simulate Bernhardt or Barrymore, the more energizing air you will get.

5. Invisible Wings

Sit on heels with head bent forward to the floor, arms resting limply in front of head. Slowly arch the back, inhale profoundly, and raise up to a kneeling position, tipping head back and bringing arms up and out at the sides in a gesture of unfolding. Imagine your arms to be wings with feathers extending about a foot beyond the finger tops, spreading like the wings of a bird taking flight. Hold a few seconds and then very gradually return to original resting position while exhaling. If this is performed slowly and aspiringly, once is enough.

Many people (especially those of more mature years) seem too inhibited and self-encapsulated even to stretch properly. Simply telling them to stretch does little good, but once a familiar picture is drawn, responsive action may follow spontaneously.

TENSING

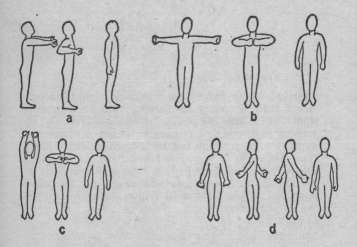

a

b

c

d

6. *The Pulley* (An Instant Invigorator)

a. Inhale and extend arms straight out in front at shoulder level.

Clench fists, palms upward, and tense upper part of body. Retaining breath, force clenched fists slowly toward chest as though pulling with utmost strength upon a heavy weight. This is really isometric.

Release, exhaling with a sigh and dropping arms into a relaxed position at sides.

b. Repeat, extending arms to the sides.

c. Repeat, extending arms straight up over the head.

d. Repeat with arms down, clenching and turning from the waist but with hips and pelvis facing forward.

These tensing positions develop lung power, squeezing the retained air deep into lung areas ordinarily unused. Beginners may become dizzy from overdose of oxygen. This is a cue not to overdo. Variation (d) requires special caution, as it can make one quite giddy if the breath is held. Breathe rhythmically.

a   b   c   d

7. *Knee Presses*

a. Lie flat on back. Inhale and double up knee, pulling it back hard against chest with both hands.

Hold five to ten seconds.

Exhale slowly and drop leg back to floor.

Repeat on other side.

Repeat, pulling up both legs at once.

b. Lie flat on back. Inhale and pull up knee, pressing it against forehead. Try to hold from ten to thirty seconds.

Exhale and relax in prone position.

Repeat, pulling up other knee.

Repeat, pulling up both knees.

In Sanskrit this is known as Vatayanasana, which means "wind-relieving pose." It does wonders to banish stomach gas and constipation, and is a boon to aching backs. Variation (b) strengthens abdominal muscles and neck.

c. Lie on back, placing hands palms down on top of upper legs. Inhale, raising head and shoulders as far off the floor as (but no farther than) midpoint of upper back. Retaining breath, push hands down toward knees and hold ten to twenty seconds.

Exhale, lie back, and relax.

d. Repeat as in (c) except that feet are raised about three inches off floor.

Stomach, neck, and back are all firmed up without a great expenditure of energy. People with weak backs receive adequate support from the floor.

One student who had suffered years from a vaguely aching back found this one particular position, head and legs up, to be most helpful of all in easing pain and tension.

8. *Knee Squeeze*

Sit on floor, exhale, drawing knees up to chest and pulling them in as far as possible with back held erect. Inhale deeply, and continuing to press knees firmly against chest, extend arms wide apart at shoulder level in broad sweep. Try not to let back slump.

Exhale and relax.

9. *Shoulder Squeeze* (or Blade)

In seated or standing position, arms straight out at shoulder level, draw shoulder blades in together as though pressing a coin between them. Hold tightly and release. The arms themselves are not moved, except by the motion of the shoulders.

Repeat five to ten times.

Do not allow arms and shoulders to wobble up and down. Shoulder blades knife only toward one another and then back.

Exercise (8) will firm up legs and lower back while (9) will do the same for neck, upper back, and pectoral muscles.

10. *Arm Lift*

Raise arms shoulder level, bend elbows, and bring hands back to shoulders, palms up; then slowly raise palms as high as possible with a slow, resistant lift. Then return hands to position on shoulders. Repeat one to five times, then bend over from pelvis and swing arms to increase circulation. This exercise is particularly effective in firming flabby underarms.

11. *The Flower*

Clench fists with thumb outside fingers, imagining them tight hard buds of late winter. Visualize the golden life force rising from the heart, pushing through the arms and up into the hands, loosening the resistant fingers like sap in the awakening spring. As fingers slowly open up, they curve back from knuckles in petal-like symmetry, expanding gradually as though the pulsing energy was forcing them into full bloom. It should require a full minute for fingers to spread wide in a complete stretch. Then for one more minute visualize the vital energy withdrawing, so that the petals fold, the flower fades, fingers relax and return to original position.

This exercise stimulates circulation in arthritic joints and is recommended for people who use their hands in massaging and healing work. If steady tension and concentration are maintained, enough power is generated for a good sweat.

Some with calcification in joints and knuckles may find it difficult at first. They should proceed gingerly in the beginning.

12. *The Roots*

Stand with feet solidly apart (about two feet) and press toes down hard. (This exercise is best done barefooted on the ground.) Breathe deeply and imagine that your body is like a tree with unseen roots extending far down to suck up the earth's own vital life currents. Feel these forces rising up legs and spine into the head and uniting the space around you with the earth below through the medium of your body. Raise arms and stretch high over head.

Curiously, some people find that this exercise makes them more appreciative of the life power in flowers and trees; it is intended to develop sensitivity to the inner self and its relation to nature.

FLEXING

13. *Rock 'n' Rolls* (Instant Invigorators)

a. *Beginners*
Lie on back. Raise knees and clasp with fingers inter-
locked behind upper legs. Gently rock back and forth
on rounded spine until sense of ease and rhythm is
attained. Feel roundness of back and shoulders and the
massaging action of the spine. Beware rolling back too
far on neck in the beginning.

b. *Intermediate*
Sit on floor, cross legs, grasp right toe with left hand
and left toe with right hand. Lower head to floor in front
without raising buttocks, feet on floor. Keeping grip on
toes, rock all the way back onto shoulders so that hands
and toes touch floor over the head. Hold briefly and return to initial sitting position with hands still holding feet.
Repeat five or more times until the body feels energized
and the muscles supple.

c. *Advanced*
Sit erect with feet outstretched. Bend forward and touch
toes. Rock back on rounded spine, holding arms and legs
out straight until toes touch floor over head (as in
Plough position). Coming forward, thrust head down
between outstretched legs, trying to touch floor with forehead. Repeat five or more times.

The Rock 'n' Rolls are not only warm-ups, but strengthen
and coordinate the whole body while massaging the neck
and spine.

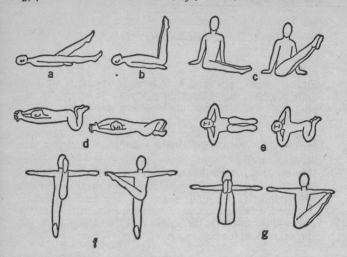

14. *The Pump* (Leg Raising and Stretching)

a. *Alternate Leg Raising*

Lie down and press small of back against floor so all
movements will proceed from center of back without
straining stomach muscles.

Inhale, and raise one leg high, keeping whole back flat
on floor and rest of the body relaxed. Move leg very
slowly and with continuous stretching as though in trac-
tion. Beginners invariably move spasmodically, jerking
up the knee, straining their faces, and letting the leg fall
back as though they had dropped it.

Repeat five to ten times on each side, alternating legs,
and breathing increasingly slowly and deeply.

With proper concentration and control this conditioner becomes an efficient way of pumping fresh blood through the
body. Performed with slow rhythm it tends to quiet nervousness.

b. *Both-Leg Raising*

Lying, inhale and raise both legs together, hands at
sides. Hold briefly. Exhale and relax. Repeat, working
up to ten or more repetitions.

When not carried beyond the point of strain, this version advances the benefits of (a) and flattens and strengthens abdominal region.

c. *Side Leg Raising*

Sitting, inhale and raise both legs three inches off the floor, hands down at sides. Swing legs together as far as possible to the right, maintaining an even distance from floor. Then raise both legs to the right as high as possible. Hold briefly. Exhale, and lower legs, keeping them on the far right. Swing back to center, and repeat on other side. Three times on each side is usually enough for this super "pump," sometimes known as "the gut buster." It firms up legs, hips, thighs, adds suppleness to strength.

d. *Knees to Side* (Feet Flat)

Lying on back, clasp hands well back over head and bend knees upward, keeping soles of feet flat on floor. Press both knees down to the floor on the right, simultaneously turning head in opposite direction to the left, so that a gentle but complete twisting is felt all along the spine. Slowly reverse position, bringing knees down on left and turning head to the right. Be sure shoulders remain on floor. Repeat three or more times on each side.

This is an ideal exercise for beginners and older people. It gives maximum stretch with minimum strain, with a safe and gentle sidewise twist relaxing muscles all along the spine and neck.

e. *Knees to Side* (Doubled Up)

With hands clasped behind head inhale and raise knees up against the chest. Exhale and lower them together, still doubled up to the floor on the right. Repeat on left side. Then swing knees across from side to side with a slow-breathing rhythm. Keep shoulders pressed flat against the floor so that extra stretch is felt in waist and thighs.

f. *Side Stretches* (Alternate Legs)

Lie on back with arms extended out from sides. Inhale and raise right leg as high as it will go. Swing right leg slowly across to the left and down, trying to touch fingers of outstretched left hand (on floor) with toes of right foot. Keep shoulders pressed flat against floor. Hold briefly, exhale, and return to original position. Repeat with left leg. No need for discouragement if toe doesn't connect with fingers. The important thing is to stretch and strengthen the back.

g. Repeat as above, using both legs together.

LUBRICATING THE EXTREMITIES

15. *Neck Rolls*

Allow head to droop forward. Inhale, raise, and turn as far as possible to the right. Hold five seconds. Exhale and return to center.

Repeat on left side.

Repeat, looking up diagonally, first right, then left.

Repeat, bringing head straight back, then lowering to chest.

Inhale, and on one breath, lifting neck high, slowly rotate head all the way around, allowing it to hang down in front, to the right, in back, and to the left. Do not turn just the face but allow head itself to relax and droop like a lily on a stem. Beginners and people who have had neck injuries will need to place hands firmly on neck for extra support.

Repeat, rotating in reverse direction.

The neck exercises may be repeated three or four times if necessary, until tensed muscles really begin to loosen up. If an unpleasant gritty sound is heard in neck, the exercise should be faithfully pursued until head revolves smoothly as though on ball bearings. Practice at odd moments, especially during prolonged desk work. Properly done, "necking" will relieve stiffness and tension in the neck and upper back.

16. *Finger Flexing*

a. Stretch arms straight out at sides, extending fingers. Rotate wrists first one way and then the other so that whole arm turns from shoulder. Repeat ten to twenty times fast.

As with neck rolls, a crunching or gritty sound will often attest to the need for limbering up in this area. A general toner-upper and tension reducer.

Stretch and press each finger in turn down toward palm of hand, trying to keep others extended.

This helps to keep hands young and flexible-looking, discourages stiff and knobby joints.

17. *Ankle Bends*

a. In standing position roll onto right outer edges of the soles of both feet. Simultaneously, break knees to the right, keeping hips and pelvis forward.

Repeat on left side.

Repeat three times on both sides.

Raise right foot and rotate from the ankle both ways as though drawing circles with toes. Repeat with left foot.

Excellent conditioners for skiing and skating, fortifying vulnerable ankles against twists and sprains. Also helpful for swollen ankles, helping faulty circulation. Improves general sense of well-being in lower extremities.

CREATIVE VISUALIZATION

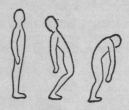

18. *Rippling the Back*

Stand erect with arms at sides. Allow knees to buckle forward. Bring pelvis forward, then stomach and chest, and finally the head, all with a loose undulating movement. Allow the head to come forward, but not too suddenly at first.

While practicing, visualize the inner energies flowing up the spinal column successively affecting each vertebra. It should stir up some psychic energy.

19. *Rippling the Arms*

Stand erect, arms extended at sides. Raise one elbow, elevating shoulder, and allow other elbow and shoulder to droop down. Hands remain at same level. Reverse positions with same undulating snakelike motions as above, but imagine energies flowing out horizontally through arms, instead of vertically.

Promotes coordination and rhythm, and is fun besides.

BALANCING

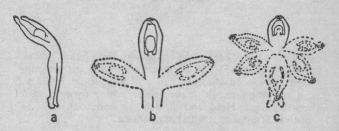

a b c

20. *The Fountain* (Instant Invigorator)

a. Inhale, stretching the whole body upward, reaching arms as high as possible over the head. Continue to stretch and hold, pulling up all along the spine. If possible, rise up on balls of feet and balance.

Exhale and relax in normal standing position.

b. Inhale, rise on toes (not too high), and hook together thumbs of upstretched hands.

Retain breath and bend as far as possible to left and right.

Exhale, lower arms, and relax.

c. Inhale, press forward onto toes, and on one retained breath rotate upper part of body in a full circle stretching from the waist. Exhale and relax.

Repeat, rotating in opposite direction.

a   b   c   d

21. *One-Leg Stands*

a. Stand erect. Catch right ankle with right hand. Inhale, pulling right foot up in back and extending left arm upward. Advanced students can pull leg far up in back, still catching foot with hand, and reaching forward with opposite arm. Hold and stretch leg and back only as much as is consistent with easy balance.

Repeat on left side.

b. Repeat, stretching just one leg back with both arms forward, balancing first on one leg and then on the other. In advanced version, body forms a T.

c. Inhale, and raise leg in front, catching hold of ankle or toes and pulling up. Both knees should be straight. Maintain pull and balance five to ten seconds, or as long as possible without hopping about.

d. Repeat as in (c), raising leg to side.

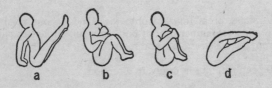

a   b   c   d

22. *Angle Balance*

a. Sit with legs extended, fairly close together, palms down on floor. Lean back slightly and raise legs together, balancing on end of spine for ten to thirty seconds.

b. Hold posture (a) with hands folded on chest.

c. Hold posture with knees doubled against chest.

d. Hold with legs out straight, hands grasping toes and bringing head to knee.

CREATIVE VISUALIZATION

23. *The Rooster*

Inhale, rise up on both toes with outstretched hands, and balance for ten seconds.

Repeat and try to balance ten seconds with eyes closed.

Repeat with closed eyes but visualize an imaginary landscape or tree or some vertical object and see if this helps in balancing. Closed-eye exercises should at first be done only with an instructor.

24. *The Stork*

Inhale and stand on foot with opposite knee bent back so that foot is knee-level from floor.

Balance ten seconds.

Try to repeat with closed eyes.

Repeat again with imaginary landscape or object of reference.

These eyes-shut exercises often reflect the efficiency of the sensory system and the cerebellum. They are usually much more difficult for older people. But they have been practiced safely by people with heart conditions, chronic degenerative disorders, or disabilities ruling out strenuous movements. These individuals often have difficulty with the extremities and may be benefited by the muscle contractions these positions necessitate.

BASIC YOGA POSTURES
(WITH VARIATIONS)

		Page
1.	Sun Salutation (Suryanamaskar)	285
2.	Headstand (Sirshasana)	287
3.	Shoulder Stand (Sarvangasana)	290
4.	The Bridge (Sethu Bandhasana)	291
5.	The Fish (Matsyasana)	292
6.	The Plough (Halasana)	293
7.	Forward Bend (Sitting) (Paschimothanasana)	293
8.	Head-Knee Pose (Janu Sirasana)	295
9.	Shooting Bow Pose (Akarna Dhanurasana)	296
10.	The Inclined Plane (Katikasana)	297
11.	The Cobra (Bhujangasana)	297
12.	The Swan (Swandasana)	298
13.	The Locust (Salabhasana)	298
14.	The Bow (Dhanurasana)	299
15.	Pelvic Stretch (Supta Vajrasana)	300
16.	The Wheel (Chakrasana)	301
17.	Leg Split (Anjaneyasana)	302
18.	The Twist (Ardha Matsyendrasana)	303
19.	The Crow (Kakasana)	304
20.	The Peacock (Mayurasana)	305
21.	The Cock (Kukutasana)	306
22.	The Scorpion (Vrischikasana)	306
23.	The Tree (Vrikshasana)	307
24.	Toe Balance (Padandgushtasana)	307
25.	Knee Stretch (Bhadrasana)	308
26.	Frog Pose (Mandukasana)	308
27.	Cow Head Pose (Gomukhasana)	309
28.	Lion Pose (Simhasana)	309
29.	Triangle Posture (Trikonasana)	309
30.	Deep Lunge (Sirangusthasana)	310
31.	Eagle Pose (Garudasana)	311
32.	Forward Bend (Standing) (Padahasthasana)	311
33.	Sitting Postures Adaptable for Pranayama and Meditation	312
	a. Easy Posture (Sukhasana)	312
	b. Kneeling Posture (Vajrasana)	312
	c. Ankle Lock (Swastikasana)	312
	d. Perfect Posture (Siddhasana)	312
	e. The Lotus (Padmasana)	313
34.	The Sponge (Relaxation) (Savasana)	313
35.	Eye Exercises	314

BASIC YOGA POSTURES

The classic Yoga postures of India are called asanas (first syllable accented). Their main purpose is development of inner power and control through habituating the body to various modes of immobility. The aim of this discipline is not listless passivity but rather an increase and conscious possession of vital forces.

The English word "exercise" implies something strenuous, an exertion, with the prefix "ex-" denoting projection out into action. Asana means just the opposite, not so much exercise as "innercise," a condition of balanced tension achieved with minimum movement and expenditure of energy.

The asanas in this section are representative of the 840,000 poses mentioned in the *Yoga Shastras*, of which eighty-seven are considered basic. As the student advances he will find the postures simplified. In the beginning extensive warming up is necessary and students move apace from one position into another, seemingly covering much ground. Later each stance is held longer and requires less preliminary adjustment until just a few asanas faithfully practiced each day insure radiant health.

There is a certain internal logic in the sequence of postures. The curving segments of the spine—cervical, thoracic, lumbar, and sacral—are systematically flexed and strengthened, every joint is mobilized, ligament stretched, organ and gland toned up through scientifically applied pressure on certain vital anatomical regions, promoting adequate circulation of blood throughout the body. Gradually the system is conditioned to increasingly strenuous demands. Then comes a tapering-off period with sitting postures which facilitate deep breathing. A final long relaxing, while lying flat on the back, replenishes inner reserves and allows time to assimilate benefits of exercises and experience a meaningful re-creation of the entire personality. Many will find it quite natural to eventually proceed on into meditation and higher aspects of Yoga.

1. *Sun Salutation* (*Suryanamaskar*)

a. Stand erect, hands folded with palms joined in front of chest. Collect yourself and think of the sun as the eternal source of light and power. Know also that you can release the radiations of your own internal sun shining forth from the heart center.

b. Inhale, raising arms high and bending back from the waist.

c. Exhale, bending forward with straight knees, and touch (or try to touch) toes.

d. Inhale, extending right leg back while keeping left foot between hands on ground. Raise head and arch back.

e. Retain breath, extending left leg behind alongside the other so that body forms a straight line resting on outstretched hands and toes.

f. Exhale, resting on floor with feet, knees, chest, hands, and forehead touching. This position is called Sastanganamaskar, meaning that eight parts of the body touch ground.

g. Inhale, pushing chest forward and up, bending back upper half of body (as in the Cobra position).

h. Exhale, raising hips with straight legs and heels pressed flat on floor. Whole body forms a triangle.

i. Inhale, bringing right foot forward, toes on a line with hands. Raise head and arch back as in position (d).

j. Exhale, with hands to toes and head down as in position (c).

k. Inhale, raising arms high over head and bending backward as in position (b).

l. Exhale, lower arms, and relax.

Continue by extending other leg back, alternating rounds. Traditionally this salutation was repeated twelve times (once for each month of the year) at dawn, each time addressing the Lord of the Sun by a different name.

Sometimes a student will practice the Sun exercise for months until suddenly the movements flow together with new fluidity and the whole suddenly flashes into his consciousness as indeed a kind of appreciation.

Those who have not yet arrived at the Sun Salutation may select one of the initial limbering exercises instead, preferably an "instant invigorator." The rocking exercises are particularly beneficial, gently massaging the back, loosening the whole body, yet not fatiguing the novice. But for those who can, the Sun Salutation will contribute the stamina requisite for practice of advanced asanas. The rhythmic alternation of forward and back bending releases tensions and the initial stretching increases muscle efficiency during later contractions. It is possible to work up from one or two to twelve full rounds depending on need. This is fine for insomnia since after twelve or more rounds the victim of sleeplessness is usually grateful for bed.

2. *Headstand* (*Sirshasana*)

Kneel down and clasp hands with fingers lightly inter-
locked on the floor. Back of head rests between hands.
Top of head—not forehead—touches floor, but all the
weight is distributed along the arms and elbows, which
press solidly down. Do *not* allow elbows to fly out at
sides; this is one of the commonest mistakes of beginners
and puts undue strain on neck. Think of arms as forming
a base shaped like a perfect equilateral triangle.

Walk forward, keeping feet on floor, knees straight,
trying to make the back as upright as possible. Head
must not be allowed to buckle under. Then sit up again
and relax. Practice until this balance seems easy and
natural. If dizziness or nausea occurs it is a sign not to
rush things. This "walk-in" is an excellent exercise in
itself, conferring many of the benefits of the headstand.

If the student tends to somersault, this indicates that the
neck and back are not straight, and some preliminary
conditioning will be necessary. Round-shouldered people
have the hardest time, since it takes longer to develop
flexibility than muscle power, but practicing the Cobra
and Bow will build up the requisite pliancy.

As soon as it is possible to support the main weight of
the body on upper arms and elbows, try to pick up feet
keeping knees bent against chest so that the center of
balance is maintained. Do not allow legs to kick out or
up. Make no sudden, abrupt, or jerky movements. If the
student must fling legs up or take a fall, the exercise is
being improperly performed, with inadequate concentration and control. It is seldom necessary or desirable to
use a wall, since anyone who requires external support
is obviously not ready for the final stages anyway.

This most difficult part can be mastered *if* the student
is willing to take it slowly and not try to raise his legs
all the way up until arms and neck can support him in
this midway position. Success requires (a) muscular development of neck and back, (b) flexibility of hips and
shoulders, (c) mental concentration and coordination.
If there is difficulty, one or more of these qualities is
usually lacking and should be developed. Often, forward
bending exercises are indicated to loosen up hip joints.

With knees still bent, raise legs slowly upward. The back is at all times perfectly straight, and only legs move up, rotating from the hips. If any difficulty is now experienced it is probably because previous stages have not yet been mastered. If one is going to fall at all, it should be while the feet are still relatively close to the door and can be brought down quickly and easily, completely relaxed. While the first stage puts demands on shoulders and arms and the second requires suppleness in the hips, this third phase demands strong stomach muscles, usually developed by leg-raising exercises.

Unbend legs completely and balance. Body should be solidly upright without swaying or bending. At the start a friend or teacher can check alignment of spine which should be so straight that a plumb line could be dropped from toe to head. If the back is crooked, nature will automatically adjust and correct it so that ultimately one becomes effortlessly vertical.

The headstand is ordinarily practiced directly after warming up, while body is at peak efficiency. It has a generally invigorating effect. Advanced students sometimes practice it as long as ten minutes, but three minutes, or less will usually prove amply beneficial.

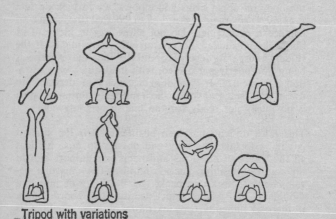

Tripod with variations

HEADSTAND VARIATIONS

Raising and lowering legs alternately and together, spreading legs and pressing together soles of feet, twisting legs around one another, pressing foot to knee, and switching hands to tripod position. When the headstand is done with legs crossed in Lotus posture it is called Oordhwapadmasana.

Children, older people, and those with necks of uncertain strength or round shoulders often are not physically prepared to practice the "classic" headstand given above, but can do very nicely with the version known as the Tripod, or Ben-Gurion, headstand. It gives the same benefits but can be practiced more cautiously, as it was by Israel's doughty elder statesman. Again visualize the triangular foundation of head and two hands. The hands are placed palms down, fingers forward, on the floor at shoulder width. Forearms should be perpendicular to the floor so that it is possible to rest knees on the elbows as in the Crow, and thus gingerly test the ability of this tripod-like base to support the body. Some students find it possible to bring one leg all the way up first and then follow it with the other, skipping the intermediate stage of resting knees on upper arms.

The headstand's benefits are numerous, reminding one that we normally start life head down.

Improves circulation to all parts of body and especially to the brain, stimulating mental powers.

Strengthens back and shoulders, putting the vertebral column into correct alignment.

Coordinates the nervous system and teaches balance.

Relieves pressure on lower back and vital organs, and restores position of vital organs by reversing gravity.

Promotes self-confidence and a sense of inner resourcefulness.

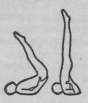

3. *Shoulder Stand (Sarvangasana)*

Lie flat on back, inhale, and raise both legs together *slowly* until whole body attains vertical position with elbows resting on floor and both hands supporting the back. Try to stay as straight as possible, pressing chin against chest. Breathe easily and naturally. Weight is centered on shoulders and back of neck. Beginners tend to wave their feet about aimlessly in the air and usually must make an effort to hold the position motionlessly, allowing gravity to work in their behalf.

Increase gradually to three minutes, and allow another half minute to come down little by little, releasing chin on way down and curving back flat against the floor. In this, as in all asanas, one does not collapse into a disorganized heap but remains self-controlled while returning to the relaxed attitude.

As the posture is practiced, the student will find his lower back strengthening to the point where he can adjust it for perfect straightness.

VARIATIONS

a. Bring one leg down over the head until toe touches the floor. Repeat with other foot, and then with both together. Knees remain straight.

b. Bring both legs down on right side of head. Return to vertical position and then bring them down on left side. Bring both knees down first on right, then on left side. Rest both knees on forehead and hold.

c. Slowly raise arms up along the thighs (inverted torso may have to bend slightly to adjust for balance) and hold. This places additional pressure on neck and shoulder area.

Sarva means "all," anga means "body," and asana is the position. Thus Sarvangasana and its variations serve as an all-purpose energizer, stretching ligaments and muscles of the cervical region, stimulating circulation, strengthening the back, toning abdominal organs, eliminating constipation, and refreshing the mind. It is a particularly salutary weight regulator, equalizing both over- and underweight people because of its stimulating effect on the thyroid. It tends also to build up chest and shoulders and to slim hips.

4. *The Bridge* (*Sethu Bandhasana*)

Although the Bridge is a separate exercise it is often practiced as though it were a variation of the shoulder stand in order to bend upper back in an opposite direction and reverse the stretching effect. It promotes added suppleness and strengthens wrists and stomach.

From the shoulder stand bring down legs one at a time to floor in front. Arms continue to support midback with thumb and fingers spread about waist. Feet remain flat on floor and are extended until knees appear almost straight so that legs and back form an evenly curving arch. Raise legs one at a time and then both together, returning to shoulder stand. Practice until it is possible to switch from the shoulder stand to the Bridge and back again easily.

5. *The Fish* (*Matsyasana*)

Lie on back with legs outstretched. Raise chest off floor, using elbows for support, bending neck backward, and arching upper back to maximum degree so that top of head rests on floor. Palms are down and elbows press against floor, but main weight should be on the buttocks. Hold fifteen to thirty seconds.

VARIATIONS

a. Raise arms, inhaling deeply, and stretch back over head until fingertips touch floor behind. Exhale and bring arms forward again. Repeat three times with breathing. This insures that position is being properly performed with weight on crown of head. Otherwise beginners are apt to rest on elbows with head hanging back loosely and not really touching floor.

b. Cross legs, arching upper back, arms crossed behind head.

c. Hold the Fish with legs crossed in Lotus posture, hands clasping toes and elbows pressing down to touch floor. Keep both buttocks and knees flat on floor as well as head. This is the classic manner of performing the Fish. It may sound impossible, but is relatively simple for anyone proficient in the Lotus.

The Fish can follow the shoulder stand or headstand to give an opposite stretch to neck and upper cervical area. It also stimulates the thyroid gland and alleviates asthma and respiratory complaints. Nearly all the basic Yoga exercises give special attention to the neck, which is considered to be especially important in contributing to good health.

6. *The Plough* (*Halasana*)

Prone on back, arms extended forward, raise legs slowly and inhale, keeping palms pressed down against the floor. Without jerking or bending knees continue to raise hips and back, bringing legs all the way over the head until toes touch the floor behind. Swing arms back and grasp toes. Breathe slowly through nose, pressing chin against chest. Bring legs slowly back to floor, straighten arms, and come to sitting position.

Repeat two or three times or else hold two minutes.

a   b

VARIATIONS
a. In Plough position stretch legs as far apart as possible and hold.
b. Bring knees down beside ears, all the way to the floor if possible. Lock body into position by clasping hands behind knees, with knees touching head. This is known as the Ear-Knee Pose.

The Plough stretches and limbers the entire spine, hips, and legs with minimum energy. It is sometimes called the "hang-over pose" not just because feet are literally hanging over the head but because even when one is feeling indisposed the Plough increases circulation to the brain and clears the mind.

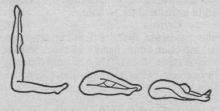

7. *Forward Bend* (*Sitting*) (*Paschimothanasana*)

In sitting position raise arms high over head, stretching spine upward and inhaling deeply almost as though yawning. Try to make the back straight. Exhale and lean forward, catching toes (if possible), and hold. Supple people can crook their first finger around the big toe and bring head down to knees with elbows touching floor. Do not bend knees. Stretch forward from the pelvis without forcing. It is not the acuteness of the angle that counts so much as the act of stretching the whole spinal region, hips, and hamstring muscles of knees. Try deliberately to relax even while stretching to (but not beyond) the border line of pain. Beginners may rock forward gently but advanced students should endeavor to remain as motionless as possible. As in many exercises, beginners will find one side more flexible than the other, and should work toward equalization. This exercise stimulates peristalsis and is almost a specific for constipation.

a and b   c   d

VARIATIONS

a. Spread legs wide apart, reaching both arms first to one big toe and then to the other, and finally catching toes of both outspread legs and leaning forward in the middle. Advanced students will eventually be able to bring face to floor.

b. For extra stretching of leg muscles draw back toes so that feet point straight up rather than out. Underpart of knees rather than hips feel the extra pull.

c. Practice toe-touching while balancing on buttocks, as in Angle Balance (see Conditioning Exercises). Bring forehead to knees and try to hold.

d. Spread legs wide apart, extending arms under knees and reaching back while head and shoulders are lowered to rest on floor in front. This is sometimes given as a separate exercise called the Tortoise (Kurmasana), and gives hips, legs, and pelvis a vigorous toning up.

Forward bending stretches most of the muscles of the body and also massages the visceral region, stimulating kidneys, liver, pancreas, and glands.

8. *Head-Knee Pose* (*Janu Sirasana*)

Sit erect with one leg outstretched, the other bent in toward the body so that the heel fits into the crotch, and sole of foot presses against (not under) the thigh. Gently press knee to floor and feel the loosening of hip joint. Raise arms high above head, inhale (as in previous forward-bending positions), and reaching forward catch toes of extended foot. Pull head down to knee and try to hold a few seconds. Advanced students will be able to touch forehead to knee and press elbows to floor without bending outstretched leg.

Repeat on other side.

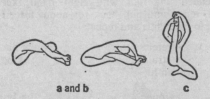

a and b   c

VARIATIONS

a. The extended leg is pointed sideways and body bends from waist to same side with ear angling for the knee. Extra stretch is given to the opposite side of chest and shoulders.

b. Place foot on top of opposite thigh with heel pressing in against the groin and bend forward as in original pose. This gives added pliability to hip joints and is the best preparation for Lotus posture. It also exerts beneficial pressure on abdominal viscera. Change sides and repeat. Advanced students can wrap arm around back and catch toes of bent foot while reaching forward. This gives extra stretch to shoulders and thoracic region.

c. With one heel tucked into crotch, catch other leg in back of knee and pull straight up until knee touches forehead, keeping back as erect as possible. Advanced students will accomplish this by catching hold of toes instead of knee.

9. *Shooting Bow Pose* (*Akarna Dhanurasana*)

In sitting posture, legs extended, reach forward and, spreading thumb around the big toe, clasp the right foot with the left hand. Pull back, bending knee so that toes are drawn up toward left ear. Simultaneously grasp toes of extended left foot with right hand, keeping leg straight, tense, and pull back for about fifteen seconds. Change to other side and repeat.

a   b

VARIATIONS

a. Pull back leg, using hand of same side while other hand clasps toes of extended foot.

b. Pull back as in first variation but straighten bent leg, raising it as high as possible.

The Shooting Bow keeps all the lower joints flexible, stretches thigh muscles, and builds up arms and shoulders.

10. *The Inclined Plane* (*Katikasana*)

Lying on back, the Inclined Plane is performed by raising the whole torso up from shoulders with arms at side, arching back. Weight rests entirely on feet and palms. Hold position with body stiff and straight, pulling spine lengthwise, allowing no sag in the middle. For variation raise first one leg and then the other high off ground. This is not as simple as it may look, but is hard to beat for firming hips, stomach, and thighs.

Although the Inclined Plane may be considered a kind of pelvic stretch it should follow immediately after forward bending exercises in order to reverse the stretching action and remove kinks from the back.

11. *The Cobra* (*Bhujangasana*)

Lie on stomach with palms pressing against floor at shoulder level, fingers forward. Successively raise head, neck, and upper back as far as possible, keeping lower half of body on floor from navel downward. Inhale slowly up, exhale down. Try to feel the snakelike motion of the spine rolling back vertebra by vertebra.

This hood pose may be retained fifteen to thirty seconds or repeated five to ten times synchronized with even breathing. It combines complete stretching of neck, shoulders, and spine.

12. *The Swan* (*Swandasana*)

From the same position as Cobra, bend knees, lift feet
up vertically and arch spine as though to bring head
back to toes. This is called the Swan because of the
lengthening of the neck.

VARIATION

Ride back on knees from straight-armed position of
Swan, sitting on heels, keeping chest and head parallel
to floor in pose simulating Chinese ancestor worship.
Reverse movement to Swan position and repeat slowly.

The Cobra and Swan improve posture, correcting round
shoulders, sunken chest, and maladjustments of spine. They
also firm chin and jaw line, tone up abdominal organs, and
like sitting forward-bending and the shoulder stand, relieve
constipation.

13. *The Locust* (*Salabhasana*)

Lie face down with hands along the sides, palms up.
Inhale and raise right foot, keeping knee straight and
the other leg down. Stretch leg out and up as far as
possible, hold briefly, exhale and lower. Change to other
side and alternate two or three times on each side. Face
should remain close to floor. This is the Half Locust and
can be performed by itself or as preparation for the
more advanced Full Locust, which is one of the more
difficult postures to perform correctly.

In the Full Locust posture, fists are clenched, hands
under groin, the body straightens, and both legs are

raised with a sudden upward thrust. Ideally, the legs should reach almost vertically into air. Hold five to twenty seconds if possible.

VARIATIONS

a. Stretch arms out in front, raise arms, head, and legs as high as possible so that full weight rests on abdomen. Advanced students may rock back and forth on stomach. The position is sometimes called the Boat (Naukasana).

b. Repeat as above with arms clasped behind back.

The Locust strengthens muscles of lower back, abdomen, and thighs, and brings a rich supply of blood to the brain, flushing the face. All pelvic organs are invigorated, aches and ailments of the lower back are relieved. This exercise follows the Cobra, thus affecting the entire spine.

14. *The Bow (Dhanurasana)*

Lie on stomach, bend knees, reach back and catch firm hold of ankles. Inhale and raise head and knees as though body were indeed a bow trying to straighten and the arms a taut bowstring. Repeat two or three times, holding five to fifteen seconds. Advanced students can rock back and forth on stomach. Ankles are spread about two feet apart; pressure of arm-pull raises knees from floor.

Afterward, continue to hold toes and press heels gently down toward the floor on either side, giving knees and lower back muscles an extra stretch.

The Bow may be varied by crossing arms so that left hand clasps the right ankle and conversely.

The Bow combines the effects of the Cobra and Locust, but is easier to control than the Locust. Its benefits are not just in the stretching of spine and toning up of muscles but in its subtle effects on glands, digestion, and circulation. Some say it develops an inner resilience and stamina which colors the entire personality. As a sequence, the Cobra, Locust, Bow, and Swan are excellent for women with menstrual disorders and the dreary back and abdominal pains which so often accompany change of life, faulty glandular action, or general sluggishness.

15. *Pelvic Stretch (Supta Vajrasana)*

The pelvic stretches are adjustable to the requirements of beginning and advanced students. They are considered to be especially therapeutic and many variations are suggested so that each individual may find something suitable.

a. Kneel down, resting firmly on heels. This heel-sitting position becomes more comfortable when the heels turn somewhat out and the toes nearly touch, forming a kind of saddle. One of the first signs of age is a stiffening in the ankles, so if this preliminary posture is difficult the student should strengthen ankles by rotating feet inwardly and outwardly for a few minutes as often as possible.

From the sitting position stretch slowly backward with arms pushing straight down for support. Raise pelvis and hold as long as reasonably comfortable. Then come forward, resting buttocks on heels and head on floor with arms extended in front. This equalizes the backward stretch. Do not sag in the middle, keep hips raised and chest and arms forward.

b. Bend back from kneeling position as before, but try to rest on elbows instead of hands, allowing head to hang back. Sometimes this is considered a variation of the Fish. Again return to forward stretching position sitting on heels.

c. The full spinal stretch, sometimes called the Supine Pelvic posture, does a great deal to develop flexibility. It resembles the previous variation except that one rests all the way back on the shoulders and head. Try to keep bent knees together touching floor, then lock arms over head. For maximum stretching from Supine Pelvic posture, press hands back over shoulders to push the head up and nearer the heels, increasing the arch in the spine.

All this is good preparation for the Wheel posture which follows, strengthening back, legs, and thighs. Breathing throughout should be even, inhaling while lifting up, exhaling on extreme back bend.

The pelvic postures are effective in firming hips and thighs, removing crepy fat deposits from the upper legs and abdominal area. The effect on glands, nerves, and vital organs is also beneficial.

16. *The Wheel* (*Chakrasana*)

This is the back bend so familiar in Western calisthenics, simple for children but extremely difficult for some adults.

Lie on back and raise torso by curving arms back over shoulders and pushing head up with hands. Be sure arms reach all the way up over the head, elbows crooked,

palms down. Try to keep feet on floor even though the
tendency will be to rise up on toes. Eventually, as posture
is held without strain, practice bringing legs off the
ground, stretching first one and then the other up as high
as possible.

VARIATION

The Wheel can also be done from a standing position.
Some people master it easily and others never, since
so much depends on extreme flexibility of back.

At the start reach arms back and try to clasp ankles with
hands. This is one version of the Wheel. Then with a
quick flip of the arms bring palms of hands over the
shoulders and down flat on floor. Once this method is
mastered, a far more graceful back bend is accomplished by raising arms high over the head and bringing
hands slowly down in back until they touch the floor.
Continue to arch the back, bringing hands in as close as
possible to the feet. It is helpful, as should be apparent
by now, to have instruction while getting the feel of this
exercise. This requires a teacher standing by.

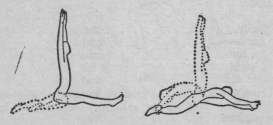

17. *Leg Split* (*Anjaneyasana*)

This is a super-stretch, developing graceful coordination. From kneeling position lift and extend left leg and

slide forward, while right leg is stretched backward simultaneously to form a split. Then raise hands high over head, inhale, and stretch backward so that spine forms arc. Hold briefly, exhale, returning legs to original kneeling position, and repeat on other side.

This exercise is even simpler from a sitting position with legs outstretched widely in front. Holding one leg firm and straight in front, lift torso up, and spreading groin, swing other leg back until torso is in the same line with both front and back leg. Squeeze groin to floor, and bend trunk forward touching extended front leg, then bend trunk back to rear leg. Bring outstretched legs back to original position.

18. The Twist (Ardha Matsyendrasana)

Sit with legs outstretched. Bend left leg at knee, bringing heel into crotch and keeping knee on ground. Place sole of right foot on floor on left side of folded left knee. Right knee is bent up to the level of the chest.

Now bring left arm alongside the outer (right) side of upraised knee and grasp toes of right foot. If it is not possible to reach toes, try to catch hold of ankle or left knee.

Finally, bring right arm around the back and reach at waist level toward inner side of right thigh. At the same time turn head and look as far around as possible over the right shoulder so that twist is felt the whole way up spine and neck. It is important that trunk remain balanced upright and not be pulled over to one side.

In describing this pose a picture is truly worth a thousand words, and the student is advised to study the illustration before passing up an especially relaxing exercise. The firm anchoring of pelvic region provides a lateral pull far more effective than that from undisciplined hip-swinging. Lungs

are expanded and become more flexible, congestion relieved
in liver and spleen, kidneys given a healthful internal massage. Both upper and lower vertebra are stretched and made
more elastic.

19. *The Crow (Kakasana)*

Squat on toes with hands on floor a shoulder's width
apart. Fingers are slightly spread and point forward.
Knees protrude two or three inches outside the elbows.
Keep lower arms straight like two pillars but allow
elbows to bend back somewhat so that knees rest firmly
on upper arms without sliding down. Keep wrists straight
as you balance with feet off floor. Try to work up to
thirty seconds or long enough for the position to seem
secure.

This exercise requires more coordination than muscle
power although it does make wrists and arms quite strong.
It is popular in classes because although it looks difficult it
can be relatively quickly mastered once the knack of getting
the knees on the elbows has been acquired.

VARIATIONS

The Sideways Crow position (Parswa Kakasana) is accomplished by balancing with both knees bent and resting the upper part of the legs over one bent elbow. When
the legs are straightened while resting on elbow the position is known as Vakrasana, the Curved pose. Legs can
also be separated to straddle the arm with one leg supporting the other.

The Crow strengthens and coordinates arms and shoulders
and develops the chest. It helps prepare for the head-

stand, especially in cases where a weak neck needs to be strengthened without direct pressure.

20. *The Peacock* (*Mayurasana*)

In kneeling position place palms of hands flat on floor with fingers pointing backward. Keep elbows firmly together so as not to exert undue pressure on ribs, and to help balance. Press elbows back into stomach just below the navel, hunching shoulders over arms to keep center of balance as low as possible. As the body is raised parallel to floor, it is supported by the forearms. Balance five or ten seconds or to the point of strain.

VARIATIONS

a. In Peacock position allow forehead to rest on floor and raise legs high in back, like the tail of a peacock unfolding.

b. Hand positions may be changed by resting on fists or fingers; this is practical only for men with powerful hands. The Peacock performed with legs folded in Lotus position appears spectacular but is often much easier, especially for women, because it helps balancing.

The Peacock strengthens back and abdominal muscles, particularly improving digestion and elimination, and tones up all the vital organs. Stimulating flow of blood to head, it serves as a facial massage.

21. *The Cock (Kukutasana)*

In Lotus posture extend arms straight down at sides and
raise buttocks off floor. Try to rock back and forth resting on palms or (if arms are short) on fingers. Then
arms are thrust down through crossed legs just behind
the knees and in front of feet. Push arms through as far
as elbows so that when rocking forward to rest on palms
the body will automatically be lifted well off the floor.

The Cock exercises wrists, hands, and shoulders. Extremely
limber people can double arms back up and grab hold of
ear lobes. This variation is called Garbhasana, the Fetus
pose, and aids the digestive powers.

22. *The Scorpion (Vrischikasana)*

The Scorpion should not be attempted until one does
the headstand. Some students master this pose by kicking up legs in back while balancing on forearms, bringing the trunk up with back arched and knees angled
forward over head. Athletic types can practice this way,
at first using a wall for balancing support. It is generally
safer, however, to begin with the headstand, gradually
raising head from floor while curving back and legs to
facilitate balance.

Advanced students find it well worth achieving for the
supreme stretch it gives the lower back and for developing
chest, shoulders, and arms. Those with uncommonly flexible
spines can practice bending knees down toward the head.

23. *The Tree* (*Vrikshasana*)

The Tree posture, like the Scorpion, requires considerable gymnastic accomplishment. It is a handstand with back arched for extra stretching and balance. Hands are first placed very solidly on floor, aligning shoulders and upper back before kicking up into position. It helps balance, strengthens the abdominal wall, and like other inverted postures militates against sagging organs.

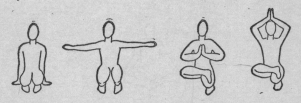

24. *Toe Balance* (*Padandgushtasana*)

In squatting position balance on toes. Then rock back and rest flat on feet, which are placed close together, with arms outstretched to maintain balance. Alternate from toe balance to flat feet several times. If second position seems difficult, spread feet and knees well apart and then gradually bring them closer together.

As legs and ankles become stronger, practice balancing on the toes of one foot alone, resting opposite ankle across thigh. If necessary hang on to some support—a chair or window sill—until balance comes more easily and hands can be joined in front of chest or over head. Some people find it easier to balance if they focus on a particular object.

This position is useful in eliminating constipation and forestalling varicose veins, flat feet, and swollen ankles.

25. *Knee Stretch (Bhadrasana)*

In sitting position press soles of feet firmly together and
gently push knees down toward floor with hands. Pull
heels in as close as possible to the crotch while keeping
knees down. Clasping toes, bend forward and bring forehead down toward floor, stretching muscles of thighs
and legs.

When the heels can be brought so far back that it is
possible to sit forward on them, the posture is called the
Ankle-Knee pose or Gorakshasana.

26. *Frog Pose (Mandukasana)*

Kneel down and spread knees, pushing them wide apart
with hands; double them so that toes meet in back. With
practice the student should be able to sit back comfortably against his feet, with the forward part of his buttocks resting on the floor.

The posture should be held for thirty seconds or as long
as comfortable. This simple exercise, properly executed,
invigorates knee, hip, and ankle joints and eases lower
back conditions such as sciatica.

27. *Cow Head Pose (Gomukhasana)*

In the Cow Head pose the student sits back between feet in a posture similar to the Frog except that the ankles turn in opposite directions with toes pointed out. Sitting comfortably, clasp hands together by reaching back over the left shoulder with the left arm, extending left hand down to meet the hand of the right arm which, elbow bent, crosses behind back and stretches diagonally upward until fingers interlock. Then repeat, with right arm reaching back over right shoulder.

Even when stiffened leg joints do not permit doubling-back, the arm phase of the exercise can be done standing up; this will keep shoulders supple and help prevent bursitis.

28. *Lion Pose (Simhasana)*

Crouch down on heels, arms out straight and resting on knees. Tense whole body, extending fingers stiffly. Roll eyes upward, tongue out and downward, and hold for fifteen or twenty seconds. If a cold or sore throat seems to be coming on, repeat two or three times during day. This exercise can also be efficaciously performed sitting in a chair.

Some teachers advocate a roaring sound to further stimulate the throat region, but this seems a little drastic. The Lion will often abort colds and incipient sore throats as it stimulates nerves of face and neck, stepping up circulation, suffusing affected membranes with invigorating blood.

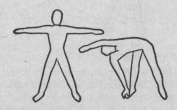

29. *Triangle Posture (Trikonasana)*

Stand erect with feet spread two or three feet apart. Extend arms at sides, inhale, and bend slowly to one side from waist until hand reaches ankle. Other arm swings in a wide arc all the way over the head to rest alongside the ear parallel to the floor. Clasp ankle firmly and stretch while exhaling. Hold five to thirty seconds and repeat on other side, visualizing legs as a firm triangular foundation.

VARIATION

Stand erect as before, with feet apart, but twist trunk from waist as far around as possible. Then, bending, touch one arm to opposite foot, the other arm first perpendicular and then becoming parallel to floor and resting alongside the ear. Feel stretch along whole side of body. Hold a few seconds and repeat on other side.

The spine receives a new kind of stretch and the abdominal organs are benefited by the gentle inner pressure. This exercise has been found to be especially helpful for menstrual problems.

30. *Deep Lunge* (*Sirangusthasana*)

Standing, legs wide apart, bend right knee and lean forward over it, bending trunk, head pressing down with hands clasped behind back. Try to bring forehead all the way down to the toes and hold approximately half a minute. Repeat on other side.

This exercise gives strength and pliability to legs and ankles and improves balance. Every skier should practice it before taking to the hills.

31. *Eagle Pose* (*Garudasana*)

Standing, lift right leg and swing it across in front of
left leg, wrapping right ankle around left calf until toes
point front on the inner side of left supporting leg. Holding this position, entwine arms in front of chest and
balance, hands at chin level. When this first balance can
be easily maintained, practice bending forward until
chest rests on upper leg and knee, keeping arms en-
twined and trying to look like an American eagle. Hold
briefly and come up slowly. Completed pose should resemble an eagle ready to swoop down on its prey.

The Eagle tones up leg muscles and thighs and develops
balance, poise, and nerve coordination.

32. *Forward Bend* (*Standing*) (*Padahasthasana*)

Standing, inhale and raise arms high over head. Bend
slowly down, exhale, and keeping legs straight bring
hands to toes with face pressing in toward knees. Try to
hold several seconds. Inhale while straightening up and
repeat two or three times.

Vary exercise by clasping hands behind back and bending from waist, bringing head down slowly first to one
knee and then to the other, accenting sideways stretch.

This standing forward bend stretches the whole body and spine, forcing blood through the system and restoring oxygen to tissues and nerves.

a	b	c	d	e
Easy Posture (Sukhasana)	Kneeling Posture (Vajrasana)	Ankle Lock (Swastikasana)	Perfect Posture (Siddhasana)	Lotus (Padmasana)

33. *Sitting Postures Adaptable for Pranayama and Meditation*

a. *Easy Posture (Sukhasana)*

The Easy posture is a simple comfortable cross-legged position. Legs are crossed in front with knees resting on insteps. Head and back should be kept in a straight line with neither sagging nor rigidity of spine. Provided the student sits quietly erect, it will suffice for breathing exercises and meditation until more advanced sitting postures come naturally.

b. *Kneeling Posture (Vajrasana)*

Kneel down with buttocks resting firmly on heels, back erect. If ankles are stiff this position should be regularly practiced until comfortable. Do not bend toes forward but rest with front of foot pressing down to floor. Can be alternated with Easy posture.

c. *Ankle Lock (Swastikasana)*

This preparation for the Lotus is worth mastering for its own sake. In this modified Lotus the ankles and legs do not tire as easily. The swastika, an ancient symbol, denotes a cross, in this case the posture of locked ankles and feet. Right leg is bent and foot crossed over with heel pulled in against left groin. Left foot is similarly crossed on top of the right ankle with sole resting between calf muscle and thigh. Feet are not pulled back as high as in the Lotus but snuggle against inner thigh.

d. *Perfect Posture (Siddhasana)*

In sitting position the legs are bent inward to crotch with soles turned upward. Heel of one foot rests on top of the heel of the other in such a way that both heels fit comfortably into the crotch. Knees should touch the floor and back remain erect though not stiff. Hands rest on knees or else are folded.

This position is conducive to meditation; hence the name, literally the Adept's pose, the Sanskrit word *siddha* meaning adept. The position used by the great saints and yogis, it remains easiest and most graceful for long-term sitting. The stretch is beneficial to legs and lower back and emotionally relaxing.

e. *The Lotus* (*Padmasana*)
Seated, bend left leg and place foot on right thigh, drawing left ankle in toward groin. Fold right leg and cross it over onto other thigh. Soles should turn upward with knees remaining on floor. Keep back straight but without rigidity since the pose itself insures erectness of spine. Hands should be placed over the knees with thumb and forefinger rounded and last three fingers extended (Jnana Mudra).

The Lotus is worth the extra effort required for mastery, both for its physical benefits and as a meditative pose. Eventually, it becomes quite comfortable and prevents the body from toppling in deep meditation. The pelvis gets a new flow of blood, and the control required calms the mind.

The Bound Lotus (Bandha Padmasana). From the Lotus posture, cross arms behind back and grab toes with fingers. The chest is stretched forward and the lungs expanded. The effect is felt throughout the body. A good meditative posture for advanced students.

34. *The Sponge* (*Relaxation*) (*Savasana*)

The Hindus call this the Corpse or Dead pose. Lie on back with arms along sides, palms up, quiet yourself and keep body loose. Close eyes and relax whole body from toes to head, breathing in slowly and deeply from the diaphragm; the exercise then becomes the American version, the Sponge.

Relaxation should be practiced after each major exercise or sequence of positions in order fully to assimilate their benefits. Literally, savasana means corpse, but in the Sponge one tries to feel porous and open everywhere like a sponge. Inhale not just with the lungs, but visualize the life-giving energies of the surrounding atmosphere being drawn in through all the limbs, pervading the whole system with revitalizing power and rejuvenating every tissue of the organism.

35. *Eye Exercises*

Beginners should work at these gradually.
a. Keeping face forward, look as far as possible to the right, moving only eyes. Then to the left. Alternate five times and close ten seconds to rest.

b. Repeat, raising and lowering eyes.

c. Repeat, with diagonal motion—up right and down left. Reverse. Close and rest.

d. Trace upper semicircles with eyes three times each way. Close and rest. Repeat with lower semicircles.

e. Roll eyes slowly in full circles three times each way around.

Always end by palming eyes—resting palms of hands on closed eyelids with fingers pointing up—for at least half a minute.

VARIATION: *The Clock*
Imagine that your nose is affixed to the center of an enormous clock. Fix gaze on successive numbers, progressing clockwise from one to twelve. Rest and then return in counterclockwise fashion back to one. Palm eyes.

PRANAYAMA: BREATH CONTROL

Pranayama means direction and control of the vital forces of the body through conscious regulation of the breathing mechanism. The word *prana* means life force, or energy. This is not just the energy of the human being but, the yogis say, the cosmic electrical currents which man and all creatures assimilate and transmit as part of the great flow of divine life.

Just as asanas are disciplines for the body and meditation a discipline for the mind, so does pranayama discipline the vital forces which join body and mind.

Breath is the great purifier, flushing the blood with oxygen which each cell requires for "internal breathing" and repair. The lungs remove not only carbon dioxide but other wastes, and the deep-breathing exercises, reaching lung areas ordinarily neglected, improve oxygen absorption and circulation. The sympathetic nervous system is also activated and the diaphragm and intercostal muscles are strengthened.

Visualization is an important factor in pranayama. As the purified blood nourishes each cell, so one imagines the vital health-giving energy coursing through his system.

Through concentration, the yogis say, the pranic forces reach the chakras or subtle nerve plexuses. There are seven of these chakras, all influenced by breath control and meditation. They supposedly regulate the psychic and spiritual forces. That at the base of the spine corresponds to the adrenals, and is known as the sacral plexus, and with the lumbar affects the sex glands. The latter are known as the prostatic plexus. The solar plexus affects the pancreas, the heart, the thymus gland; the thyroid, the mid-brow, and the cerebral centers tie in with the pituitary and the pineal glands. They are the highest centers.

With meditation and breath control the energies of the three centers below the diaphragm (base of spine, sacral, and solar plexus) are rechanneled into the higher centers (heart, throat, brow, and head). The solar plexus is the great clearinghouse for the instinctual forces, being closely tied in with emotions, the unconscious mind, and the sympathetic nervous system. The Ajna center—the mid-brow or "third eye"—is said to integrate the five lower centers. It is nearly always considered safe to concentrate on the

Ajna center, but seldom on the solar plexus, in spite of what one hears about yogis studiously contemplating their navels, for the Ajna center is the source of the higher intuitive powers.

There is nothing unnatural, and everything natural, about breathing exercises. They teach the student to breathe as nature intended, enlarging lung capacity, expelling old, stale air, and imposing a new vitalizing rhythm. Deep breathing has a generally calming effect on the whole personality, reducing jumpiness and nervous tension. The creatures that breathe more rapidly than man tend to be more restless and short-lived. Monkeys have almost twice the respiration rate, whereas the long-lived elephant and tortoise are slow breathers. Animals, as well as children and primitive peoples, breathe somewhat diaphragmatically, relaxing the stomach, as do civilized people during sleep when the system must refresh itself.

It is not necessary nor even desirable to be constantly thinking about how to breathe, any more than about how to stand or sit or walk. If a few simple breathing and stretching exercises are regularly performed, correct breathing habits will become automatic.

Manifold breathing exercises are not necessary. A variety are taught to develop proper breathing habits in the first place and for special cleansing and revitalizing purposes. In the practice of pranayama, progress develops from mental concentration, control, and the power to visualize. The criterion of success is elementary. One should feel better and grow more vital and resilient day by day.

Concentration while breathing is all-important. Any student wearing a watch with a second hand can make this test: For ten seconds focus attention on that moving hand, allowing no other thought to enter mind. At the end of this time notice breathing. Most people will find that it has slowed down, and that it always does slow down when they are absorbed in some engrossing pursuit. One of the first things the Yoga student learns to do in moments of stress—or in rallying energy—is to deliberately slow down his rate of breathing. Nervousness decreases and composure is induced.

The Yoga student, stressing diaphragmatic breathing, must always bear in mind:

1. Inhaling, let stomach relax and balloon out. Exhaling, pull stomach in. The diaphragm constricts and rises during exhalations, relaxes and falls during in-

halations, causing the air to reach the lower lung where it is widest and most capacious.

2. It is more important to breathe out than in. There is no use rushing outside and absorbing great bursts of air if all one does is push the stale air deeper down into the lung pockets. Pulling in the stomach and exhaling, empty the lungs thoroughly. Since nature abhors a vacuum, fresh air will then rush in.

Ideally, one should breathe completely expanding first the lower, then the middle, and finally the top of the lungs, just as one would fill a cup. With diaphragmatic breathing complete utilization of the lung capacity will follow automatically. Do all breathing in and out through nose.

SIMPLE DIAPHRAGMATIC BREATHING

Lie flat on back with knees pulled up, feet slightly apart. Inhale deeply and allow stomach to relax and expand like an inflated balloon. Exhale and pull stomach in so that the diaphragm rises and presses upward against rib cage into thoracic cavity. Continue until rhythm seems easy and natural.

Continue to breathe diaphragmatically but after filling lower lungs concentrate on filling middle and upper lungs as well; note difference in capacity.

Exhale, visualizing the air pressing out first from the lower and then from the upper chest cavity. Observe how the breath seems to move up through the body with a wave-like motion.

This simple exercise relaxes the body, calms the nerves, and helps the student to gain conscious control of his automatic response mechanism.

As simple as it is, this deep diaphragmatic breathing has relieved asthma, emphysema, and other respiratory problems, including shortness of breath. In asthma clinics, therapists will place a toy duck on a child's stomach and instruct the child to make the duck rise and fall as though it were sitting on the water.

As an aid in subduing nervousness, visualize a calm blue sea with waves rhythmically rising and falling. With each rising motion inhale and with each falling motion exhale, until the breathing is very slow and regular and the body completely relaxed.

SITTING-UP DIAPHRAGMATIC BREATHING

Sit erect, placing one hand on stomach and the other on chest. While inhaling, allow the lower hand to move *out*, with the stomach. Exhaling, lower hand should move in, as the stomach does. Top hand should not move at all. The back must be straight and there should be no heaving of shoulders and chest. Heaving the bosom may have been considered romantic in Victorian days, but it is a wearing way of getting your air. Try to move only the muscles of the stomach region. Upper breathing will follow naturally later on.

Do not overdo these exercises. They should serve simply as periodic reminders to the subconscious mind, which will with sufficient prompting take over the breathing function automatically.

DYNAMIC CLEANSING BREATH

Sit cross-legged on the floor (a chair is permissible) with head erect and spine straight. Inhale deeply, relaxing stomach muscles, drawing air to the very bottom of the lungs. Diaphragm presses downward pushing the abdomen out. Purse lips as though about to whistle. Exhale, blowing out with considerable pressure until every bit of breath is gone. Simultaneously, suck stomach in hard, pressing air out from below. Muscles should contract like a tube of toothpaste being rolled up neatly from the bottom. Repeat three to five times or until the body feels warm.

This exercise is helpful in conveying to new students the value of diaphragmatic breathing, since the results are so immediately effective.

VITALIC BREATH

Breathe in through the nose in a series of sharp sniffs until lungs are completely filled. Then blow out explosively through the mouth with a sound like a loudly whispered "haa." This clears and strengthens the lungs.

THE BEAUTY BREATH

Stand erect with arms upraised, inhaling deeply. Bend forward from the waist, retaining breath, and hold from five to fifteen seconds or until face feels flushed and a sense of warmth suffuses the whole body. It is all right to bend the knees a little so that the head comes way down. Exhale, return to standing position with arms down, and relax.

Repeat three to five times. Breath should never be held before system is eliminating wastes regularly and body has become elastic.

Students who find the above exercise strenuous can begin by sitting cross-legged on the floor and bending forward from the waist while holding the breath and exhaling.

THE HEALING BREATH—
CREATIVE VISUALIZATION

Lie on back and place both hands, palms down, upon the solar plexus (in region of the navel). Inhale slowly and visualize life force (prana) flowing down the spine and into solar plexus. Retain the breath a few seconds and imagine this vital energy being drawn into the hands so that they seem to be blotting it up. Exhale slowly and place hands on forehead, visualizing this shimmering but gently cooling light with soothing irradiation.

Repeat five to ten times.

ALTERNATE BREATHING
(ANULOMA VILOMA PRANAYAMA)

Alternate breathing, considered by some the most important of the breathing exercises, is usually practiced after the asanas or just before meditation.

The first thing to learn is how to hold the hands in a Mudra, the traditional way of closing the nostrils. In this ancient gesture the thumb and last two fingers are held up while the first and second fingers are pressed down into the palm of the hand. This allows room for the nose and is very comfortable.

Beginners inhale four counts (each count equal to one second) through left nostril, gently closing right nostril with right thumb, using Mudra. Exhale eight counts through right nostril, closing left with last two fingers. Inhale four counts through same right nostril, closing the left. Exhale eight counts through left nostril, closing the right. This is one round. Repeat five rounds.

Exhalation always lasts twice as long as inhalation, to empty the lungs thoroughly each time and make room for the new supply of air.

Intermediate students should add an interlude of holding the breath between inhalation and exhalation. Begin with four counts inhaling, four retention, and eight exhaling. Then gradually (over a period of months) increase the retention time to eight, twelve, and finally sixteen counts.

The ideal ratio for alternate breathing is considered to be 1:4:2—inhaling, retention, exhaling. Begin with three rounds and work to five.

Specialized students can work very gradually and cautiously to 5:20:10 and 6:24:12, up to what is generally an upper limit of 8:32:16. It is not necessary to go beyond the minimum ratios if they prove suitable.

Increase ratio as capacity comfortably increases. The essential is rhythm and regularity, not trying for a breath-holding record. There should never be the slightest sense of strain, since the aim is to soothe frayed nerves and restore tranquillity. This is a purification exercise, cleansing the nasal passages and getting one used to breathing through the nose.

THE RECHARGE—KAPALABHATI
(ADVANCED BREATHING)

Sit on the floor in erect posture with the spine straight but not stiff or tense. It is best to sit in a Lotus or modified Lotus (ankle lock) posture so that the trunk is firmly anchored, but any cross-legged posture will serve to keep the body from restless movement. Inhale and exhale a few times deeply—through the nose only—in order to establish the proper rhythmic motion of abdominal muscles: pushing these muscles out when breathing in, pulling in while breathing out. Exhale forcefully, pulling abdominal muscles in as hard as possible and driving air from lungs with a powerful push from the diaphragm. It will take some practice to strengthen these muscles so that they can do the job properly. Emphasis should be on exhaling. Do not worry about bringing air into the lungs since they will have to fill up the vacuum anyway. The point is to force as much as possible of the old air *out*. Be careful not to take air in or out through mouth.

Only the abdominal muscles move, not those of upper chest, shoulders, or head. The face remains serenely peaceful, reminding one of the ancient adage "The brow of the sage is unwrinkled." There should be no blowing or snorting through the nostrils but a free flow of air. It is imperative that this exercise first be practiced under guidance, since uninstructed beginners invariably get it all wrong, and it should not be overdone.

Ten to fifteen expulsions are usually enough in the beginning, but they can be comfortably increased.

As soon as the mechanics of inhalation and exhalation have been mastered, an interlude of breath suspension can be added for the very advanced. Following the round of sharp expulsions take a very deep breath and suspend it to a count of sixteen; then build up very gradually, stressing comfort at all times. This is not intended as a breath-holding competition, but an opportunity to experience the illumination which this exercise may eventually produce.

Ordinarily, smokers are not permitted to practice Kapalabhati because it could blow the tar and nicotine deeper into the system. In classes, heavy smokers are asked to "take it easy" since the Recharge will set them to coughing.

Kapalabhati should be, practiced before the alternate breathing, to clear out the throat and nasal passages. Its stimulating effect upon the body accentuates the subsequent soothing and harmonizing influence of the alternate breathing. Customarily, they are given together after the asanas and just before the final relaxation. Simple diaphragmatic breathing and the cleansing breathing should be done to warm up the body before any physical tune-ups.

THE BELLOWS (BHASTRIKA)

Sit in a meditative pose on the floor, preferably the Lotus or ankle lock. Inhale and exhale as in the Recharge, but with heartier breaths. The main difference is that

(1) As much emphasis is placed on inhalation as on exhalation, producing a considerably slower rhythm.
(2) The entire respiratory system is brought into play with middle and upper lung area being filled as well as the lower section used in diaphragmatic breathing.
(3) There is a retention period of a second or two, and the breath is expelled through the mouth.

Most students will find ten expulsions ample, as the exercise is explosive and puts considerable pressure on the lungs.

ADVANCED PRANAYAMA— BANDHAS OR MUSCULAR LOCKS

With advanced students only, the asanas and pranayama are often augmented by the bandhas or muscular locks— bandaging the muscles together—applied during retention of breath. The tensing of certain inner muscles, the yogis say, stimulate the three vital plexuses—in the throat, abdomen, and base of spine. These deliberate contractions assertedly increase muscular tone and coordination and galvanize the whole nervous system. They are said to produce an electrical current or force called "Kundalini

Shakti" (the Serpent Power) which rises through a subtle central channel of the spine, Sushumna Nadi. When locks are properly applied (especially after the Recharge and the Bellows), this vital pranic energy or kundalini mounts toward the higher chakras, unfolding ever expanding levels of consciousness as it rises. Students often experience a sensation of heat, which shows that the dormant energies have begun to stir.

ANAL CONTRACTION (MULA BANDHA)

This can be practiced in almost any position but is generally associated with the sitting posture. The anal (two circular bands of muscle which close the entrance to the rectum) sphincters are forcibly contracted several times in quick succession. As control is gained over these lower muscles, the abdomen can be pulled in simultaneously, pushing the diaghragm up toward the thoracic cavity, while the chin is pressed against the base of the throat.

Extremely beneficial to the lower areas, this will tone up the reproductive organs and remove constipation. This practice is also known as Aswini Mudra.

ABDOMINAL CONTRACTION
(UDDIYANA BANDHA)

This exercise is generally practiced independently of the other bandhas under the name of Stomach Lift. It is sometimes performed in a seated position, or even lying with knees upraised, but most students find it easiest when practiced standing up.

First stand erect and inhale deeply. Bend slightly forward, press palms of hands firmly against the thighs, and exhale forcefully, emptying the lungs as completely as possible. The diaphragm must be made to rise up and press against the rib cage, as though the stomach were about to touch the backbone.

When it is no longer possible to keep from breathing in, straighten up and let the abdominal muscles relax. Repeat seven or eight times, remembering that there must be two separate motions of the abdomen, first *back* and then *up*.

Once the basic lift has been mastered, practice raising and lowering the abdominal muscles five to ten times on a single exhalation. Obviously fat people and those with sagging muscles will not be proficient at first, but trying it will tone muscles and melt away the waist-line. It should always be practiced on a empty stomach.

The stomach lift massages the entire abdominal region internally and is particularly beneficial for people with digestive problems.

THE CHURNING EXERCISE (NAULI KRIYA)

Technically, this is one of the six Kriyas or internal cleansing exercises, but it is usually given with the bandhas since it is learned as a continuation of the stomach lift.

The first stage involves learning to isolate the two oblique muscles of the abdomen, which run from the ribs to the pubic bone. They are made to stand out together by taking the position of the stomach lift and then forcibly contracting both sides of the abdomen with a forward-downward thrust. This is called the Central Contraction or Madhyama Nauli.

Next, the left and right oblique muscles are made to ridge out separately by pressing down with the hand upon the corresponding thigh in a stooped position until each muscle tightens to form a visibly vertical band. These can then be successively manipulated with a churning or rotating motion which can continue as long as the breath can be comfortably suspended. Repeat three times.

CHIN LOCK (JALANDHARA BANDHA)
Jala means brain. *Dhara* means the upward pull.

While practicing retention of breath, press chin firmly against chest so that it fits into the jugular notch, and hold as long as the breath is comfortably retained.

This position theoretically exerts an upward pull on the nerves passing to neck and brain, not only stimulating this extremely sensitive area but sealing the air at the throat and containing the pranic energy. The chin lock is often applied simultaneously with the anal contraction. This closing up of passages at the top and bottom of the spine is supposed to unite the positive and negative currents of the body (called prana and apana), intensifying awareness. One may begin to feel like a sort of pressure cooker as the vents are sealed off, and care must be taken to proceed slowly, guarding against overstimulation.

YOGA MUDRA

More a seal than a lock, Yoga Mudra is particularly effective in meditation and during suspension of the breath. Inhale deeply, tilt head slightly back. Lightly close ears with thumbs, eyes with index fingers, nostrils with middle fingers, and gently press together upper and lower lips with remaining two fingers. Concentrate either on seeing a light behind the eyes or else on hearing the "sound current" within. Yogis very often practice meditating on the sound of the *aum*.

PURIFYING EXERCISES (KRIYAS)

Certain preliminary yogic practices designed to purify the respiratory, digestive, and nervous systems are called Kriyas, or cleansing exercises. Some of the more relevant, such as the Recharge (Kapalabhati) and Churning (Nauli) are described in other sections. Others, such as Dhauti and Basti, which involve such exotic practices as swallowing a tape; learning to irrigate bladder, rectum, and stomach; belching; and touching tongue to forehead, have traditionally been associated with Eastern therapeutic teachings.

The Hindu culture has always been ritualistically concerned with an ideal of purity and cleanliness. In America, on the other hand, the same woman who keeps a dozen kinds of soap, bleach, and scouring powder on her shelves will think nothing of besmirching her lungs with cigarette tar and her mind with dirty gossip, and of edifying her little boy with monster comic books.

The advanced Yoga adept may find it useful to know how to empty and rinse out his stomach with warm water, to belch up unpleasant gases, or take a Yoga-style enema, but the ordinary practice of asanas and pranayama should suffice to keep the average Westerner as pure as he wants to be.

Students with sinus conditions or postnasal drip or who feel a cold or sore throat impending sometimes find the exercise known as Neti helpful. This involves sniffing in through the nose a quantity of lukewarm water to which a pinch of salt has been added, and expelling it through the mouth, taking care not to force it into the upper nasal passages where it may irritate delicate membranes. Indian yogis sometimes use a soft gauze tape or tiny rubber tube to clear out nasal passages. People with neurotic tendencies often become obsessed with maintaining the "cleanliness" of stomach, intestines, and rectum, which ordinary Yoga automatically takes care of. Because of this preoccupation with the grotesque, Yoga is often misunderstood in the West. Nobody carrying out a normal Yoga routine, with only the most rhythmic movements, can long maintain digestive problems or continue constipated.

TRATAKAM

Although technically one of the Kriyas, the gazing exercise known as Tratakam purifies the inner vision for meditation and is popular among Yoga practitioners. It involves gazing fixedly at a particular object or point of focus. For this purpose colored disks about six inches in diameter may be cut from construction paper and mounted on white backgrounds. Place these circles at a distance of about ten feet and gaze at each one fixedly for a minute or more each. This is fundamentally an eye exercise, but may be used as an aid to meditation.

Natural objects such as the moon, a star, sunset, or flower may also be used as objects for gazing. Afterward, close eyes and try to recapture the picture with inner vision. People with some natural clairvoyance often find that gazing at a candle while in a relaxed mood stimulates a train of visual imagery. Try to gaze as long as possible without blinking, rest eyes, and repeat.

TIPS FOR TEACHERS FROM THE TEACHER

One of the happiest results of Marcia's Yoga classes has been the way they have spread. Some students have found a new family togetherness in sharing their interest with husbands, wives, or children. Others have started small groups and have been amazed at their influence. Several have become professionals. In the hope that no one will allow an unbecoming (and unyogic) modesty to interfere with possible service, the following suggestions are offered by my guru.

1. If you are teaching, never stop learning yourself. No system is complete, no level of achievement more than a steppingstone to the next. However ordinary you may be, Yoga can make you extraordinary, but only so long as you keep on trying. Unless you are willing to set an example, there is no guiding spirit to enliven the group, regardless of how much technical knowledge you impart. The principal function of the teacher is to help the student realize his own sufficiency and insufficiency. Yoga postures are simply ways of allowing Nature to function, an unobstructing of the channels of circulation and communication within the personality.

2. Encourage the student's faith in his own capacity by pointing out demonstrable improvement from week to week. Progressing visibly in the exercises, he values increasingly the intelligence and well-being of the body. Similarly, he can progressively enhance his appreciation of the wisdom of the inner self, which makes him a finer, more sensitive person as he responds increasingly to its call. A qualified teacher can throw out the guidelines whereby the student can help himself.

3. Always veer on the side of caution. Even an expert cannot be sure what physical or psychological problems another human being may have. A child may appear stiff, for instance, but it may only be inner tension. Creative visualization may work out these tensions.

Even when a student's chest is concave, muscles soft, shoulders collapsed, and face twitching, it is not necessarily helpful to try and straighten everything out all at once. Ultimately outer improvements can come only through helping him by gradual stages to achieve self-confidence. Do not underestimate the importance of just standing by with friendly encouragement even when the student doesn't seem to be accomplishing much.

4. At the same time, don't permit the inevitable psychological resistance of the beginning student to get you down. Be prepared for indefinable aches, excuses for nonattendance, and discouragement or blockages. Even though you can't expect to hold all the people who begin, help them to understand that even their resistances are part of the reintegration process and a positive sign that the discipline is making inroads.

5. No matter how large a class you may be teaching, give each student an individual word or pointer to let him know you care not just about his progress in Yoga but about him as an individual. Constant repetition of exercises patiently done will often reveal sudden dramatic results.

6. Try creating a receptive mood for the end result you are striving to attain. Be more interested in the means than the end. In Yoga there is something for everyone and you can never know when or where the seeds you cast out may germinate. Let those who cannot take the discipline eliminate themselves. *You* accept all who are willing to try.

7. Always allow at least a few minutes before classes to collect yourself and raise your awareness to as high a pitch as possible. Never end the final ten-minute relaxation (during which you do not wander off but sit quietly in a meditative posture) without taking each student individually into your heart and praying for his health and well-being. End with some prayer or invocation.

8. Plan your schedule so there is time to talk with students about any special needs and problems. Although the teacher must maintain a certain impersonality and dignity, people must know he or she is accessible. The harmony between teacher and student is as vital as any other harmony that Yoga imparts—though it is a harmony of principle, not personality.

TRAINING PAGES

Beginning Students
Intermediate Students
Advanced Students
Moderate Workout
Yoga Therapy

Exercises should be performed so that effort is involved without strain. This routine, with gradually increasing time-counts can be followed for a month to three months, depending on beginner's age and condition. As much time should be taken resting between exercises as exercising. While these exercises affect every part of the body, the important thing is to breathe deeply and rhythmically and bring the mind to bear on doing the exercise correctly. It is the effort that is important, not the result, in the beginning. Alternate exercises are indented below to add variety to the routine, and they may be substituted or added as the student progresses. Remember, you are the best judge of how much you can do. There is no hurry! Do as many exercises as you can at first without tiring. Work toward a complete schedule.

	Page
Simple Diaphragmatic Breathing	317
Dynamic Cleansing Breath	318
The Hugging Exercise	267
Invisible Wings	267
Rock 'n' Rolls	273
The Pump	274
Knee Squeeze	270
Knee Presses	269
Chest Expander	265
The Pulley	268
Arm Lift	271
The Blade (Shoulder Squeeze)	270
The Pendulum	266
The Stork	281
The Rooster	281
Angle Balance	280
Ankle Bends	277
Neck Rolls	276
Shoulder Stand	290
The Plough	293
The Fish	292
Forward Bend (Sitting)	293
Cat Stretch	265
The Fountain	279
Finger Flexing	277
The Cobra	297
The Swan	298
The Locust	298

The Bow 299
Pelvic Stretch 300
Forward Bend (Standing) 311
Triangle Posture 309
Easy Posture 312
Kneeling Posture 312
Eye Exercises 314
The Sponge 313

INTERMEDIATE STUDENTS

As the student develops, being in better condition, he does less of the warm-ups and more of the postures. Control is stressed more in this stage, as the student finds that his body—and mind—are gaining a new awareness of its limitations and powers. Again, depending on individual capacities, he may continue in this grouping for a year or so before going into advanced work, tentatively exploring advanced exercises from time to time to test his readiness. Remember, there is no hurry! Busy people can do half the routine one day, the other half the next. It is better than not doing them at all.

Page
Vitalic Breath 318
The Beauty Breath 319
Sun Salutation 285
Headstand (Attempt) 287
Shoulder Stand 290
The Bridge 291
The Plough 293
The Fish 292
Neck Rolls 276
Forward Bend (Sitting) 293
The Inclined Plane 297
Head-Knee Pose 295
Shooting Bow Pose 296
The Cobra 297
The Swan 298
The Locust 298
The Bow 299
Pelvic Stretches 300
The Twist 303
The Crow 304
Cow Head Pose 309
Frog Pose 308

Toe Balance   307
Knee Stretch   308
The Stork   281
    The Rooster   281
    One-Leg Stands   280
Deep Lunge   311
Triangle Posture   309
Kneeling Posture   312
Perfect Posture   312
Ankle Lock   312
Stomach Lift   323
Alternate Breathing (4:8:8)   319
Eye Exercises   314
Yoga Mudra   325
The Sponge   313

ADVANCED STUDENTS

After a year or so, the average student up to his middle
years should be able to complete the following routine. As
in other stages, the effort rather than the result is all-important, and detachment should be cultivated along with
control. There is still no hurry! Relax between exercises.
As in the intermediate stage, the routine can be split up.

                                                     Page
Sun Salutation (four times)   285
Headstand   287
Shoulder Stand   290
The Bridge   291
The Fish   292
The Plough   293
Forward Bend (Sitting)   293
Head-Knee Pose   295
The Tortoise   294
Shooting Bow Pose   296
The Cobra   297
The Locust   298
The Bow   299
The Wheel   301
Leg Split   302
The Twist   303
The Peacock   305
The Cock   306
The Scorpion (very advanced)   306

The Crow   304
  The Sideways Crow   304
The Tree (Handstand) (very advanced)   307
Knee Stretch   308
Cow Head Pose   309
  Frog Pose   308
One-Leg Stands   280
Eagle Pose   311
Deep Lunge   311
Triangle Posture   309
  Forward Bend (Standing)   311
Perfect Posture   312
The Lotus   313
  The Bound Lotus   313
Kapalabhati (Recharge)   321
Bellows   322
Alternate Breathing (4:16:8)   319
Eye Exercises   314
Tratakam   327
Locks (Bandhas)   322
Churning (Nauli)   324
Yoga Mudra   325
The Sponge   313

MODERATE WORKOUT

Some Yoga each day is better than none, and even a limited
schedule can convey remarkable results in physical and
emotional betterment. This middle-aged writer, for instance,
took from twenty to thirty minutes a day with the following
routine and appeared to prosper. But remember, rest between exercises is as important as the exercise itself. And so
is the habit of deep rhythmical breathing.

                                                     Page
Simple Diaphragmatic Breathing   317
  Dynamic Cleansing Breath   318
The Pump   274
The Blade   270
Sun Salutation   285
Neck Rolls   276
Shoulder Stand   290
The Plough   293
The Bridge   292
Pelvic Stretch   300

The Fish 292
The Cobra 297
The Swan 298
The Locust 298
The Bow 299
Forward Bend (Sitting) 293
The Crow 304
Triangle Posture 309
Perfect Posture 312
Stomach Lift 323
Kapalabhati 322
Alternate Breathing (4:8:8) 319
The Sponge 313

YOGA THERAPY

		Page
Asthma	Simple Diaphragmatic Breathing	317
Backache	Cat Stretch	265
Bad Posture	The Cobra	297
	The Locust	298
	The Bow	299
	The Twist	303
	Perfect Posture	312
Bursitis	The Pendulum	266
Circulation	Headstand	287
	Shoulder Stand	290
Colds, Sore Throat	The Lion	309
	Headstand	287
Constipation	Shoulder Stand	290
	Forward Bend (Sitting)	293
Eyestrain	Eye Exercises	314
Fallen Arches	Toe Balance	307
Flabby, Crepy Underarms	Arm Lift	271
Gas Pains	Knee Press	269
	Stomach Lift	323
Hangover	The Plough	293
Menstrual Problems	Triangle Posture	309
Round Shoulders	Chest Expander	265
	The Blade	270
Sciatica	Frog Pose	308
	Perfect Posture	312
	The Lotus	313
Sinus Trouble	Headstand	287
	Shoulder Stand	290
Stiff Neck	Neck Rolls	276
	The Twist	303
Sunken Chest	Alternate Breathing	319
	Diaphragmatic Breathing	317
Thyroid Problems	Shoulder Stand	290
Varicose Veins	Eagle Pose	310

GLOSSARY OF SANSKRIT TERMS

ASANA: A physical posture conducive to meditation and bodily control. The third of eight stages of Yoga.

ASHRAM: A dwelling place (traditionally secluded in the forest) in which a teacher (guru) devotes his life to imparting spiritual guidance to his students.

ASHRAMA: One of the four stages of life through which, according to Hindu tradition, an enlightened man passes. These are: (1) student, (2) householder, (3) retirement to forest, and (4) renunciation of desires and ambition.

ATMAN: The true Self, as contrasted with the limited ego or separate-seeming personality. Also called Universal Principle, Supreme Consciousness, Divine Soul.

AUM (also OM): Most sacred of Mantras or Words of Power. Considered as the name of God and source of all vibration. This mystic syllable is known also as the Pranava, meaning that which pervades Life. It is sounded in meditation to purify and align the various parts of the personality and to stimulate psychic centers.

BANDHAS: Muscular locks done during some breathing exercises to seal in and unite the pranic forces. The three main bandhas are: (1) jalandhara bandha, the chin lock, (2) uddiyana bandha, the abdominal contraction, and (3) mula bandha, the anal contraction.

BHAGAVAD-GITA: "Song of God." The best-known Indian scripture. It is an allegory concerned with the art of spiritual living, and an exposition of Karma Yoga, the path of right action.

BHAKTI: Devotion to God as source of all God. Also worship of and communion with the divine spirit in every form. One of the main branches of Yoga.

BIJA: Literally, seed. A syllable used as a focal point for meditation, representing a deity or particularized divine quality.

BRAHMA: The Creator. One of the principles of the Hindu trinity of Brahma, Vishnu, Siva. Not to be confused with Brahman.

BRAHMAN: Ultimate reality. The Holy Power which manifests as the whole of Creation yet remains eternally One and transcendent. The omniscient divinity that one endeavors to realize in meditation.

BRAHMIN: Highest of four castes into which Hindu society is divided; a member of this priestly class.

CHAKRAS: Literally, wheels; vortices of psychic energy. These vital centers situated along the spine and in the head serve as points of reception for constantly circulating "pranic forces" which galvanize the individual into action. Also called Lotuses because composed of whirling streams of energy which radiate outward in petal-like emanations.

The chakras do not exist in physical matter but are regulators of higher psychic and spiritual forces which condition all bodily responses.

Location	Sanskrit Name	Corresponding Gland	Plexus	Number of Petals
1. Base of Spine	Muladhara	Adrenals	Sacral	4
2. Lumbar region	Swadhisthana	Sex glands	Prostatic	6
3. Solar Plexus	Manipura	Pancreas	Epigastric	10
4. Heart	Anahata	Thymus	Cardiac	12
5. Throat	Vishuda	Thyroid	Laryngeal	16
6. Brow	Ajna	Pituitary and	Cavernous	2 (96)
7. Cerebrum	Sahasrara	Pineal	Cerebral	1000

CHIT: Consciousness.

CHITTA: The instinctive mind, which is to be controlled in meditation.

DHARANA: Concentration. Sixth stage of Yoga.

DHARMA: Duty of being true to oneself. Right expression of innate qualities.

DHYANA: Contemplation. Seventh of the eight stages of Yoga.

GAYATRI MANTRA: Most ancient and sacred of Hindu prayers. An invocation to the sun as symbol of the divine mind which illumines and bestows understanding.

GRANTHIS: Literally, knots. Three points of obstruction in the spine which block the free flow of pranic forces and hence limit consciousness. The purpose of Hatha Yoga is to break through these knots, effecting a release and liberation of energies.

GUNAS: The three qualities of which the universe is composed, and which also constitute progressive stages of development. These are inertia (tamas), activity (rajas), and rhythm (sattva).

GURU: A spiritual guide or teacher.

HATHA YOGA: That branch of Yoga dealing with purification and disciplining of the body. *Ha* means sun and *Tha* means moon, referring to positive and negative life forces which are brought together and unified through postures and breathing exercises.

IDA: A channel on the left side of the spinal column through which the nerve current (prana) flows. It is said to be a conveyor of negative electrical force in contrast to its opposite (pingala), which is positive. These subtle energies are said to correspond to ascending and descending tracts of the autonomic nervous system.

JIVA: The personal soul, a unit of Life.

KARMA: Law of cause and effect, carrying over from a previous life on a mental and moral plane. "As ye sow so shall ye reap."

KARMA YOGA: A yogic discipline of duty and selfless service.

KOSHA: Literally, a sheath, vessel, or container. The human mechanism is said to consist of the following five koshas or bodies:

1. Annamaya kosha: Gross physical body
2. Pranamaya kosha: Subtle or etheric body
3. Manomaya kosha: Desire-Mind body
4. Vijnanamaya kosha: Higher mind, body of wisdom
5. Anandamaya kosha: Body of bliss

KRIYAS: Internal cleansing exercises.

KUMBHAKA: Literally, a pot. Retention of breath during pranayama.

KUNDALINI: A fundamental power or electrical force awakened through exercise, breathing, and concentration on nerve centers. Kundalini is pictured as lying coiled like a serpent at the base of the spine until deliberately raised up through the various chakras to radiate from the top of the head. This deliberate awakening of kundalini should be practiced only under expert supervision.

MANTRA: A word for God, phrase, or terse invocation (usually a Sanskrit formula) repeated to produce physical and psychological effects. Mantra Yoga is a discipline (closely related to Bhakti Yoga) featuring use of such Words of Power.

MUDRA: A position taken by fingers or limbs symbolic of an inner quality or intent, capable of producing vital currents.

NADAM: The sacred word *aum* heard internally. Sound current.

NADIS: Channels (corresponding to nerves) of pranic energy. Nadis supposedly form an invisible network of

vital forces energizing the physical body. Where many
such subtle conduits meet, one finds a major chakra, or
psychic center.

The three main nadis, *ida, pingala,* and *sushumna,* have
their physical counterparts in the sympathetic nervous
system and the spinal cord. Kundalini, awakened, rises
up the sushumna nadi from the base of the spine to the
head, revivifying the whole system.

NIYAMA: Religious observances. Second stage of Yoga.

OM: See *aum,* the Sacred Word.

PANTANJALI: Compiler of classic *Yoga Sutras* several centuries B.C. First authoritative text on Raja Yoga.

PINGALA: See Nadi.

PRAKRITI: The world of matter.

PRANA: Vital energy present in and activating all which
lives. In an ultimate sense prana is the sum of all energies
of the universe.

PRANAYAMA: Regulation of breathing. Fourth of the eight
stages of Yoga. Involves not just control of respiration
but deliberate direction of psychic energies or prana.

PRATYAHARA: Cultivation of introspection through withdrawal from objects of the senses to more subjective
perception.

PURAKA: Inhalation.

PURUSHA: Pure spiritual consciousness without material
limitation.

RAJA YOGA: The science of controlling the mind through
meditation, helped by Hatha Yoga.

RECHAKA: Exhalation.

SAMADHI: Divine Union. Superconscious state which is the
goal and final (eighth) stage of Yoga.

SAMNYAMA: A combination of concentration, meditation,
and contemplation (the final three stages of Yoga)
fused into a single process of complete understanding.

SHAKTI: Divine power of Nature.

SHANTI: Peace. Often intoned three times, preceded by the
syllable *aum* at the conclusion of prayer, meditation, or
recital. Often used as a benediction.

SUSHUMNA: The central channel of pranic energy corresponding to spinal column. See Nadi.

UPANISHADS: Scriptural works of India. That philosophic
portion of the Vedas dealing mainly with man's relationship to God.

VEDANTA: Literally "the end of the Vedas," the summit
of knowledge conveyed in the ancient scriptures of India.

VEDAS: The sacred teachings of India, containing the

prayers, ritual, and philosophy upon which its ancient faith was founded.

YAMA: Ethical training, in preliminary stage of Yoga.

YOGA: Union. From Sanskrit root *yuj*, meaning to join. A controlled effort toward self-integration and self-realization so that the individual spirit may merge with the Universal Spirit in a spirit of oneness.

YOGA, Kinds of:

The principal Yogas, or paths of self-realization, all ultimately converging and blending, like diverse paths to the same mountaintop.

1. KARMA YOGA, the way of right action, duty or selfless service without thought to results. Leads to a perception of the workings of the divine will in all outer events.

2. BHAKTI YOGA, the way of worship and devotion to Supreme Being. Through love the devotee transmutes all personal emotions into adoration of and absorption in a God whose nature is compassion for all creation.

3. JNANA YOGA, the way of knowledge. Through scholarly reflection and discrimination the aspirant learns to reject that which is illusory, to identify with one immutable Truth underlying all phenomena—God-union.

4. RAJA YOGA, a way of meditation, through controlling the random wandering of the mind, in which mastery is achieved over the whole apparatus of thought and consciousness.

RAJA YOGA in turn includes:

a. HATHA YOGA, the way of controlling the mind through mastery of the psysical and vital bodies by means of asana and pranayama.

b. MANTRA YOGA, the way of inner communion through chanting of Words of Power, especially repetition of names of God, of which the principal one is the mystic syllable *aum* or *om*. Based on the idea that all objects are subject to vibration or sound.

c. KUNDALINI YOGA, the way of arousing latent powers to produce mental illumination and superconscious perception. This involves breathing and concentration on chakras, or vital nerve plexuses, in spine and head in order to liberate the great dormant forces in human nature.

YOGA, Stages of:

1. Yama. Internal Purification.
   a. Harmlessness
   b. Truthfulness
   c. Nonstealing

    d. Continence
    e. Noncovetousness
 2. Niyama. Observances.
    a. Purification
    b. Contentment
    c. Strength of character
    d. Study
    e. Self-abnegation
 3. Asana. Postures for disciplining body.
 4. Pranayama. Control of vital forces through regulation of breath.
 5. Pratyahara. Withdrawal. Cultivation of an attitude of introspection.
 6. Dharana. Concentration.
 7. Dhyana. Contemplation.
 8. Samadhi. God realization through meditation.

YOGI: One who practices Yoga. Sometimes called yogin. Feminine form is yogini.